CONTENT

CW00547091

INTRODUCTION

A JOURNEY TO ZERMATT is a voyage of discovery. However many times a traveller may be tempted to explore this most famous resort, a picturesque village at the foot of the Matterhorn, there is always something new to see. The Matterhorn seems to change with every passing moment but remains forever the most breath-taking sight.

However many photographs, paintings and descriptions, the reality exceeds all expectations.

I have attempted to paint a portrait of the region, of its inhabitants and their many achievements. It is therefore dedicated to all the people of Zermatt, without whose kindness, support and hospitality this book could not have been written.

Hence the title

From Zermatt, with Love ...

A WELCOME

The earliest official document in which the village is mentioned as 'Pratobornum' dates from the year 1280 AD. Even today the official seal of the village bears the name 'VALLIS PRATO BORNI', from which the German translation of the name of Zermatt derived. It is historically assumed that the German name was used on documents for the first time in the years 1495 and 1544 AD.

Until the end of the 18th century our Alps were feared and avoided, most likely because of the threat posed by growing and advancing glaciers during the Middle Ages. Nevertheless, the enjoyment found in the mountains by adventurous Englishmen and nature loving romantics from France, Germany and Switzerland, became more and more understood, despite the comments of the Bernese author Gottlieb Gruner who called Zermatt in 1790 'the most dreadful wilderness of Switzerland'.

The hotel dynasty of the Seiler Family began in 1853. The Burgerschaft came on the scene as second hotel empire in 1879 with the construction of the Grand Hotel Zermatterhof. It may sound macabre and peculiar but it is a statistical fact that the first ascent of the Matterhorn in 1865 with the tragedy of the descent resulted in an upward leap in the number of visitors to Zermatt. The numbers shot up again dramatically both in 1891 when the Visp-Zermatt-Bahn was opened and in 1898 with the commissioning of the Gornergratbahn. The winter season began to take on importance once the three skiing areas of Theodul/Klein Matterhorn, Gornergrat and Blauherd/Rothorn had opened. The upturn of tourism was enormous. Zermatt became the most popular resort of Switzerland.

Zermatt is different from other resorts. Even the sound of the name 'Zermatt' evokes a certain 'toughness'. In their minds eye many would-be visitors imagine a landscape which is topographically softer with more rounded contours. But how can a place be delicately formed when it has as immediate neighbours 29 out of Switzerland's 38 peaks with a height of 4,000 metres or more? How could that be, when the peak which is the most famous of them all, and which makes respectful shudders run down the visitor's spine, is so close to Zermatt that it is almost within touching distance of all living rooms in the village?

I wish Mrs. Elisabeth Upton-Eichenberger's informative book with the appealing title *From Zermatt, with Love* every success and hope that it will find an interested readership from a wide range of countries and walks of life.

The book gives the guests of Zermatt immediate access to much valuable and stimulating information about our world famous resort. Holidays at the foot of the Matterhorn are an experience in each season, all the year round. Zermatt extends a very warm welcome to you!

Robert Guntern
January 1995 Gemeindepresident Zermatt

AN INVITATION

The book, From Zermatt, with love ... by Elisabeth Upton – Eichenberger is close to the heart of the Burgers of Zermatt not least because it traces the history of the birth of our Burgergemeinde. The chapter which includes three of our legends reflects the traditions and ancient ways of life. The descriptions of the walks, of the Chapels and the climbing tours which take place amongst the magnificent surroundings of the Alpine landscape portray our natural heritage.

We shall give a warm hearted welcome to all the guests who make the journey to Zermatt into the beauty of the mountain world watched over by the Matterhorn, the symbol of our village.

[signature]

Hr E. Aufdenblatten
President of the Burgergemeinde Zermatt

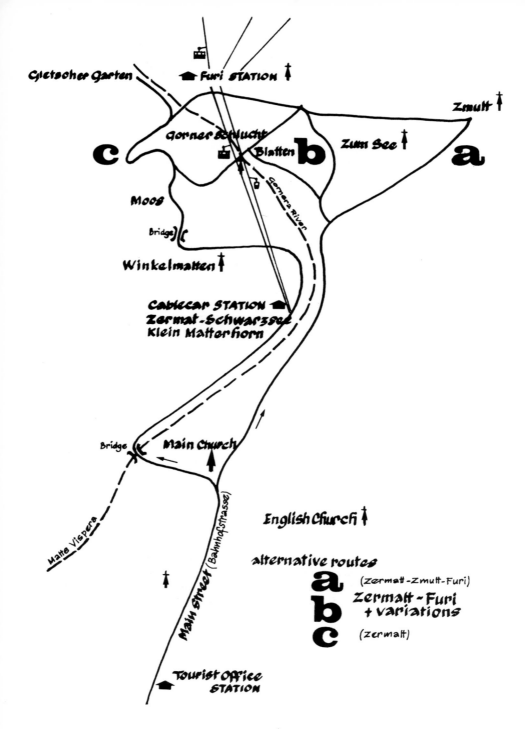

Gletscher Garten

Furi STATION

Zmutt

Gorner Schlucht

Blatten

Zum See

c

b

a

Moos

Gornera River

Bridge

Winkelmatten

Cablecar STATION
Zermat-Schwarzsee
Klein Matterhorn

Bridge

Main Church

English Church

Matte Vispera

Main Street (Bahnhofstrasse)

alternative routes

a (Zermatt-Zmutt-Furi)

b Zermatt - Furi
+ variations

c (zermatt)

Tourist Office
STATION

4

A WANDER THROUGH THE VILLAGE

ZERMATT IS A remarkable village; wonderful to explore and savour. While many visitors feel compelled to rush off into the mountains surrounding the village, it is worthwhile to take time out first and explore. Whether shopping, eating, observing, or just simply relaxing, many a fulfilling day can be had touring the village. Devoid of the motor car, Zermatt offers a truly peaceful and tranquil setting. It is not just a village for sportsmen, it also serves to inspire artists and to reinvigorate the spirit.

A bright red mountain train brings its passengers into the long, covered station of Zermatt. The main building of the 'Gär', as the local inhabitants still call it (a word borrowed from the French 'gare'), is traditional. Everything else looks new and efficient.

A board equipped with telephones and press buttons enables the visitor, who has come without prior booking, to see at a glance which hotels have rooms to let, make a choice and an instant booking.

A few steps, and onto the 'Bahnhofplatz', bustling with activity on a typical sunny summer's day. Electro taxis, solar battery powered buses, and horse-drawn carriages await their passengers. Two grand coaches, one blue, one maroon, bring the memories of the past splendour of Victorian travel into the present. Benches around 'the square' provide both resting and meeting places. One bench, the one opposite the Gornergrat Railway Station, which is situated across the road from the main station, can be particularly recommended: it is the bench with a view of the Matterhorn summit.

The buildings surrounding the Bahnhofplatz are part of a new development which houses the Zermatt Tourist Office, the place to get a plan of the village. Not far from it are the new Public Telephones offices which provide a model of efficient telecommunication.[1] There are shops and newspaper kiosks.

A last look at the new station complex shows the architectural philosophy of modern Zermatt. The buildings are constructed in chalet style, their façades draped in summer with hanging geraniums, the height of the roofs curtailed and governed by local by-laws. Zermatt is determined to retain the charm of an Alpine village, and the style of the new buildings reflects this.

In Whymper's days,[2] shops were huddled together, side by side: a pharmacy, a general store and many souvenir shops. The famous guide, Melchior Anderegg, who achieved notable first ascents and took the first woman up the Matterhorn, was a sculptor. He, too, had a shop in the main street where he sold his wood carvings as well as climbing items. Today, echoes of the past remain in the souvenir shops of Zermatt, which, amongst many other countless items, still sell wood carvings and rustic linen.

Another fine Swiss tradition is well represented: jewellery shops with exquisite,

---

1. The public telephone facilities consist of individual glass booths with independent dialling facilities connected to a manned central board where telephone charges are paid after the last call, i.e. no coins, no change needed.

2. See the chapter 'The Matterhorn'.

hand-crafted collectors' pieces. All the renowned brands of Swiss watches are to be found, next door to florist shops and confiseurs, with home made chocolates and truffles, mouth-watering gateaux and Torten. Butcher shops display their local specialities of dried sausages, dried ham and fillet of beef, sold in cheerful and impeccably clean premises. Pharmacies and Perfumeries are side by side with photography shops and banks. Sports shops offer a large choice of the latest sports equipment and fashionable clothing. Swiss quality stainless steel, copper cooking ware, famous Swiss army knives with personalised engravings are on sale. The visitor is spoilt for choice.

Hotels, Restaurants and their open air '*Terrassen*' line the Street and there are flowers everywhere.

Another new building development, further up, on the right hand side, has an arcade which leads through to the modern Post Office. This building contains the famous specialist Swatch Shop, a bank, boutiques, and newsagents. Above are the luxury suites and apartments which are linked by an underground passage to the Hotel Mont Cervin opposite. This Hotel, first built in 1852, is one of the original three grandees of the Golden Age of Mountaineering.

A side street comes in from 'Unterdorf', the lower village. It is a delightful, narrow street, where original old Stadels,[3] bunched together, can still be seen.

Further along the main street we come to the Guide Office and Ski School Bureau. Behind this chalet building are the Seiler Monument and the historical Seiler Garden, with Zermatt's largest open air 'terrasse' in front. The Alpine Museum (due to be rehoused) and the English Church are at the rear, both worth a visit.

3. Stadel = small stable and/or barn.

The street narrows past one of the oldest hotels in Zermatt, the Hotel de la Poste, built in 1883, with a traditional 'Stübli'[4] on the other side, before widening out between the Grand Hotel Zermatterhof and the Hotel Monte Rosa.

The Zermatterhof was built in 1879 on Church land and is the property of the Burger Gemeinde.[5] It has a spacious and lovely shaded garden in front, a tennis court on the side, and stands well back from the street.

Directly opposite is the Hotel Monte Rosa, built in 1855. It was Zermatt's first hotel and looks very much as it did when Edward Whymper stayed there before his first ascent of the Matterhorn. There is a commemorative plaque on the outside showing the climber in a serious and thoughtful mood.

All the original hotels of Zermatt have been updated and refurbished whilst retaining many of their traditional characteristics, old paintings and other memorabilia.

Across from there is the Parish Church with its pink cobbled square in front of the entrance steps. Shops, 'Old Zermatt' cafés and restaurants, as well as a hotel, line the Church Square next to the Gemeinde Haus (Council House).

The Church Square is the place for open-air concerts. Zermatt is very proud of its smartly turned out brass band. The Association of Mountain Guides also has its own band, and music plays an important part in village life.

On the corner, beside the Church, is a magnificent fountain with bronze cast marmots playing above the water. This is one of several fountains in Zermatt with bronze animal sculptures: one, at the entrance of the Zermatterhof, portrays an endearing frog, another a proud ibex.

The Church Square represents one of the major crossroads of the village. Straight on, the street leads towards the Matterhorn and the part of Zermatt called 'Oberdorf', the upper village. This is where some of the oldest houses can be seen. It is well worth walking up the street, towards an old farmhouse facing south, to look at the Matterhorn. The view of the grand summit rising above the roof-line of Oberdorf chalets provides one of Zermatt's most photogenic scenes. A beautiful, carefully tended kitchen garden in front of the farmhouse grows rows of vegetables mixed with flowers in a perfect blend of colours.

Turning left at the Church, the street passes the cemetery, the lovingly kept resting place of many past generations of Zermatters and of climbers who lost their lives in the mountains.

Further on, a bridge spans the river Vispera, whose milky waters come down from the high peaks and the glacier world beyond the village. From the bridge, there is a stunning full view of the Matterhorn, a favourite place for photographers.

Beyond the bridge there are more hotels, restaurants, 'Stüblis', sports shops as well as food shops. Straight ahead the road rises, the starting point of the walk up to the Sunnegga mountain station (2,288m).

There are thoroughfares flanking the river on both sides, with seven bridges connecting hotels, meadows and gardens. Round trips, crossing back to the main street via the Carrefour Séchaud for instance, can be made through the side streets, mostly on the flat: a wealth of village walks with something new to discover

4. Stübli = homely, casual café/restaurant: a locals' and visitors' meeting place.

5. See chapter: 'The Birth of the Burger Gemeinde'.

everywhere.

Quaint old houses, Stadels, fountains, cobbled streets, bars, cafés, restaurants, small hotels, the exclusive as well as the secluded, the old Zermatt nestles next to the Zermatt of today.

Unlike many other resorts throughout the Alps, Zermatt has retained the atmosphere of a mountain village. It has kept much of its traditions whilst moving with the times and thus achieved an almost impossible balancing act. Behind the old façades are comfortable homes, and hotels of all categories, with some providing completely up-to-date facilities and luxuries.

Good food, be it local specialities or international cuisine, is served in the restaurants and 'Stüblis' as well as in the hotel dining rooms.

For those who want it, for the young and not so young, there is plenty of night life, from traditional Swiss musical evenings to rock groups and discos. It is worth investigating all of the 'Zermatt Scene' which spreads well beyond the main street.

There are many restaurants, mainly lunch-time places all over the mountainside. With the extensive network of modern transport available, most of them are easily accessible and may be reached on a *downhill only* walk. A short climb, however, can also make the visitor feel that the delicious, sometimes sophisticated cuisine, as well as the 'waist line killers', have been earned and well deserved ....

The village keeps the tradition of celebrating Corpus Christi (Fronleichnam) in June. This is the day when the Mountain Guides, wearing their special uniforms, bring their ropes to be blessed in a moving open air service. There follows a procession through the village which everyone is invited to join.

On 15 August, the religious festival of 'Maria Himmelfahrt' is celebrated with sung Mass at the Parish Church. A string ensemble accompanies soloists and choir in a setting of the Mass by Mozart or Haydn. There is a large folklore procession, and people from all the neighbouring villages come, wearing their traditional costumes and carrying baskets of flowers. Little old carts, with bundles of hay, old-fashioned haymaking tools - all to the sound of at least ten different bands - horse drawn carriages, Saint Bernard dogs, a group of people dressed to represent the golden age of mountaineering and, last but not least, Zermatt's old historical fire engine! Down by the tennis courts are large tents with refreshments, musical entertainment and dancing.

The first of August is the Swiss National Day. Flags fly. Bonfires, beacons for signalling from mountain to mountain, illuminate the skyline. Children carry lanterns, and there is a magnificent display of fireworks.

The whole village is in a party atmosphere!

OPENING HOURS FOR BANKS AND SHOPS

Shops close between   12.00h and 14.00h.

Sundays are observed as a day of rest. Food shops are closed, except for bakeries.

Other shops and services may be open for some of the day.

It is always possible to hire sports equipment.

Visitors should check opening times.

Bank opening times: 08.30h - 12.00h   14.30h - 18.00h.

Banks are closed Saturdays and Sundays. There are numerous cashpoints.

PUBLIC HOLIDAYS

Sunday closing times apply to all major Christian religious festivals as well as to the following *bank holidays*, some of them local only:

19 March	St. Joseph's Day.
Towards the end of June	Corpus Christi (Fronleichnam), a variable feast.
1 August	National Day.
15 August	Maria Himmelfahrt.
3rd weekend in September	Eidgenössischer Bettag (National day of Prayer).
1 November	All Saints.
8 December	Maria in Empfängnis.

CHEAP RATE TELEPHONE CALLS

Switzerland	Monday to Friday	17.00h – 19.00h and 21.00h – 08.00h
	Weekends	21.00h Friday to 08.00h Monday
Europe	Monday to Friday	21.00h – 08.00h
	Weekends	21.00h Friday to 08.00h Monday
Canada, USA	7 days a week	23.00h – 10.00h

HOTEL POST, ZERMATT

Tel. 028 67 19 32   FAX 028 67 41 14

Ten distinct bars and restaurants beneath 21 charming rooms, the Hotel Post, Zermatt is one of the oldest and funkiest hotels in all the kingdom of the Alps.

Every room is individually decorated with ease of living and instant familiarity in mind, each is unique and as comfortable as your living room. At the Post you feel at home immediately!

Three Italian restaurants, six bars and a take-away pizza / cappuccino bar offer you all categories of restaurants, discos, jazz clubs, bars, and snack bars right on the premises.

From the stylish eclectic atmosphere of the *Pink Elephant Jazz Bar*, to the up-beat dancing of the *Village Disco*, to the intimate retreat of *David's Boathouse* bar you don't have to leave the house to paint the town!

All under one roof!

SPECIAL EVENTS IN ZERMATT

INTERNATIONALER MATTERHORNLAUF –
INTERNATIONAL MATTERHORN RUN

This has long since become an annual event. The 12th Matterhornlauf, a mountain run for everyone, took place on 28 August 1994 and after the Zermatt tennis championships earlier in the season the run is the next high point in the Zermatt summer sport programme. The routes – UPHILL ALL THE WAY:

Zermatt – Zmutt – Stafel – Schwarzsee for Runners and Tourists
Furgg– Furggbach – Schwarzsee for Schoolchildren.

The categories are as follows:

Total height ascended: 1,001m
12 km run 'Runners'

Total height ascended: 1,001m
12 km run 'Tourists'

	Year of birth	Not divided into groups,
Ladies II	up to 1959	Time only is recorded and a
Ladies I	1960 to 1974	certificate is handed out at the finish.
Young people	Since 1975	
Seniors	1955 – 1974	
Veterans I	1945 – 1954	
Veterans II	1935 – 1944	
Veterans III	up to 1934	

Over the last five years each participant to reach the end of the run has been presented with a medal in the sought-after 'Zermatt 4,000m Peaks series'. After the engraving of the Liskamm (4,527m) to commemorate the 1993 Matterhornlauf, the 1994 medal features the twin peaks Castor (4,228m) & Pollux (4,092m). There are 38 peaks of 4,000m and over surrounding the village of Zermatt.

Dozens of local hotels offer prizes of free weekends for two to the winners, and there are cash prizes for the three fastest runners in both the ladies' and men's classes.

A look at the winners' lists from the first run in 1982 onwards gives a clear indication of how fierce the competition is between locals and visitors from all over the world. The Matterhornlauf has to be the total antithesis to downhill ski events, in that, apart from footwear, no special clothing and equipment is needed, and the pull of gravity hinders rather than helps. Compare this with ski racing where high-tech clothing and skis play a major part in performance, as gravity accelerates the descent. For spectators, too, the simplicity of the Matterhornlauf set in the magnificent scenery and warmth of the late summer must make this a memorable contest to witness, a chance to cheer on their favourite runners and to encourage those who find the going hard but want to make it to the end. A special day on which to enjoy to the full a holiday amid such awesome surroundings, combined with the thrill of the competition.

SWATCH WATCH

CELEBRATION OF THE 100 MILLION SWATCH WATCHES SOLD WITHIN 9 YEARS OF THE START OF PRODUCTION

In the centre of Zermatt, beside the Parish Church, there stands a blue box-topped column looking like something between a post-box and a Dalek with a platform attached to it. There may well be a queue of young and old, waiting to step up and have a look. For this is the kaleidoscope presented to the village as a thank-you and in remembrance of the three days at the end of September 1992 when Zermatt was host to the 'Swatch the World' congress, attended by over 40,000 fans, makers, and guests of SWATCH. Swatch SA felt that the gift to Zermatt of a kaleidoscope demonstrated the aim of their philosophy. On looking through this magical instrument, village and mountains are perceived in almost dreamlike sequence, giving a fresh and mythical quality to scenery that has been painted, photographed and sketched thousands of times and is recognised by people the world over. To peer into the kaleidoscope is to regain a childlike wonder at the beauty of our earth.

Why has this world renowned Swiss company chosen to establish in Zermatt one of the two new generation Swatch Stores in Switzerland and decided upon Zermatt as the venue for its celebrations?

Because this magnificent, authentic temple of nature - the Matterhorn - has been a symbol of Switzerland and of the Alps from earliest times. It embodies in particular solidity and uniqueness, both virtues of the Helvetians or the Confederates of Helvetics.

Because Zermatt's tradition of welcoming hospitality would ensure an unforgettable stay for the thousands of Swatch fans who came from all over the world to celebrate this multi-cultural event.

Because the marvellous community of Zermatt was a place from which Swatch could transmit a credible message to the outside world in the unveiling of their new creation, the 'SWATCH THE PEOPLE', a tribute to all peoples and the earth they live on. The design of the bracelet and face of SWATCH THE PEOPLE unites the skies, the earth's strata, flora and fauna, as well as human beings from east and west, north and south. These ideals inspired Alessandro Mendini, the designer, together with Swatch Design-Lab, to create a watch celebrating our wonderful multi-racial planet as it revolves towards the millennium.

But the kaleidoscope was presented to Zermatt at the *end* of the '100 MILLION CELEBRATION', that is, at the end of the biggest party the village had ever seen. The party was fun, full of innovation and love of life. Like the SWATCH watches, there was nothing stuffy about the events: ski acrobatics, clowns, comedians, theatre groups, exhibitions, sideshows, concerts, a 'pop' son et lumière created by Jean Michel Jarre and displayed with the village and the Matterhorn as backdrops, and fireworks. The visitors' book, measuring 1.2m x 0.8m, 1,000 pages thick and weighing 250kg, gave the Swatch fans a chance to inscribe a happy, funny dedication to a great event. - What fun it would have been to be there!

HOTEL EDEN **** ZERMATT

For the highlight of the year let us carry you off to paradise.
Enjoy the atmosphere of refinement at the Hotel Eden in the heart of Zermatt under the personal management of the family.
Feel at home in our elegantly furnished bedrooms and enjoy our delightful hotel and garden.
Relax in our full size swimming pool after skiing or walking and then treat yourself to a sauna, turkish bath, jaccuzzi or sun-bed.
You can feel it doing you good!

Familie Ch. + K. Lutz-Aufdenblatten,
CH-3920 Zermatt
Tel : 028 67 26 55
FAX : 028 67 62 40

HOTEL GARNI
Metropol ✦ ★★★
ZERMATT

FAMILIE OTTO TAUGWALDER
TEL : 028 673231   FAX : 028 672342

Out hotel is surrounded by greenery and offers stunning views over the mountain world of Zermatt. A large, quiet and sunny garden area, perfect for total relaxation, is only three minutes' walk from the heart of the village.
We pride ourselves on the individual care we give our guests who are our friends.
The Hotel Metropol is a modern and comfortable Garni Hotel,
but we cook simple Swiss dishes in the evening for our guests who wish to stay "at home".

Welcome to Hotel City Garni.
Our aim is the wellbeing of our guests.
Family atmosphere and all rooms en suite with TV
Ski Instructor/Mountain Guide
Chris Petrig
3920 Zermatt
Tel: 028 672071
Fax: 028 675686
By us it is always an
"Auf Wiedersehn"

‹HOTEL ★★★★
BEAU-SITE ZERMATT

Modernes, erstklassiges Haus mit Hallenschwimmbad, Sauna • Ruhige, sonnige, zentrate Lage
Telefon 028 67 12 71 • Fax 028 67 23 28

Direktor P. Maissen-Glutz
CH-3920 Zermatt

La Crêperie

You will find us
on the Bahnhofstrasse
or opposite Migros
by the Ice Rink in the «Bistro-Café-Bar».

THE ENGLISH CHURCH IN ZERMATT

T HE MUCH LOVED English Church in Zermatt, dedicated to St. Peter, is of great historical importance. Today such a building project would be unthinkable. The Church, lovely in its sobriety, was a product of its time. Nowadays, Churches have moved closer together, and Anglican services may take place within any ecclesiastical community, in keeping with the new ecumenical ideals. This was not so in Victorian days, the Golden Age of Alpinism.

Church-going took place then on a very much more regular basis, and when people travelled abroad, they missed their own church. Many of the British pioneers who came to Zermatt brought their families, wives, children and other relatives with them. Women took part in the sporting activities and ventured on to the glaciers (... wearing long skirts). Thus, the number of English-speaking tourists was quite considerable. Most, if not all of them, wished to attend their own church services. A Church was needed!

This was a sentiment which the people of Zermatt could only too well relate to, for their Church was, and remains, at the heart of the community. It was not therefore surprising, but none the less most generous, that both Mr. Clementz of the Hotel Mont Cervin and Mr. Seiler of the Hotel Monte Rosa opened the Contributions Book at the start of the climbing season of 1865, to raise funds for the building of a new church. Subscriptions could be paid into the care of either hotelier, or at the offices of the Colonial and Continental Church Society.

As Mrs. Cicely Williams points out in her excellent booklet about St. Peter entitled *A Church in the Alps*: British tourists were fortunate in having such sympathetic support from Mr. Seiler and Mr. Clementz.

Mr. Clementz was an important and influential politician as well as the proprietor of the Hotel Mont Cervin. Mr. Seiler was a maestro of hotel-keeping and held a high rank in the Swiss Army. Their support counted for a lot and drew people along.

1865 was to be an unforgettable year in the history of Alpine climbing: the conquest of the Matterhorn an apotheosis. So it was. The Matterhorn was climbed for the first time on 14 May 1865.[1] The tragedy which took place during the descent plunged the climbing world into great sadness. Zermatt suffered as at first tourists stayed away. All at once 'glorious mountaineering' was reduced to 'unnecessary risk-taking amongst threatening summits'.

The Matterhorn tragedy could have meant the end of the project to build an English Church in Zermatt. Fortunately this was not the case. Subscriptions to the Church fund were received almost immediately after the accident. The families of Lord Francis Douglas and Douglas Hadow, who had perished on the Matterhorn, sent contributions to the fund. There was soon enough money to purchase an additional piece of land.

Tourism and Alpinism recovered and grew from strength to strength. As a result, five years later, on St. Peter's Day, 29 June 1869, the foundation stone of the

1. See the chapter 'The Matterhorn'.

Church was laid. The building started at once. On 29 June 1870, one year later to the day, the church opened its doors for the first service.

The Church of St. Peter was officially consecrated on the 6th day of August 1871 by Bishop Edward Parry, Suffragan Bishop of Dover. It was a great occasion in which everybody took part. There were fireworks, both in Zermatt and half-way up the Gornergrat at the Riffelberg Hotel, then called Riffelhaus. As ever, the hospitality of Zermatt towards its guests was most generous and warm-hearted.

Not only was there an English Church in Zermatt, but there was also a churchyard which could receive the bodies of the climbers the mountains claimed. The remains of the Revd. Charles Hudson, who was killed on that fateful first descent from the Matterhorn, were moved from the large cemetery next to the parish church and laid inside St. Peter's, beneath the holy table.

By the middle of the 1920s the churchyard was full, and the British climbers who died on the mountains were again buried in the village cemetery. It may be because so many were killed in the prime of life, including a surprisingly large number of women, that the churchyard today has an aura of nostalgia and moving regrets for what might have been.

Night's candles are burnt out
and jocund day stands tiptoe on the misty mountain tops.

This couplet chosen from Shakespeare's *Romeo and Juliet* is inscribed on the tomb of Edward Broom, famous climber and member of the Alpine Club. The sensitivity of the words mirrors the poetry of the mountains, and visitors always seem drawn to this tomb.[2]

The interior of the Church with its white-washed walls is perhaps surprisingly simple, almost plain, were it not for the plaques which honour the memory of famous climbers. They do not so much decorate the walls as bring the history of mountain climbing alive, through the deaths remembered thereby.

The English Church is now open during both the summer and winter season, but there is no resident Chaplain. The Chaplains who conduct the services come for a period of two weeks at a time. They are appointed by the Intercontinental Church Society. The Chaplains have an important role to play within the tourist community. Even with an ever-changing congregation, there are many needs to respond to, besides conducting services. The Chaplains are present and available on a daily basis to give their comfort, support and help whenever it is needed. St. Peter's Church is alive and well, a warmly supported Church in the Alps. It is often said to draw even the most 'doubting of flocks', in a desire for spiritual elevation which springs from the mystery and grandeur of the mountain world.

Our thanks go to the Intercontinental Church Society and to Canon Gordon Reid, Vicar General of the Diocese of Europe,
for talking to us.
We would also like to acknowledge Mrs. Cicely Williams's book
A Church in the Alps, the reading of which has greatly helped our research.

2. The grave lies on the right hand side of the path leading to the main door of the Church.

17

SEILER HOTELS
ZERMATT

For an unforgettable vacation!

The leading hotels of Zermatt
offering traditional swiss hospitality
combined with high standards of comfort and service.

Several restaurants with different fares - piano-bars
indoor pools with sauna, fitness, massages, etc.
garden - kindergarten - meeting facilities.

Welcome to one of the Seiler Hotels!

Mont Cervin and Residence *****
Tel. (028) 66 88 88
Fax (028) 67 28 78

Monte Rosa ****
Tel. (028) 66 11 31
Fax (028) 67 11 60

Schweizerhof ****
Tel. (028) 66 11 55
Fax (028) 67 31 27

Nicoletta ****
Tel. (028) 66 11 51
Fax (028) 67 52 15

Riffelalp ***
Tel. (028) 66 46 46
Fax (028) 67 51 09

Swiss Rock
Tel. (028) 67 68 80
Fax (028) 67 50 45

International code for Switzerland: 0041

THE ALPINE MUSEUM OF ZERMATT

A TOUR OF THE Alpine Museum of Zermatt, off the main street by the Seiler Garden, is a **must** for the visitor who wishes to comprehend what the village stands for and has experienced in the last 200 years or so. With over 18,000 tickets sold per annum the museum is financially self-sufficient. There is plenty for children to see, too, such as meeting (stuffed!) ibex and marmots, eagles and owls eye to eye and delighting in the homely Zermatt kitchen with its ancient equipment.

Zermatt's Alpine Centre was formed in 1944 with the eventual aim of building an Alpine Museum in the village. As with any museum, a nucleus of exhibits had to exist to show the need for such a place and to give it commercial viability from the start. The precursor of the museum was located in the Hotel Mont Cervin. The hotel's **Seiler Collection** contained paintings, and photographs of the guest Alpinists and their guides, a chronicle of the conquests of the peaks from the first ascent of the Klein Matterhorn by H.B. de Saussure in 1786 to the epic climbs of the 1930s. Hotel guestbooks, manuscripts, as well as memorabilia were plentiful, especially of the first ascent of the Matterhorn (14 July 1865) by Edward Whymper, Revd. Charles Hudson, Lord Francis Douglas, D.R. Hadow and the three guides, Michel Croz of Chamonix, and the Taugwalders (father and son) of Zermatt, and its tragic aftermath.

The need for a museum became acute in 1957 because of the planned demolition of that part of the Hotel Mont Cervin which housed the Seiler Collection. The Alpine Museum was constructed within one year, at the cost of 70,000 Swiss francs, and opened its doors in the summer of 1958. The Seiler Collection was incorporated into the exhibits, including the 'Whymper Room'.

The prehistoric stone axe from about 3,000 BC which was found in the Garten towards the Theodul Pass is the museum's most precious exhibit.[1] The collection of Roman coins, horse shoes, chains, etc. disgorged by the glaciers may be found upstairs. The human bones found near the railway station date from about 1,000 BC.

Especially fascinating are the relief models of the valley of Zermatt and the Matterhorn area created by topographer Xavier Imfeld.

There is a picture gallery of the famous who were attracted to Zermatt and its Alps: royalty, politicians, the military and scientists. The captions to the paintings and photographs make the visitor pause and think about the adventurous men and women from far away and from Zermatt, whose lives were marked, and sadly often lost, by their exploits in the area.

The first floor of the Museum is partly taken up with the kitchen of a 17th century chalet, the family home of the Taugwalders, the first Zermatters to stand on top of the Matterhorn (father and son accompanied Whymper on his ascent). What could be more evocative than this room, authentic in all details? Perhaps the cheesery exhibited nearby, which has been moved lock stock and barrel from a

1. See the chapter: 'The Glacier Garden of Dossen'.

19

chalet in Eggen on the Findleralp?

In the ski section the visitor may well marvel at the first snowshoes and skis with their leather thong bindings and rudimentary sticks. A striking contrast to the modern equipment which helped local ski aces to win their place in the Museum's gallery of the famous.

In the Alpine Museum of Zermatt reposes the reality behind the myth, and tokens of the courage, elation and sorrow brought about by man's fascination for one mountain, the Matterhorn.

ZERMATTERHOF

★ ★ ★ ★ ★

GRAND HOTEL ZERMATTERHOF, *Discover the Splendour*
Tel: 028 661100 Fax: 028 674842 Telex: 028 472145

St. Mauritius - The Parish Church of Zermatt

THE PARISH CHURCH of Zermatt is unlikely to get a mention in a specialised guide to Fine Arts, nor would Zermatt attract visitors for the sake of studying the architecture of St. Mauritius. The design by Adolf Gaudy, native of eastern Switzerland, is conventional, conformist rather than controversial, in keeping with the architecture of the beginning of our century. But the church is living witness of faith and prayer. Many hundreds of people, from Zermatt itself and from all over the world, come here for silent prayer or to attend divine services.

St. Mauritius was constructed between May and October of the summer of 1913, just before the first world war. The Great War, together with a subsequent 'flu epidemic, held up any interior work until 1920, when the church was first painted. The architect favoured dark, tomblike shades, and the nave, crypt and baptistry combined to create a muted atmosphere to the whole.

All this changed in the course of the great renovation in 1980. Light and airy colours were chosen to express the religious tenets of the Baroque period: Rejoicing on this earth, and hope of eternal life. The ceiling is adorned with a fresco depicting Noah's ark in a contemporary setting, which was designed and executed by the Florentine painter Paolo Prente. The decorations are in keeping with the three Baroque altars, richly ornamented with traditional figures of saints, which dominate the interior of the church. These were carved out of pitch-pine by craftsmen from the Goms Valley in the Valais between 1730-1752. This wood is very soft and easy to carve and contains a special resin, which not only gives off a typical scent, but also keeps the voracious woodworm at bay, ensuring almost 'eternal life' for the three altars.

The tower, 53.8m high, holds 6 bells, which may be rung in many subtle combinations to announce to the mountains and valley the joys and sorrows in the life of the village. The golden cockerel atop the tower is an excellent weather forecaster: In the anxious wait for snowfalls, which are the pre-requisite for a successful winter season, it is the weather cock at 'south-west' which announces that snow is on its way!

The installation of the new organ completed the renovation. The instrument has 2 manuals and 25 stops and a mechanical movement with tracker action.

The cost of the renovation carried out between 1980 and 1982 came to nearly 4 million Swiss Francs, ten times more than the original cost of the building at the start of the Century. As no church tax is levied in the canton Valais, there were no official funds to draw upon. Amazingly, all the monies needed were donated by inhabitants and guests of Zermatt.

Our thanks go to Ivo Kronig, the Librarian of the Public Library of Zermatt, Historian and Theologian, to whom we owe the text.

THE BIRTH OF THE BURGER GEMEINDE

I N 1991 ZERMATT celebrated 200 years of the coming together of the small independent hamlets of Mutt,[1] Wynchilmatto, and Hoffen and the inhabitants of the region of Aroleyt. The families who lived there were accordingly referred to as the 'Hoffero', 'Aroleytero', 'Wynchilmattero', and 'Muttero': names of a strong, sturdy people.

1791 saw the birth of what is today the parish of Zermatt. Counting meadows, mountains and glaciers, Zermatt with its surface area of 24,366 hectares is the third largest parish in Switzerland.

The history of Zermatt begins in far distant days. We pick up the threads in the 15th century, at the period when Zermatt changed its name from the original Latin name of Prato Borno to Zer Matt. Prato Borno reflects the use of Latin until beyond the late Middle Ages as the language of the Law. 'Prato' in Latin means meadow, or rather 'in the meadow'. Borno is much more difficult to translate, and experts have failed to agree on its meaning. The late Georg Julen who, as one of Zermatt's great historians, was asked to write the history of the Burger Gemeinde in celebration of its 200th anniversary,[2] translates it as 'Matte im Quellgebiet', which means 'meadow in a region of springs'. Zermatt lies indeed in an area rich in springs and water – the Findelbach, the Gornera and the rivers Furgg, Mutt, and Trift all have their source around Zermatt.

In the 15th century the hamlets expanded, and the families went ever further to graze their cattle and cut the meadows for hay. As a result the inhabitants grew closer together, and proximity led to arguments. At last, 'on the 28th day of the Month of Christ in the year 1476', the representatives of the individual hamlets came together and shared out their natural heritage. The meadows, the grazing land, the forest: in short, both the fertile and the barren land, were divided into four, so that each hamlet had its own clearly defined area. A fifth area, from Triftbach to Aruflue, from *Grund zu Grat*, from 'Bottom to Summit', was declared communal ground, or as the people called it then: 'Grindero Gwältsami'. Everyone was allowed to use that common land to graze, to fell a tree, or take out a tree stump, and to hunt for their own personal use. It was forbidden to *sell* any of the produce unless everyone agreed to it.

The barren land was then of great importance, just as it is today. It was the hunting ground and provided extra meat for the families. On the divided land sections, each family could only hunt on its own allocated area. This was not an easy thing to administrate, and arguments soon took place.... Things became even more complicated through marriage settlements. A Wynchilmattero, for example, found himself owning a piece of land in Mutt or Hoffen, if he married a girl from one of the other hamlets. Most of the disputes, however, seem to have taken place between the three more or less united hamlets of Mutt, Wynchilmatto and Hoffen

---

1. Mutt acquired the letter Z in the front of its name, meaning 'by' or 'to', and today the hamlet on the way to the Schönbiel Hut is known as Zmutt.

2. Georg Julen: *Burgergeschichte von Zermatt - Prato Borni.*

against the 'loners' of Aroleyt, who liked to do their own thing.

At last, on 8 March 1555, there was a reconciliation between the people of Zermatt, and a new document was drawn up. The hunting rights over the fifth share of the land, the 'Grindero Gwältsami', were given back to those original owners who could prove their previous ownership. The others lost their hunting rights and were confined to the single area allocated to their specific hamlet. In the 'Grindero Gwältsami' area, those entitled to hunt could take any of the animals which lived there: chamois, hares, deer, ibex, martens, vultures, and partridges. Marmots could not be hunted by the people from Aroleyt, and in return the other three could not hunt the Aroleyt marmots.[3]

In the year 1476, as we saw, the land had been first allocated and divided into small 'parishes', i.e. Hoffen had 39 families, Wynchilmatto 43, Aroleyt 46, Mutt 54.

Zer Matt counted about 900 souls, the number diminishing later on. Although the villagers had the right to run their own affairs to the extent of drawing up legal documents, they were not free citizens. The people of Zer Matt were in the hands of various aristocratic families, who had obtained land and properties originally from the Bishop of Sion. This dated back to the year 999, when Rudoph III of Burgundy had made over the Valais to the then Bishop of Sion, making him sole overlord. In time, parts of the land passed into the hands of ambitious aristocratic families, both local and from neighbouring countries. By the middle of the 16th century the 'Matters' owed their allegiance to three aristocratic families: 115 of them to the De Werra of Visp and Lenk, 39 of them to the Platea or Armengart from Visp, and 35 of them to the Perrinis. The people of Zer Matt also owed the Church of St. Niklaus (or Chanson, as it was then called) a debt, the so-called 'corn tithe', i.e. a tenth of the harvest of barley, corn, rye, etc. The overall situation was complete anathema to the proud and independent minded people of Zer Matt. As the fortunes of the aristocratic families faded, the Zer Matters seized their moment and their chance, and set about buying their freedom.

The De Werras were the first to sell out. On the 1st day of the month of Christ 1538, 115 families bought their freedom for what amounted to 9450 working hours.

On 4 April 1562, 35 families bought their freedom from the Perrinis.

Finally, on the 23rd day of the month of Christ 1618, 39 families bought their independence from Franz de Platea.

The overall cost was 1,800 Möser pounds. A further 4,140 Möser pounds were spent on buying their freedom from the Church. This represented 99,900 working hours at contempory rates, namely 1 'batzen' or 'penny' per hour (13 batzen per Möser pound). This huge sum was paid out within the space of eighty years, from 1538 to 1618. It was an enormous sacrifice, and a testimony to the capacity for work and self-sacrifice by the individual for the good of the community.

3. The original document written on parchment is held in the Burger archives of Zermatt.

THE BIRTH OF THE PARISH OF ZERMATT
AS IT IS TODAY

The legal document drawn up in 1555 lasted for over 200 years. By then the individual hamlets had grown ever closer together. Hoffen (Dorf) and Wynchilmatto were almost one village. The people became closer, even though perfect peace did not always prevail. At last, even the people of Aroleyt were ready to join the others. It was decided to come together and form one parish out of the four existing factions.

The date was 14 June 1791. On 22 April 1792 a further order was agreed upon to consolidate the Parish, under which the forests were added to the common ownership of the burgers. At that time everyone who lived in Zer Matt was a 'Burger of Zermatt', a free citizen who had bought his land from 'Grund zu Grat', from 'Bottom to Summit'. Proud and independent mountain people.

This was not to be the end of a fairy tale, where they lived happily ever after, in peace. They were to be conquered once more and this time by Napoleon. Europe was torn apart by wars, and the people of Zer Matt also had to send soldiers to the army of the Kaiser. Some never returned, having lost their lives on distant battle fields.

Later, in the years between 1802 and 1810, the canton of Valais became an independent republic. But one morning, in the year 1810, the '*Moniteur*' published the following decree:

Art. I: The Valais is united to the Empire.

Art. II: The territory shall form a department under the
            title '*Le Département du Simplon*',

Zermatt became the 'Mairie de Zermatt'. The justification for this act was that the road up the Simplon Pass had cost a vast amount, and that it was a communication line which served more than sixty million people. Napoleon saw it as his duty to ensure and secure this all important thoroughfare by imposing law and order in the Valais.

THE ZER MATT WAR DUES

Although Zer Matt is hidden at the end of a valley, it did not escape the long arm of Napoleon's greedy 'Préfet'. Enormous war dues had to be paid. It was quite impossible to gather all the money demanded, even though every family had to contribute. Pewter wares were added to the money, to try and make up the sum. In the end, even the Church's communion Chalice had to go.

The President of the Burger Gemeinde, Alfons Zumtaugwald, went down to Visp to pay part of the war debts which were owed by the Zer Matters, or Matters as they were called. When he arrived in Visp there were many people there already, waiting to pay their dues. He came forward and explained that he had come a long way, and that the journey back to Zer Matt would be long and arduous. Could he pay first?

Alfons Zumtaugwald proceeded to put money and chattels on the table. The 'Préfet', looking at the waiting queue of people, realised that time was not on his side. He glanced at the heap of money and pewter and thought 'it looked about right'. He pronounced Zer Matt's war debts 'paid off in full'. The Chalice, however, had remained hidden inside Alfons Zumtaugwald's coat or, more likely, his smock. That treasure at least was saved, much to the joy of everyone in Zer Matt who gave their President a hero's welcome.

The people of Zer Matt remained impoverished for a while, but slowly recovered through more hard work and dedication.

After the battle of Leipzig in 1813 the Allies invaded Switzerland, and the Valais was freed under a provisional government.

On 12 September 1814 the Valais became part of the Swiss Confederation (Confederatio Helvetica), as its twenty-fifth canton.

THE LANGUAGE OF ZERMATT

IN ZERMATT, in October 1993, a new book was published with the aim of recording all the old names given to fields and other places in the Zermatt area. These were used by farmers and hunters and later also by Mountain Guides, climbers, and walkers to identify precise locations: paths, meadows, hillocks, rocks and rock ledges all had a name.

The names which have thus been recorded are in the old language of Zermatt.[1] In a previous book written by the late Georg Julen and published in 1984, '*Wörterbuch der Zermatter Mundart*' (a dictionary of the Zermatt dialect), the names applied to and other individual places have already been explained, and the correct pronunciation established. For this latest book the area of Zermatt was divided into five sections. Each section was extensively photographed and the various hamlets, fields, forests, etc. identified on the photographs by a letter and by an explanatory legend. This carefully prepared book acts as a historical record of place names and as a repository of the old language but also as a visual geographical record of times gone by.

Today more than ever perhaps, people are conscious of the need to keep their cultural heritage and traditions and it is this need which gave birth to the book in question. It was a labour of love which involved not only the people whose names appear in the book but the village as a whole. Everybody who could possibly do so contributed to the project by remembering nearly forgotten names and their exact location.

The origins of the old language of Zermatt are obscure and expert opinion differs on the subject. Today, the people of Zermatt still speak their own dialect. It is closely related to Swiss German but it has a number of words which are unique to it. Often, an additional 'a' at the end of a word, pronounced as in Latin and Italian (the neighbouring country's language) gives the language a poetic sound.

In the Swiss German dialect vowels double up, as for example: u + e and i + e. Both vowels are pronounced to lengthen the words - drawing them out in a singing way.

Example: Gut = German for good. In Swiss German it becomes: guet, the 'u' pronounced liked the 'oo' in 'pool', followed by 'e' as in 'per'.

In Zermatt the 'u' becomes like a French 'u': a pointed sound, with the phonetic symbol (y), and the second vowel 'e' is kept and pronounced.

'Gueta Tag' in Zermatt means literally: 'Good Day!' phonetically written 'gyete tag'.

Not such a strange language once you know how it works!

There is no doubt that the unique characteristics of the 'Zermatter Dialect' give the resort an added flavour, and one can well imagine how rich the local legends

---

1. The title of the book is as follows: Orts und Flurnamen der Gemeinde Zermatt by Klaus Julen, Oswald Perren, Alex Taugwalder, Leo Schuler and Beat Perren with Air Zermatt. As a non profit-making project, any revenue from the book will go to the parish library and/or to the Nursing and Old People's Home built in 1987, to ensure that no 'Zermatter' need leave his/her native village, family, and friends.

sound when they are told in their mother tongue.

The people of Zermatt are well aware that they cannot expect their visitors to learn their language in just a few days or even weeks! Thus French and English are learned at school from an early age. Communication is generally not a problem for visitors to Zermatt.

Everyone will try to help.

Margrit Lochmatter
Haus Bolero, Zermatt
Tel: 028 67 33 50
For your holiday apartment
New comfortable flats
With fireplaces and in-house sauna
View to the mountains
A few minutes walk to the Klein Matterhorn Cable Car Station

LEGENDS

HISTORICAL BACKGROUND TO THE LEGENDS

L EGENDS USUALLY HAVE an element of truth in them, and the best thing is that everyone can choose the part they want to believe in. Legends hold many keys to the past as their roots lie in the way things were and in what people believed in. Witches, gnomes, and ghosts existed. The power of the mountain world nurtured fears which were exorcised by making stories out of them. The stories were told before they were written and reflect the language and the characteristics of the people: their sense of humour, their bond with nature which stemmed from the working existence. They kept cattle, sheep and goats as well as pigs and grazed them on the mountain meadows. They tilled terraced fields and grew oats up to a height of 2,200m. They went into the forests to fetch their fuel, mindful of what they took from the land.

Always present in the background of the Zermatt legends is religious faith.

The long winter months, when the village was often cut off for weeks at a time by heavy snowfalls, encouraged story telling. Although Zermatt has changed beyond recognition since those days, the art of story telling has not died out. Many local people, especially after a good glass of Fendant, can tell a very good tale.

It can be very rewarding to delve into the historical past of Zermatt and to find clues regarding the origins of the various legends. In the case of the legend: 'Karl and his Womenfolk', there is evidence that some of the men of Zermatt left the village and went off to fight in distant lands. Extracts from the Church Register provide a wealth of information.

That communications must have been slow to reach Zermatt is obvious – Zermatt, a village at the very end of a steep Alpine valley in the days before roads and rail. It took six years for the news of Johann Anton Aufdenblatten's demise to get to Zermatt. He died in 1732, and the news reached the village in 1738.

The legend of 'Karl and his Womenfolk' is, like many legends, told in different ways. In one version, Karl the Sacristan comes across as brave and decisive from the beginning. In the other, it is the women who provide the courage and the inspiration which led to victory.

The women of Old Zermatt did not have an easy life. Farming was hard in the Alps and the women accomplished many tasks. As a tribute to their courage we have chosen to tell the second version. Part of the earthy character of the language is inevitably and sadly lost in translation. In an effort to retain as much of the atmosphere of Old Zermatt as possible, we have tried to keep the English text in line with the German words. Some additions to the stories were made possible, as we were privileged to listen to the legends told to us by the people of Zermatt. There are over forty such legends, and we have chosen three of them as an example of what they all offer.

KARL AND HIS WOMENFOLK

This story took place in times of great hardship. All the men of Zermatt had gone to war and only the women, the vicar, and the Sacristan remained in the village. No news came from outside. The women and the girls took care of the housework, of the cows, the goats and the sheep. They did everything.

But one night, refugees came over from the Aosta Valley into the village and brought news that the 'Augsttaler' (inhabitants of the Val d'Aosta, on the south side of the Theodul Pass) were arming themselves to come and loot Zermatt and its entire valley.

'They've assembled in Valtournanche and they know that the men have left Zermatt. They'll be here in two to three days. There are lots of them and they're well armed.'

The women rushed over to the Sacristan to tell him what the refugees had said. The Sacristan was helpless. He did not know what to do in the absence of the men of Zermatt. He sat down on a rock and cried. There is a saying that the rock is still wet from his tears to this day.

But then the women got together and spoke out:

'Why should we cry? Let us fight. We'll defend ourselves. Let the 'Augsttaler' come. They'll see what they're up against. Haven't we got two arms and don't we work like men? We'll defend ourselves like the men. You lead us Sacristan, and we'll go to war with you.'

The women and the girls assembled as fast as they could, armed with scythes, flails and hayforks and set out to meet the enemy with Karl the Sacristan bravely in the lead. No one wanted to leave, however, without first going into the Church to pray.

The procession climbed up past Hermetje (an area above Furi and Aroleid), towards the Gandegg Hut. The brave women and girls from Zermatt struck camp on the last meadow where grass still grows before giving way to scree and rock.

In the meantime, the 'Augsttaler' began to have doubts about the rumours regarding the absent men of Zermatt and sent spies across the Theodul Pass to make sure that the coast was clear. Suddenly the spies spotted the crowd of women sitting on the grass, chatting away. Only, they could not tell from a distance that they were looking at women. They could not work out what was going on and they caught fright. They ran back and reported to their captain who decided to send a party of negotiators to try and come to an agreement with Karl the Sacristan. 'What kind of soldiers have you got here?' they asked him.

'They are very brave men from the Visp Valley who have heard about your disgraceful deeds and who are ready to beat you on the battle field.'

'But why have they all got such big breasts?'

'It is their courage which swells their breasts,' Karl the Sacristan replied, 'and you either negotiate now or you'll all be dead.'

There was nothing for them to do but to negotiate and the 'Augsttalers' left and went home over the Theodul Pass.

It was with great joy that Karl the Sacristan was able to relay the news of the victory to his valiant flock. All were filled with happiness and gratitude to God. They knelt and prayed, and whilst they were praying their weapons, the scythes, the flails, and hayforks turned green and the meadow looked like a garden flowering, which it still does to this day.

The deeds of these brave women and girls have lived on amongst the people of Zermatt and are told again and again in the story of 'Karl and his women folk'.

THE STRANGE DREAMS OF A MAN FROM FINDELN

A Zermatter[1] who lived in the region of Findeln, on the grassy slopes below the Findeln Glacier, had dreamt three times already that he would find his luck on the great bridge of Sion, down in the Rhône valley.

One day, as he went to the market in Sion he remembered his dreams and thought of the fortune he was to meet on the bridge. As he had time on his hands after concluding his business at the market he set off to look for the bridge. The bridge in question is not an easy one to find because the 'Grand Pont', as it is called, meaning the Great Bridge, is nothing other than a road under which runs the river Sionne before flowing into the Rhône.

Our Zermatter searched everywhere for the large bridge, looked around and asked people he met. Everyone just seemed to laugh at him. Suddenly a man walked up to him and said

'What are you looking for?'

'I'm looking for the big bridge'.

'Why on earth would you want to find that bridge?' asked the man.

So the Zermatter told him about his three identical dreams. The man burst out laughing and called him a fool. 'I, too, had a dream.' He said. 'I dreamt that in Findeln there is a 'Stadel'[2] with a treasure buried in the walls. I don't even know where Findeln is and I don't think about a treasure any longer. Now, don't be a fool and go home.'

The Zermatter went home. The Stadel in Findeln belonged to him. He demolished the wall and found quite a lot of money hidden there. He was able to repair his house, buy cattle and a few more things and lead a life free of worries, together with his wife and children.

The number of legends related to the Findeln area is vast. This is where the poor souls of the departed make penance. Why there and not on the other surrounding glaciers? No one knows.

Stranger still is that the legends which are told about the Aletsch Glacier[3] are often the same as the ones told about Findeln.

1. Zermatter = inhabitant of Zermatt. 'Ich bin ein Zermatter' means I am from Zermatt and implies 'I belong to Zermatt' or even that 'Zermatt belongs to me - I carry it in my heart'.

2. Stadel = small stable and/or barn.

3. The Aletsch Glacier is Europe's largest glacier. It flows at the back of the 'Jungfrau', one of the great jewels of the Bernese Alps, from the canton of Berne, into the canton of Valais.

THE LEGENDS OF AROLEID

There are two legends concerning the origins of the name Aroleid – two legends which in turn inspired the Swiss poet and novelist Gottfried Keller to write a poem bearing the same name: Aroleid.

One of the legends tells how in times gone by many eagles nested in the Zmutt Valley on a rock in the first meadows, which acquired the name 'Arofluh' – Aro or Aru being the word for 'eagle' in the local dialect. The eagles of the Zmutt Valley sometimes stole or harmed young lambs and brought sorrow – 'Leid'. Thus the meaning of Aroleid: the eagle's harm, the harm the eagle caused.

Another legend tells the story of a young mother who was working in the fields, her baby lying on the grass near by. Suddenly an eagle swoops down and carries off the baby. He deposits his precious prey on the other side of the Zmutt River and prepares to devour it. But people working in that area managed to free the baby and return it, unharmed. The place where the Eagle set down the baby became known as Aroleid.

The legends are sad, but not too sad, at least when compared to Gottfried Keller's poem. The legends are simple stories, and although the shepherds lose a few lambs, in the second legend the child's life is saved and we have a happy ending.

The reason why this tale inspired such a sad poem lies perhaps in the name Aroleid, a poetic name, tinged with the sadness of a romantic song. The name has a certain magic which lives on. Even one of the great ski runs from Schwarzsee down to Furi – more or less straight down underneath the cable car – is called Aroleid. The region, however, where the legends take place is BELOW Furi. It includes the area around the hamlets of Blatten and Zum See, an area correctly named AROLEIT from the Latin. Gottfried Keller adopts the same 'mistake' as the legends and allows the nostalgic and romantic echo of the word Aroleid (with its 'softer' ending) to weave its way through his poem.

The poem itself may appear simple and straightforward at first glance: the death of a shepherd up in the mountains, on the edge of a steep moraine; his wife, filled with bitter sorrow, perhaps unable to grieve in a proper manner because her husband's body is never found – a fate not uncommon in the then untamed mountain world. Then comes the second tragedy: the one told in the legend. The child is stolen by the eagle and carried off, never to be seen again. In the poem, no one is there to save the child: no happy ending.

The reader may almost be taken in by this apparent simplicity but then questions form themselves. Is it possible that an eagle, however strong and powerful, could push a man down a mountainside, except perhaps by terrorizing him? A mystery surrounds the death of the shepherd. Was the eagle there at all, let alone responsible for what happened? There is no doubt about the presence of the eagle in the second tragedy: The poet addresses himself directly to the reader to describe the scene of the abduction of the child by the Eagle. The woman, however, sees only the last of the swaddling band floating away – the last image of her child who will never be returned to her, not even in death, and because of this there can be no real mourning.

AROLEID
A POEM BY GOTTFRIED KELLER

Im Wallis liegt ein stiller Ort,	*In the Valais there lies a silent place*
Geheissen Aroleid;	*Known as Aroleid,*
Es seufzt ein Gram im Namen fort	*A lingering sorrow sighs in the name*
Seit lang entschwund'ner Zeit.	*From times long since vanished.*
Ein Berghirt hing in Tod'sgefahr	*A mountain shepherd hung on the verge of death*
Am steilen Firnenrand,	*On the steep edge of the moraine.*
Ihn stiess hinunter dort der Aar,	*The Eagle pushed him down from there*
Wo keiner mehr ihn fand.	*To where no one ever found him again.*
Auf grüner Matte sass sein Weib;	*Upon a green field sat his wife;*
Das Kind ins Gras gelegt,	*Lay the child upon the grass,*
Sass sie und schaut' mit starrem Leib	*She sat, her body rigid and looked*
Hinüber, unbewegt,	*Across, motionless.*
Hinüber, wo im Dämmerblau	*Across, where in the dusky haze of blue*
Der Berg zur Tiefe schwand	*The mountain faded towards the abyss*
Und mit des Gipfels Silberau	*And with the summit bathed in silver*
So still am Himmel stand.	*Stood silently against the sky.*
Voll bitt'rer Sehnsucht sprang sie auf	*Full of bitter longing she leapt onto her feet*
Und ging im Mattengrün	*And went into the green of the field*
Mit schwankem Schritt und irrem Lauf	*With swaying steps and a crazed run*
Und heissem Augenglühn.	*And hot burning eyes.*
Da schreit ein Kind, ein Flügel saust	*There screams a child, the roar of a wing*
Wohl über ihrem Haupt -	*Well above her head -*
Mit ihrem Kind zur Höhe braust	*With her child soars into the heights*
Der Aar, der es geraubt.	*The Eagle who had stolen it.*
Noch sieht das Wickelband sie weh'n	*She sees the last of the swaddling band floating*
In der krystall'nen Luft,	*In the crystalline air*
Dann sieht sie's wie ein Pünktlein steh'n	*Then she sees it like a dot*
Im Ferneblauen Duft,	*In the distant fragrant blue.*
Dann nichts mehr, nie, so lang sie lebt!-	*Then nothing more, ever, as long as she lives!*
Sie nahm kein Trauerkleid;	*No mourning she wore,*
Doch von dem Leid, das dort noch weht,	*But from the suffering which there remains*
Der Ort heisst Aroleid.	*The place is named Aroleid.*

'No mourning she wore'. Nothing for her as long as she lives.

There is no consolation in Keller's poem and yet, the use of colours, the carefully chosen tones of blue and silver, create a landscape bathed in a kind of haze which exudes ethereal beauty and lifts the poem out of despair into deep poetic sadness and we, the reader, are left with a glimmer of hope - perhaps it was just a bad dream .....

GOTTFRIED KELLER

Gottfried Keller (1819 - 1870), Swiss poet and novelist, was born and died in Zürich. At the age of twenty one he left Switzerland for Munich to become a painter. He was not successful, but no doubt his love of painting sharpened his powers of observation and played an important part in his subsequent writing career. The poetic and artistic use of colour and coloured atmosphere in his poem 'Aroleid' which is included here in this book reflects this.

Gottfried Keller went back to Germany to study at the Universities of Heidelberg and Berlin where he read History, Philosophy and Literature. On his return to Switzerland he was elected Secretary of State for Zürich, a post he held until his death.

Perhaps his most important work is 'Der Grüne Heinrich', which is autobiographical.

As far as poetry is concerned, he published two volumes: one entitled simply 'The Poems' (in 1846) and the other 'The New Poems' (in 1851).

He also published a book on Legends entitled 'The Seven Legends'. It is his interest in legends which manifests itself in the poem 'Aroleid' based on the Zermatter legends.

DAS FACHGESCHÄFT

IN

ZERMATT

**perren-
barberini
photo
optik
papeterie**
zermatt 3920

Landeskarte der Schweiz 1: 25 000
Specialist maps published by the Federal Office of
Topography available here.

THE MATTERHORN.

SPORTS FOR EVERYONE

TENNIS

THE NINE TENNIS courts of Zermatt are situated at the heart of the village with the Matterhorn in full view, looking on, distant and benevolent in an encouraging mood. In spite of their central location the tennis courts are quiet and in a small world of their own, almost a kind of secluded oasis. Here, Zermatt has kept the look and atmosphere of a small village.

There are spectator benches – Zermatt's traditional red painted benches – around the courts. A children's playground with swings and a climbing frame is close by; table tennis and a café and restaurant facilities are also within the complex.

The tennis courts were restored in 1992 and covered with synthetic lawn carpeting and a layer of quartz sand. This substantial investment has brought great advantages for the players. Not only is the surface quick drying which allows play to resume within half an hour after rainfall, but it also reduces the risk of injury. The surface is designed to 'give', and thus to prevent an extreme stop which jars the back and knees.

The tennis centre offers coaching facilities and everyone is welcome, children included.

In the high season of July and August, courts need to be booked a day ahead. There are no weekly bookings, which ensures greater flexibility and opportunity for all players and guests of Zermatt. Guest tournaments are held every Thursday in July and August. Entries are requested by 4 o'clock on Wednesdays, the day before the event.

The Tennis Club also organises three to four competitive events a year where the participants are qualified tennis players, holding a licence.

For further information please telephone the tennis centre on (028)·67 36 73. Many hotels also have their own tennis courts, including indoor facilities.

All these splendid amenities make Zermatt one of the great tennis centres of the Alps.

MOUNTAIN BIKING

Mountain biking is one of the fastest growing sports.

Zermatt provides scenic and varied mountain bike trails which are clearly marked with official signs. This has been done in order to avoid 'a conflict of interests' between walkers and mountain bike enthusiasts, and to ensure safety for all concerned. According to Swiss road traffic regulations, a trail must be at least

2m wide before it may be used by bikers and walkers alike.

It is also important to remember that all bikes must be equipped with the appropriate accessories the law requires. Most important are lights and a bell. In a car-free resort such as Zermatt, guests tend to feel unthreatened by traffic and are therefore mostly unaware of the potential danger of the speedy mountain bikes.

Zermatt is a wonderful place for mountain biking.

Route A: Cycling to the top of Schwarzsee and back, that is to say as close to the Matterhorn as you can get, is very exciting.

Route B: Mountain biking across the valley from the Matterhorn: Zermatt-Ried-Patrullarve-Tuftern- Sunnegga-Wildi-Moosjesee-Gant-Grindjisee-Stellisee-Fluhalp or Blauherd. Return via the same route. NB: there is no connecting trail between Blauherd and Sunnegga.

Full size views of the Matterhorn provide a stunning backcloth to enhance the experience of biking in Zermatt.

Mountain biking is a real fitness sport and Zermatt is a an inspiration to fitness.

A map showing the mountain bike trails may be obtained from: the offices of the Municipality of Zermatt, the tourist office or specialist shops.

HELI SKIING IN SPRINGTIME

SPRING SKI TOURING - A GUIDE'S RÉSUMÉ

As a rule spring skiing begins mid-February and ends mid-May. There exist many options for the enthusiast to ski off-piste in the spring:

Day-tours (with guide) with ascents of one to three hours to be followed by long descents over extensive, imposing glaciers. To give a few of the choices available:

From	Ascent	Descent
Klein Matterhorn	to Schwarztor	via Schwärzegletscher
Klein Matterhorn	to Schwarztor	to Italy
Klein Matterhorn	to Breithorn	via Theodulgletscher
Stockhorn	Schwarzberg - Weisstor	Saas - Almagell
Stockhorn	Cima di Jazzi	Findelgletscher
Sunnegga - Blauherd	Pfulwe	Täsch

Ski-tours lasting several days, and which pass through the solitary world of the glaciers.

Helicopter skiing at over 4,000m.

To maximise descent time, a helicopter air-lift to the starting point may be the answer.

Seven out of the 48 official helicopter landing pads in the Swiss mountains are suitable for heli skiing, and out of this number, four are situated near Zermatt:

Departure Zermatt	Monte Rosa	4,200m
Departure Trift	Aeschihorn	3,600m
Departure Täsch	Aeschihorn	3,600m
Departure Täsch	Alphubeljoch	3,800m
Departure Saas Fee	Alphubeljoch	3,800m
(in the neighbouring valley)		

More than one flight can be arranged on any one day, eg:

1st flight	Aeschihorn and departure to Trift
2nd flight	Trift to Alphubeljoch and descent to Täsch
3rd flight	Monte Rosa and descent to Zermatt

All routes given above are off-piste and harbour many dangers. They should be followed only under the protection of a Mountain Guide who will be able to propose alternative routes, should the weather close in.

**For all information contact the Bergführerverein,
Zermatt (Mountain Guides' Association)
Telephone from UK 00 41 28 67 34 56
or Zermatt Skischule, telephone from UK 00 41 28 67 54 44**

SUMMER SKIING

Zermatt offers the largest area of summer skiing in the Alps. When the cable car to Klein Matterhorn (arrival platform at 3,820m) was finished in 1979, it opened up a whole new expanse of glacier area, amongst stunning scenery, to summer skiers. A network of ski-lifts ensures a good variety of runs as well as some excellent training slopes, especially in the valley-like landscape between the Gipfellift and Testa Grigia.

This area is often used by various national ski teams in their training for the next winter season. It is not uncommon to see the Swiss National Team hurtling down the slopes, each racer's every move monitored by a video camera, and carefully watched by the trainers. Good spectator sport ....

Summer skiing can be an ideal time to introduce beginners or children to this thrilling sport. A warm or hot sunny day offers extra encouragement for the beginner and there is no stiffening of the limbs due to winter cold. The Zermatt ski school organises 'summer ski school packages' for all skiers, including children from six to sixteen years of age. The classes, however, can only operate with a minimum participation of four to five persons. Private tuition is also available.

A word of caution: it is worth remembering that sudden drops in temperature, should the weather turn, can make a difference of 20°C. Flexible, layered clothing, hat and gloves are always recommended. Apply sun cream (total block advised) at **all** times, and wear sunglasses which are indispensable to avoid permanent damage to the eyes.

But overall, Zermatt enjoys a good climate with low rain fall. Here, there should not have to be unending speculation about the weather, but cheerful optimism that it will remain fair.

Throughout the summer season a sudden drop in temperature, combined with a fresh snow fall, provides perfect, winter like snow and skiing conditions. On days like these, when the snow clad mountains become inhospitable for climbers, summer skiing provides an exciting alternative. In any event, skiing included in a summer holiday is fun and provides good sport.

The Ski School office is open from 17.00h to 19.00h in July and August. The summer ski-lifts usually operate, depending on the snow and weather conditions, daily until approximately 14.00h. For further information contact the Ski School by telephone:

From UK 00 41 28 67 54 44, from Zermatt 67 54 44
or write to the Secretary, summer Ski School, CH3920 Zermatt.

Remember to check that your insurance covers you for summer skiing.

For the reluctant walker a morning on the ski slopes and an afternoon combining the deckchair, the swimming pools, and the tennis courts form the basis of a wonderful holiday.

GOLF WITHOUT A GOLF COURSE

This is what awaits the participants in the Eagles Cup, the golf tournament of Zermatt. Although there is no golf course in Zermatt itself, golf is a great favourite with many of the inhabitants. This gave birth to the idea of alternative golf.

No greens and no putting!
Natural golf played amongst the most beautiful mountain scenery,
in the wild and unspoilt territory of rocks, streams and Alpine meadows.

The first of the competitions, aptly named the Eagles Cup, took place in 1992 from Schwarzsee down to Stafelalp, at the foot of the Matterhorn. Eighty people, men and women, from as far afield as Australia, the United Kingdom, and Germany took part. It was an unqualified success.

From then on, the Eagles Cup has been played each year, although the venue has been altered. The competition now takes place on the Gornergrat side, from Rotenboden[1] down to Riffelberg. It is played on a **nine hole course of 3.5km with no green until the final hole**. Each player is restricted to three clubs.

In 1994 the competition was won by a young man from the Swiss canton de

1. Rotenboden is the last train station below Gornergrat.

Vaud, out of over one hundred participants. In this tournament, one of the players – an Englishman this time – had a hole in one, the first in the history of the Eagles Cup.

With the increasing success of the event, a decision may have to be made to limit entries, or to spread the competition over two days. At present, the Eagles Cup takes place at the weekend, with a reserve day.

Zermatt also has mini-golf facilities and **an indoor driving range**.

A holiday in Zermatt need not be a holiday without golf.

For further information contact:

Julen-Sport
(opposite the top end of the tennis courts)
Tel. from UK 00 41 28 67 43 40, fax 67 79 55.

or contact the Tourist Office in writing.

Our thanks go to our golf consultant, Mrs. Judith Lunt.

SWIMMING

Swimming pool facilities are an important part of the sporting scene in Zermatt.

Fifteen hotels have their own swimming pools, of which eight at least are open to the general public, enabling flat dwellers as well as hotel guests to relax after a day's walking, biking, or skiing, or to cool down after the excitement of a tennis match ....

Other facilities included in some hotels and in all the de luxe first class establishments are: whirlpool, sauna, and steam baths, jet stream and fitness gyms. Swimming lessons are available in the Hotel Schweizerhof on an individual or group basis.

There is open-air swimming in the Leisee at Sunnegga Here you may paddle and swim in the waters of a sparkling mountain lake, which lies in the palm of a green plateau. The lake rests on a viewing terrace of its own, with the Matterhorn and the mountain giants of the western chain of summits in full view.

A perfect place for a picnic and for sunbathing whilst absorbing the beauty of the surroundings and filling one's lungs with pure Alpine air.

PARAGLIDING

The sport of paragliding is not even 10 years old. It all began in the mid 1980s, when French parachutists, for fun, walked off the steep cliffs of their Atlantic coast, parachutes propped open, to glide using the support of the thermal air streaming up along the cliffs. On hearing about the doings of the French, Laurent de Kalbermatten of Monthey in the Lower Valais was first intrigued, and then enthusiastic enough to go into the commercial production of paragliders.

The new sport caught the imagination of adventurous men and women alike and went on to become a 'boomsport' in 1988. At that time the many paragliding schools in Switzerland could not accommodate the numbers of applicants. At present there are over 30,000 delta- and para-glider pilots in Switzerland, and the numbers are growing.

The appearance of paragliders has changed completely over the years. The challenge of getting the correct balance between safety and performance is renewed with each technical development and the introduction of new materials.

Zermatt has attracted paragliders for some years, but the difficulties of the high altitude region should not be underestimated. When strong winds are blowing (such as the Föhn), all flying has to be suspended. This is a frequent occurrence, and paragliders are strongly advised to inform themselves about the characteristics of the Zermatt area before taking off. There are many active thermals in the region. Flights lasting several hours and reaching altitudes of 4,000m are commonplace between late spring and early autumn, in breathtaking scenery, majestically dominated by the Matterhorn. The flight from the Unter Rothorn to Zermatt in the tandem glider with an instructor remains an unforgettable experience. No training is needed for an enthusiast to become airborne under the care of an experienced pilot. The only requirements are that the passenger be equipped

      with warm, windproof and waterproof clothing
      with solid footwear, such as walking boots
      and with a good pinch of courage!

Areas for paragliding flights:

Route:	Unter Rothorn (3,100m)	Riffelberg (2,550m)
Starting place:	close by the mountain station	below Hotel Riffelberg
Landing place:	Galerie Bahnhof Zermatt (1,600m)	Galerie Bahnhof Zermatt or Furi
Starting direction:	south, west	south, west, north
Please note:	Observe exclusion air corridors.	rarely used in winter due to crosswinds.

For details please apply to

TOM'S 2PLACE
LICENSED TANDEM PILOT
ZERMATT
TELEPHONE 028 67 35 89

SPORTING CLIMBING
AT THE KLETTERGARTEN

Departure Point: ZERMATT - GORNERGRAT BAHN (Exit Riffelberg)

The Klettergarten of Zermatt is in the area between Gagenhaupt and Riffelhorn. The climbing routes are on a rock face which can be reached by abseiling 30m, or 20m abseiling plus some Kletterei (a 50m rope is recommended).

The Klettergarten has 8 routes graded from IV to VII+. The routes, over excellent rock, vary from between 80m to 140m in length and are well secured with pinions.

The area has the great advantage of catching the early sun. The dew dries quickly and the rock soon feels warm and inviting. It is a great privilege to be able to indulge in sporting climbing in surroundings of such immense grandeur and beauty: one of Europe's most spectacular panoramas of ice-covered summits, the Matterhorn in the distance, followed by the giants on the west side of the Zermatt valley.

The sport owes much to Philipp Biner, Kurt Lauber, Robert Andenmatten, Andreas Perren, and Gianni Mazzone: the Mountain Guides who, together with Anjan Truffer were mainly responsible for opening up the routes and introducing to Zermatt yet another 'boomsport', namely
SPORTING CLIMBING.

THE GEOLOGY OF ZERMATT

G EOLOGY IS A VAST, specialist subject, and the geology of the Zermatt area is so rich and complex that one chapter alone can hardly do it full justice. For the uninitiated, the spectacular mountain scenery, with snow and ice capped summits, jagged peaks and, above all, the Matterhorn, can be the catalyst for a life-long interest in geology.

The Alps were created, 90 million years ago, as the result of the collision between the African and European tectonic plates. Zermatt displays better than anywhere else in the Alps the effects of that collision. Here, the lines of fusion between the two continents took place at the level of the mountain ranges, and the scars, or geologically speaking, the sutures, are clearly visible.

Few regions in the Alps contain such a wealth of minerals and rocks. Since the beginning of modern science geologists have probed the visible surface in search of greater knowledge and understanding of the various rock structures and their chemical composition. (In geological terms, relatively shallow digging).

The mountains we see are only small protruding teeth, whose roots and history go deep into the earth's crust, where their secrets have remained for so long. The last forty years, however, have seen the development of 'in depth' geology. Through the use of new techniques, seismic instruments have brought a wealth of information to the surface.

Tremors and explosions create sound waves which penetrate deep into the earth's layers. The *echoing* sounds reach the surface, where they are captured by sensitive instruments which are capable of recording up to 20 signals per second. Up to 400 'Geophones' (!) can be used in the registration line. Millions of these signals, combined together and analysed, enable the scientists to build up a precise picture of deep regions, impossible to observe by eye. The last guesswork aspect of geology is disappearing, to be replaced by a precise science.

As a result of this significant progress, a National Research Programme was set up in 1985, entitled 'Exploration of the Geological Depth Structure of Switzerland', for short PNR20. The project took off in 1986, and hundreds of earth scientists began their search to discover the fundamental and hidden structure plans of the Alps. In doing so, they explored the whole of Switzerland's underground base. The budget: 14.5 million Swiss Francs. The brief: an in-depth search of the continent, from the North Cape to Tunisia, down to a depth of 60km.

In May 1994, the first findings were published and immediately created a sensation. Geologically speaking, the Matterhorn is of African origin, i.e. it was part of the African plate.

It has now been proven that the African plate slid over and above the European plate, during the collision of the two continents, 'giving birth' to the Alps, a process which spanned 60 million years. The two geological plates were pushed together, interlocked, and folded within the 'convergence zone', rose and exposed themselves to erosion.

At the same time, the new researches confirmed that the Alps are growing by

1mm a year, as they are subjected to continuous pressure, even though the collision is nearly at an end. At this moment in time, the African plate is still moving north and the Central Alps are moving south, contrary to the general direction of the 'push'.

FOR THE VISITOR to Zermatt the geological fascination lies in the visible world. Most, if not all, come to Zermatt to see and admire the Matterhorn: a giant amongst mountains, which rises alone in solitary splendour. It has the shape of an eye tooth, with the point seemingly sheared off, to allow, or perhaps even invite, man to stand on the top. Invite man? Not so long ago, until the last century, mountain people believed that demons and ghosts inhabited the high peaks. Mountains were not to be climbed, for who knew what mystery they harboured?

FOR THE GEOLOGIST, the Matterhorn is nothing but a 'Gigantic Ruin'.[1] Modern scientists have known for a long time that it is the process of erosion which shaped not only the Matterhorn, but the entire Alpine landscape.

IN ZERMATT

Even to someone for whom a rock is a rock, the infinite variety of colours, the shapes and tortuous or clean lines within the rock faces attract and hold the eye.

On the way from the hamlet of Zmutt to the Schönbiehl Hut, in line with the Obergabelhorn, we counted and identified eight different sorts of metamorphic rock fragments and a couple of rocks from the original African crust within one square meter. The rich variety of colours creates a natural mosaic. Here the sun picks out the glistening silver of the 'Muscovite schist'[2] and the white of marble with particles of crystal.

Other rocks, in other places, reveal their true colours in the rain or under water. The green of the 'Serpentine Rock', whose other name is simply 'green stone', and the brown colourings of ionised grey schist, acquire a life of their own. The beds of clear mountain streams, as opposed to the milky glacier rivers, are like shimmering cascades of multi-coloured rocks.

It is by observing all the different rocks in the Zermatt region that the geological picture of the area emerges, as well as the evolution of the landscape.

ON ONE SIDE, in the Monte Rosa region, granite rocks belong to the European continent.
ON THE OTHER SIDE, in the Matterhorn region, the Dent Blanche, Obergabelhorn, Wellenkuppe, Zinalrothorn and, at the end, the Weisshorn, belong to the African plate. Here the predominant colours are brownish and light green with white dots.
IN BETWEEN, in the regions of Zmutt, Riffelberg, the Theodul Pass, Breithorn, Strahlhorn and Adlerpass, we find green rock (Serpentine rock). On the Ober and Unterer Rothorn, as well as to the west of the village of Zermatt we find greyish schists, i.e. Bündnerschiefer,[3] all of which stem from the ocean deposits, as do the

1. Source: Peter Bearth *Geologischer Führer von Zermatt*, published by the Alpine Vereinigung Zermatt.
2. Schist = crystalline rock formed in layers.
3. Bündnerschiefer: named after the canton Graubünden (in French, Grisons) where it occurs in great quantities.

mud-like sedimentary rocks.

The in-between area of the Zermatt region stems from the bed of a former ocean, named Tethys (after a Greek goddess) which lay between the African and European plates. During the collision of the two continents and the Tethys region, the whole complex was 'brought down' to greater depths by about 50km. The sea-bed originally consisted of mud and pillow lava (volcanic lava which solidified in 'cushion form'). Most of it was transformed beyond recognition into metamorphic rocks such as Serpentine rock, Bündner and Muscovite Schist. The cushion form of the original lava of the ocean bed is still recognisable in the silhouette of the Rimpfischhorn. An example of volcanic rock from the ocean bed of the Tethys can be seen in Zermatt in the park area just below the church, above the river.

TO SUM UP, the internal structure of the mountains in the Zermatt region is due to the collision of the African and European plates. The landscape which we see today, on the other hand, is the result of glacial and water erosion. Glaciers grind the rock down to flat, polished surfaces. Water penetrates into every crack it can find, alternatively freezing and thawing, creating temperature stress: a physical force which slowly causes the mountains to disintegrate.

With thanks to Dr. P. Lehner for his help in putting a great deal of material at our disposal, Dr. P. Heinzmann for collaborating with the texts, and Mr. Willy Hofstetter for his help and support.

Swiss geological survey maps, published in Bern, are available from specialist book shops.
They can also be ordered direct from the Swiss Hydrological and Geological Survey, 3003 Bern, Switzerland.

For a general and practical guide to Swiss geology:
Gesteine bestimmen und verstehen, Ein Führer durch die Schweiz by Peter Heinzmann and Franz Auf der Maur, published by Birkhauser, Basel.
The book is currently only available in German. An English translation is under consideration.
For further information please contact Dr. P. Heinzmann at the Swiss Hydrological Survey address (see above).

ZERMATT AND LAPIS LAZULI

THE MOST POPULAR jewellery made from indigenous semi-precious stones in Switzerland is made from polished lapis lazuli, a complex silicate containing sulphur, of bright blue colour. In Switzerland this mineral occurs – apart from tiny crystals – only near Zermatt. Poor quality crystals of it may be found at 3,400m on the Stockhorn (already part of the Monte Rosa massif), but a seam 100m long and 50m wide was discovered in 1958 below the ridge between Hohtäli and Stockhorn during drilling for the cable. car Gornergrat-Stockhorn. The seam contained wide bands of the most beautiful lazuli rock. There followed a boom in lapis lazuli jewellery.

A few decades before, one of the most competent and loved Mountain Guides of Zermatt, Alexander Taugwalder, had discovered these gentian-blue jewels glowing below the rocky ridge. Sadly Taugwalder fell to his death in an ice avalanche on Monte Rosa in 1952. A shimmering blue cross of lapis lazuli marks his grave, which can be found in the stillness of the cemetery in Zermatt.

We are indebted to Mr. Willy Hofstetter for introducing us to
the late Gerhard Gnehm's documentation.
We would also like to thank Mr. Alfred Kronig of Zermatt for showing us
some splendid examples of lazulite rocks.

THE GLACIER GARDEN OF DOSSEN

YVO BINER OF Zermatt, hotelier and amateur geologist, has always been close to nature and fascinated by the magnificence and mysteries of the surroundings he was born into. It is because he recognised what he saw when he came across a 'glacial pot-hole', that we now have one of the most interesting and accessible geological 'parks' here, in Zermatt. Chance and childhood memories played a great part in this discovery of the glacial pot-holes, which form one of only three known sites in Switzerland.[1]

This is how it all began:

As a young boy, Yvo's father took him on a 'glacier excursion'. It was not something he normally did, and quite why he decided on the outing has always remained one of life's little puzzles. At some stage during their trip on the Gorner Glacier they went into a heavily crevassed area. They jumped across many crevasses, but some of them were too wide for that. Yvo's father had to cut steps into the ice, down into the gaping holes, to where the crevasse narrows, in order to surmount the crossing. Yvo was very scared at times, in spite of being with his father. Afterwards what remained, however, was the memory of the ice and the water: crevasses of blue ice, rivulets, and streams running on the surface of the glacier; stones and rubble strewn everywhere and occasionally the presence of a large angular rock; the contrast between the smooth polished ice inside the crevasses and the pockmarked surface of the glacier, like sandpaper to the touch.

This experience encouraged him to use any spare time exploring the mysteries of the glacial world.

One day in 1966 Yvo Biner, by then an established hotelier, took one of his guests up to the Dossen area to show him the old rock fall where, according to history, the columns for the Chapel at Winkelmatten were extracted from the rock. This is when he stumbled upon a large glacial pot-hole and immediately identified it as such. With a pick-axe and a spade he freed it from the remaining soil until it stood, uncovered for all to see. He contacted the director of the famous 'Glacier Garden' of Lucerne, Dr. F. J. Roesli, who confirmed Yvo Biner's interpretation. It was a most exciting find and one which would lead to many more. Yvo Biner himself dug in the area, carefully removing forest top soil. It was hard work, requiring a great deal of physical strength. At the same time he had to make sure not to damage the edge of the pot-holes. He found a great number of them of various sizes and shapes, beautifully sculptured. The most remarkable of them are deep, smooth, polished cauldron-like formations.

What causes the formation of a 'Glacial pot-hole'?

Because many pot-holes were found with a smooth polished millstone in their middle it was often wrongly assumed that the presence of one such stone, constantly whirled around by water, enabled the formation of a pot-hole. This assumption is now known to be wrong. A polished millstone can be an accessory

1. The Glacier Garden of Lucerne is probably the most famous of these sites.

to the erosion process but not the sole cause of it. Too many empty pot-holes have been uncovered for this to be otherwise.

Jets of glacier water laden with rubble, pebbles and sand, water which has penetrated from the surface of the glacier down to its rock base, is responsible for the glacial pot-holes. The water also picks up the rubble which has collected inside the pot-holes during its resting period, namely during the freeze up of the winter months. The whirling waters start working their new load of stones and dig a deeper and wider pot-hole as soon as the great thaw begins.

Where the water flows along a smooth surface of the rock bed of the glacier, it flows at a slow pace, and there is no whirlpool action. It is when other factors intervene, such as a sudden thaw, or when the water comes across an obstacle in the river bed, that a rotating whirlpool action might arise.

How does the water penetrate through the thick layer of ice down to the rock base of the glacier?

Once the temperature rises in the spring and the sun shines fiercely on to the glacier, the thawing process begins. The winter snow softens and begins to melt into pools or into ever deepening small rivers, according to the gradient of the glacier. The temperature of the water is degrees warmer than the ice itself. It attacks the ice and helps the thawing process which gathers momentum as a result of it.

Streams pour down crevasses, often creating internal lakes at the base of the crevasse. Even where a narrow crevasse closes up again through the movement of the glacier, the constant flow of the water can go on through a system of inner funnels.

Eventually the waters flow out, at the mouth of the glacier, as it is called. Sometimes there is an ice cave, which can be huge and contain several chambers, or maybe a simple arched ice bridge. The waters flow out in a noisy rushing torrent, white in colour. The whiteness is caused by a thin cloud of rock dust which gives the water its 'milky' appearance.

The erosion process which results in the appearance of a glacial pot-hole varies greatly and it is therefore difficult to date a pot-hole's age. Some take years or centuries and seem to have been worked by the glacier at different phases of glaciation. Geologically speaking, however, when we look into a glacial pot-hole we look into the recent past and into a living process, as the formation of new glacial pot-holes can still take place. At the Glacier Garden of Dossen it has been possible to date these even in the absence of precise scientific data regarding the movements of the Gorner Glacier. This represents one of the most exciting aspects of this glacier garden: we know for certain that the large glacial pot-holes date from about 10,000 years ago or even more. Again, fate intervened in favour of the geologist. Large, century-old larch trees grow in the area of Dossen and one of these (whose trunk was partially rotten) had to be cut down. It was then discovered that it had grown on top of a large glacial pot-hole. By counting the rings in the trunk of the tree it was possible to establish that the tree was at least four hundred years old which meant that the pot-hole which preceded it was more than four hundred years old, and therefore did not result from the most recent glacial periods of the 17th and 19th centuries.

Yvo Biner worked from 1966 (the date of the discovery of the first glacial pot-hole) till 1974 on the Glacier Garden, at which point it was opened to the public. He painstakingly removed layers of forestry top soil and freed the glacial pot-holes for us all to see and enjoy. He made the paths and erected the protection railings, enabling us to look on one of nature's greatest phenomenon: single pot-holes, the largest one discovered measuring 3.40m in depth and 2m to 3m in width; twin pot-holes, one connected to the next; a good dozen pot-holes in all, large and small, a fascinating sight.

The access to the Glacier Garden is very easy. It is about a 45 minutes' walk along an earth road which was built by the Grande Dixence Electricity Company when it collected the waters of the river Gorner above Dossen. The start of the road is just below Furi station, at the bridge which crosses the Gorner river.

The Glacier Garden is opposite one of the designated family picnic areas in Dossen. For further information enquire at the Tourist Office.

The Quarry of Dossen

In the vicinity of the Glacier Garden you may come across the remains of the old soft stone quarry. A path winds its way past the quarry of 'potstone', a metamorphic rock so soft that you can scratch it with the blade of a knife. The existence of this bed of potstone amongst the great mass of serpentine rock on that side of the mountain enabled the art of stone pottery to develop as far back as 2,000 years ago.[2]

Legend and reality are fused together in the 2,000 year old history of the quarry of Dossen. The story goes that there were men of Herculean strength in Zermatt. A family named Furrer counted several such men. One of them, Anton Furrer, is supposed to have carried great columns of stone dug out of the mountainside at a place called Mischisand near the river Gornera below what is today the Glacier Garden. The columns were destined for the Chapel at Winkelmatten as support for the porch.[3] To reach Winkelmatten one had to cross over a smooth rock area. It is recorded that Anton Furrer took off his shoes and socks in order to ensure a safe and strong grip on the rock surface and *carried* the columns, as it was the only way to cross those rocks. The columns were later replaced but they can be seen today in the garden north east of the main Church. To this day one can also see the 'caverns' from which the columns were extracted. One of them is 15m deep, about 1m wide, and 2m high.

2. The soft stone known as 'Lindfluh' in Zermatt was worked into pots and cooking utensils. Workshops were on the site of the quarry itself and at Furi as well as in Zermatt. (Many fragments were discovered when the Hotel Monte Rosa was extended.) Because the 'Potstone' holds and diffuses heat it was also used to make heating stoves. One such stove would have been enough to heat an entire living accommodation.

Examples of stone pottery, all of it from either Dossen or the workshop at Furi are housed in the Alpine Museum of Zermatt, a 'must' for every visitor.

Opening times: summer 10.00h – 12.00h and 16.00h to 18.00h. Closed Saturdays.

3. The Chapel of Winkelmatten is a short distance above the village of Zermatt, about 100m off the Zermatt-Furi road, before the bridge on the way to Moos.

CHALETS AND STADELS

ONE OF THE most attractive features of Alpine villages is the houses and their gardens, where flowers and vegetables grow side by side. Warm and picturesque, the villages have retained their old world charm and intimacy, the atmosphere of days gone by.

As the mountain train winds its way up to Zermatt from Visp, the architecture changes - town houses giving way to wooden buildings and chalets. The very old houses, Stadels[1] as well as the tall, narrow village houses, are immediately recognisable. They are all built of solid, hard-wearing larch-wood, darkened by decades or even centuries of strong sunshine. The unadorned façades have very small windows, designed to conserve as much heat as possible in winter. The sober lines have a great purity. Today's architecture has had to adapt to changing times, losing some of these

aspects. The style of design today is general rather than regional and has resulted in a certain loss of local identity. Chalets and houses have larger windows, usually divided into small squares, to blend in with the old buildings. All have balconies and window boxes, which in summer-time are ablaze with flowers. Geraniums are the main favourite, but petunias, tiny yellow and white daisies and many other flowers are also used to turn the balconies into small, brightly coloured gardens.

The traditional roofs of the old family farmhouses and stables were covered with local slates. This tradition has survived, and there is even a revival of it. In many cases, as tiled roofs wear out, they are replaced by slate. In the smaller villages on the route from Visp to Zermatt, every roof is a slate roof. The same can be said of the beautiful hamlets up on the Alps around Zermatt, which have been restored. Thus they are in keeping with the century-old tradition of using local materials, trees and rocks, to produce a subtle, special kind of harmony between man and nature. The stone suitable for roofing varies in colour as well as density from area to area. The original roofs of Old Zermatt came from the region of Stafelalp and neighbouring quarries. There, the slate is pale grey with brown to green tinges. It is of high quality, hard-wearing and tough. Today, the slate comes from the village of Kalpetran,

1. Stadel = small stable and/or barn.

further down the valley, and is darker and slightly softer, or it comes from Skt. Niklaus and Eisten in the Saas Valley, which is similar to the slate from Stafelalp.

In time, the slate roofs weather. In autumn, they collect the copper-coloured larch needles. Lichen becomes established, so that deep orange and soft bright green patterns decorate the slate.

The Construction of the Roofs

Almost perfectly shaped squares of stone are laid flat, horizontally in a straight line, starting at the bottom, from the middle point. The subsequent lines are hung point downwards to create a diamond shaped pattern, rising up to the apex of the roof.[2] A raised double layer of narrow pieces of slate seals the top of the roof. A snow pole, i.e. a round log, is fixed along the base of the roof to keep the snow from sliding off.

The original stone roofs were single roofs. Today, only the 'Stadels' (barns) are built in this way. Modern constructions have double roofs for insulation. The first roof is made of pine, and the slates are then laid in the traditional manner, leaving a gap of about 10cm between the two. The new double roofs are so well constructed and strong that they never need to be repaired.

It is a tradition that when a new chalet is built and the first roof is constructed, a small pine tree, garnished with ribbons, is fixed to the gable. The local priest is asked to come and bless the house, and there is a traditional feast of wine, local cheese and air-dried meat, to which all who worked on the house are invited. From this point onwards it is considered that the house, if not finished, is at least a shelter, providing some form of protection from the elements.

2. See sketch of Stadel with slate roof.

INSPIRATION MOUNTAIN RAILWAYS
THE BVZ AND THE GORNERGRAT BAHN

THE ORIGINS OF THE BVZ
(BRIG-VISP-ZERMATT)

HE SECOND HALF of the 19th century saw the construction of railways almost everywhere, including the main line between the lake of Geneva and Brig, following the Rhône valley. The next logical step was a mountain railway track to Zermatt, a brave and audacious plan, but a plan which was based on astute economic forecasting. By the 1880s Zermatt already welcomed in the region of 12,000 visitors a year, and the only way to reach the end of the valley was on foot, by mule, or carried in a sedan chair.[1] If so many people, inspired by the romantic movement and the golden age of Alpinism set out on what could be a hazardous journey, how many more would venture into the Alps in the comfort of a train?

So it was that in 1886 Charles Masson from Lausanne (La Banque Masson, Chavannes et Cie) and Konrad Gysin (Basler Handelsbank) were granted the concession to construct a railway from Visp to Zermatt. The authorities made two provisos:

1) A longer summer season than had originally been planned, i.e. from May to October.

2) Local inhabitants were to benefit from concessionary fares.

The first train ran on 3 July 1890 as far as Stalden. In August of the same year the service was extended to Skt. Niklaus thus progressing beyond the 'wild section' of the journey.

On 6 July 1891, the first train pulled into the station of Zermatt: a steam locomotive and wagons running on an adhesion/rack rail track, 100cm gauge, which covered the distance between Visp and Zermatt in 2 hours 40 minutes. The new railway operated with four steam locomotives, bearing the inspiring names of the summits visitors came to view and discover: Matterhorn, Monte Rosa, Mischabel, and Gornergrat.[2]

There were 12 carriages bringing the total of available seats to 592. Added to that were 3 luggage vans and a further six goods vans.

The first season saw the arrival of 33,695 visitors to Zermatt. The railway was a huge success!

This required a fifth steam locomotive, the St. Théodule, followed by others, the Weisshorn, Breithorn and last of all the Lyskamm in 1980, making a total of 8.

1890 was also the year in which two other applications were made, for the construction of the Gornergrat railway, and a project to reach the summit of the Matterhorn.

---

1. The old mule track can still be seen above Stalden between the hamlets of Mühlebach and Kalpetran: a lovely place for a walk which captures the atmosphere of the pioneering days.

2. The steam locomotives were built by the Swiss Locomotive Manufacturing Industry, Winterthur.

Gornergrat-Bahn Zermatt

A world famous beauty spot surrounded by 29 4000m mountain giants

THE 1890 MATTERHORN PROJECT

To conquer the Gornergrat 'by train' was a daring project, but the Matterhorn? The Matterhorn does not appear willing to receive uninvited visitors. It looks beautiful, remote and private. For any engineer to envisage a plan to civilize the mountain must have required tremendous courage, imagination, and optimism. In short, this is how the scheme looked: a continuation of the steam railway was to give way to a funicular at a 55% incline. Then a rack and pinion railway at a 33% incline led for 4.5km along the Hörnli south slope and Furgg glacier to the underground station at 'Whymper's Hut' (altitude 3,140m). Another funicular, this time at an average gradient of 75%, covered the remaining distance of 2.3km with one last change at the half-way point, ending 20m below the summit, where there was to have been a restaurant, viewing galleries, and dormitory facilities.... It never happened.

THE GORNERGRAT RAILWAY

The railway up to Gornergrat did become reality and was the *first electric rack and pinion railway in Switzerland*.[3] Seven years after the Visp - Zermatt line was opened, the Gornergrat railway was inaugurated, on 20 August 1898, operational from June to early October.[4]

There were already three hotels on the way to Gornergrat: the Riffelalp Hotel which opened in 1884, replacing a previous guest-house. The new railway ran some 500 metres from the hotel and the then owner, Alexander Seiler Junior, had to create a means of access through the forest.[5] The only way to acquire the necessary land was to apply for a tramway concession, which he obtained. In 1899, the 468m long Riffelalp tramway was constructed. It travelled on a 0.80m gauge track, for a duration of 3 minutes, at a speed of 8 km/h. Thus, the tramway held two records: it ran over the shortest known distance, and at 2,200m was the highest tramway in the world. Sadly it is no longer in existence since the day a fire destroyed the Riffelalp Hotel whilst it was being restored. A new hotel stands there today, still in the ownership of the Seiler family, and luggage is transported by 'speedy buggies'.

The second hotel, the Hotel Riffelberg, situated above the tree-line on a wide balcony of Alpine meadows, was first built in 1854 by three Zermatters named Kronig, Welschen and Ruden.[6] In 1864 it was extended to increase the beds from 18 to 48. Today, it is the largest of the 'mountain hotels'. It has 60 beds and remains in the hands of the Burger Gemeinde.

The third hotel was the Hotel Belvédère, built in 1896, which also belonged to

---

3. The concession to construct the railway was granted in 1892 to Messrs. Imfeld and Heer. Imfeld was later to give up his share of the concession to the architect August Haag who took over the project in partnership with Karl Greulich.

4. The season of 1929/30 saw the beginning of an extended winter service to Riffelalp.

5. The view of the Matterhorn seen through the trees of Riffelalp forest is unforgettable.

6. Pfarrer Josef Ruden (1817-1882) is one of Zermatt's legendary figures. Zermatt owes him a family chronicle and the inspiration to build its very own hotel: the Zermatterhof.

the Burger Gemeinde. It was pulled down to make way for the Kulmhotel in 1910, the hotel which still stands at the top of Gornergrat, above the last train station, in line with the Stockhorn cable car system. To the hotel was added in 1966 an observatory dome followed by a second one at a later date; this gives a very distinctive shape to the roof of the building which stands out from as far away as across the valley.

In November 1993 the Gornergrat railway took another big step forward in the history of its technical development. It acquired 4 new double drive locomotives and carriages[7] and invested 25 million Swiss Francs in the project. The new engines travel at double the speed, i.e. from 14 km/h uphill to 28 km/h and from 15 km/h to 21 km/h downhill, 'smoothly gliding' along the track and increasing the transport capacity to 2,400 people per hour. Substantial construction work had to be undertaken to make this possible, such as the lengthening of platforms and the strengthening of the 50m high and 90m long Findelbach viaduct, as well as the construction of five new electrical transformer stations.

The Gornergrat Bahn is a success story. The rewards are well deserved for they are the fruit of much courage in the planning and execution of the original project.

A great vision rewarded.

THE BVZ TODAY

Economically speaking, the history of the mountain railways reflects many difficult periods. The first world war saw a collapse of the tourist industry, and the end of the war did not signify a sudden surge in the amount of visitors. Travelling in the inter-war years was made difficult by complicated travel documents and formalities. Recovery was slow.

Meanwhile Zermatt wanted to establish itself as a winter resort. The success of this depended largely on running the railway from Visp to Zermatt during the winter season. There were great difficulties in doing so, as the valley leading to the great mountains and the ski slopes was largely untamed and much more dramatic than it is today. The Visp river carried large volumes of foaming water before the construction of the great hydro-electric schemes. There were floods as well as avalanches which caused much damage to the railway track. Supplementary protection work had to be undertaken to ensure the safety of the railway track, requiring large investments. Besides, in the 1920s steam was being replaced by electricity: a new turning point in the history of the mountain railway and the development of Zermatt.

In the winter of 1927/28 the Seiler Hotel, in those days the Hotel Victoria, decided to open for the first time for Christmas and New Year. On that occasion the railway ran as far as Skt. Niklaus and the guests continued their journey by horse-drawn sledge.

---

7. The locomotives were built by SLM (Schweizerische Lokomotiv und Maschinenfabrik AG) with ABB responsible for the electrical parts.

The following winter a first attempt to run one train a day between December and the end of February was successful, thanks to a mild winter.

Heavy snowfalls in 1930/31 suspended all services beyond Skt. Niklaus and Zermatt. On a temporary basis, horse drawn carriages ferried people as far as Randa. From there the train journey could be resumed thanks to the electricity supplied by the Findelbach hydro-electric scheme, the first such scheme to be built in the Alps.

At the same time as avalanche protections were being built, the planning of the conversion of the BVZ to electricity was well under way. The chosen solution was as follows: 11,000 V, 16.66 HZ, the same as the mountain railways of the canton Grisons Rhätische Bahn and paving the way for an eventual complete railway connection between the two regions. An extension to the narrow track railway line between Visp and Brig was constructed at the same time as the electrification project. The Furka-Oberalp followed suit, and 25/26th June 1930 saw the inauguration of the **Glacier Express**, the narrow gauge mountain train which connects the southern Alps of the Valais to the eastern mountain regions of Switzerland. It is possible to travel from Zermatt to Skt. Moritz and back on an unforgettable day's travel without changing carriages, except maybe for an 'excursion' to the restaurant facilities (but be sure to book your seat *and* meal in advance).

From 1 October 1929 onwards, the railway line Brig - Visp - Zermatt, the BVZ, was totally electrified. The 8 steam locomotives were replaced by 5 electric locomotives. The romantic appeal of the steam engines has, however, remained, and it is still possible to indulge in memories of the past **and travel on a steam excursion**. The Breithorn, the only remaining steam locomotive, will happily puff along on much sought after special journeys.

1933 marked the beginning of an all year timetable. This did not signify the end of technical and other developments. Beside constant improvements in protecting the train line, the railways have had to adapt to changing times. The opening of the road beyond Skt. Niklaus as far as Täsch in 1972 brought about big changes. Most of the train travel now takes place between Täsch and Zermatt, as the majority of visitors drive their cars as far as Täsch. This has resulted in one of the major developments of recent years: the operation of the 'Pendel Zug', a special shuttle train service between Täsch and Zermatt. The trains operate at 20 minute intervals and carry over 1.5 million travellers per year: 66% of the total train users.

1986 saw the introduction of 'step free carriages' on the shuttle trains which enable travellers to wheel their trolleys from the platform onto the train in Täsch and off the train on arrival in Zermatt (and vice versa).

In 1987 an all powerful snow-plough was added to the impressive list of equipment.

In 1990 five new locomotives, Brünig FO, replaced the 1929 machines, 'crocodiles'.

HOTEL RIFFELBERG, *Discover an Original Mountain Palace*
Tel: 028 672216 Fax: 028 673994

KULM HOTEL RESTAURANT, *Discover a Great View*
Tel: 028 672219 Fax: 028 672286

THE JOURNEY FROM VISP TO ZERMATT

To travel from Visp to Täsch is much faster by car than by train. Furthermore, the car journey enables visitors to stop at leisure. The train journey, on the other hand, leads one slowly through the valley and its changing character, from lowland to Alpine scenery, and therefore allows one to savour every moment.

From Visp to Stalden, the valley is similar in character to the Rhône valley. Vines grow as high as the village of Stalden in a hot and dry, nearly Mediterranean climate. Large villages have crept up the mountain slopes and nestle on well cultivated plateaux. Amongst the highest vines in Europe are grown above Visp to produce 'Glacier wine' at an altitude of 1,100m. After Stalden the valley divides into the Skt. Niklaus valley on the one hand, leading to Zermatt, and the Saas valley, leading to Saas Fee, on the other.

The section between Stalden and Skt. Niklaus consists of a gorge and narrow steep-sided slopes. It is the wild section of the journey with the train running close to the river, to rock and eroded mountain faces. Beyond the village of Kalpetran appear the scars of the slate quarries which supply the material for the age old roofs of the Zermatt valley.

Beyond Skt. Niklaus the valley opens up again until Täsch, with many villages along the line. Slopes seen from the train, viewed at leisure from right and left, rise up to become glaciers, a signal for visitors that they are entering the real Alpine world.

Past Täsch the train once again enters a narrow valley, with tunnels and galleries to reach Zermatt. Where is the Matterhorn? Step outside and across to the Gornergrat railway station. From there you will see the summit of the Matterhorn inviting you to walk up the village and admire it in full view and total splendour - just as you expected.

Were it not for the constant care and modernisation of the railway system which ensures an efficient service on the Brig - Visp - Zermatt line, would Zermatt today still be a car-free resort? The answer to this question highlights the debt owed to the mountain railway, the familiar little red snake which winds its way up the valley with endless perseverance and a courage all of its own.

SUNRISE ON THE GORNERGRAT

During the summer season there is a weekly trip to observe the sunrise on the Gornergrat, departure times according to sunrise. Breakfast available at the Hotel Gornergrat-Kulm.

64

INSPIRATION SUNNEGGA

ERMATT'S FIRST SKI-LIFT went from the village, through the forest, up the west facing slopes, to Sunnegga. It was erected in 1942, in the early days of winter tourism. The Sunnegga ski-lift was then the only means of uphill transport apart from the Gornergrat Bahn.

Five years later, in 1947, the ski-lift was replaced by a chair-lift, and the ski-lift itself was moved up the mountain from Sunnegga up to Blauherd: one stage higher, as it were. The new chair-lift could carry 300 people an hour. In 1960 this figure was doubled to 600.

This chair-lift Dorf - Sunnegga (from the village to Sunnegga) was a romantic experience. Each chair carried two people at a time and, unlike the chair-lifts of today, the passengers had their backs to the mountain and faced the view over the village, to the Trift Valley, with the Matterhorn on the left and the Weisshorn on the right.

As winter tourism took off, long queues began to build up at the bottom of the chair-lift. Decisions had to be made regarding the future.

The first plan was to build a Gondelbahn (4 man cabins) next to the ski-lift. This, however, would have meant clearing a second track on the wooded mountainside resulting in deforestation with ensuing avalanche dangers. There was opposition to the plan because of this serious risk to the environment as well as the cost of running two operations side by side.

The second plan was to replace the chair-lift with a Gondelbahn. This would have meant the closure of the existing transport system, i.e. the chair-lift, for nearly a whole year. Besides, the projected maximum transport capacity of the Gondelbahn of 1,500 persons per hour was not sufficient to cover the predicted increase of tourism in Zermatt. This scheme was rejected outright.

The idea of building an underground track funicular/railway was first mooted by the Gemeinderat in 1975, when the vote went against the project, albeit by a small margin, producing an inconclusive result. Because of the closeness of the vote, preliminary planning work on both schemes under consideration continued.

It came to a general vote on 13/14 December 1975, a date which was to mark a turning point in the history of Zermatt's transport system. This is how Zermatt voted for the building of an underground track railway from Zermatt to Sunnegga: 605 'Yes' against 510 'No'. Result: the building of the Zermatt Alpine Metro, as it was first called, was to go ahead, and the Gondelbahn project was abandoned.

The concession was granted by the federal authorities in the summer of 1976. Planning permission was given on 24 November 1976. The list of advantages for the 'metro project' was impressive and proved to be an accurate forecast:

(a) The best ecological solution.
(b) Fast moving trains means fast transportation. The trains can carry 2,540 persons per hour.
(c) Excellent overall security, i.e. no climatic interference.

(d) Emergency access to train passengers at any stage of the journey via a parallel running staircase.

(e) People travel 'on the ground', i.e. the metro offers a real alternative to the airborne travel of Gondelbahns, chair-lifts and cable cars.

(f) Low running and maintenance costs.

(g) No snow clearing problems and ensuing costs.

(h) Finally, the trains can operate in any weather conditions.

Work began in the summer of 1976. The actual tunnelling began early November 1976. The underground area for the entrance/ticket hall and access to the trains was first hewn out of the rock. The upward sloping tunnel from the back of the hall was cut at an ever increasing angle until it could accommodate the 11m long boring machine used to cut the main section. The ejected rock spoil was reduced to rubble with a breaker, washed along a channel to waiting lorries and carted away to a tip on the Täsch Wand. Some of the debris was used as hardcore for the construction industry.

At a meeting in early 1977 the newly elected 'Gemeinderat' (Parish Council) had to put the building of the project Zermatt-Sunnegga on the agenda. One of its tasks was to check the costings. These revealed a substantial shortfall. At the same time, the Burger Gemeinde[1] found itself in a changed position, which precluded it from participating in the project as originally planned.

1. Burger Gemeinde or Burgerschaft: the historical association of the original inhabitants (i.e. the original settlers of Zer Matt), which still exists today. Gemeinde: the modern equivalent of a parish according to the present Swiss constitution.

There was no alternative but to suspend work. An extraordinary meeting was called, at which the question was asked: 'Do you wish the project to continue with a majority participation of the Zermatt Gemeinde?' The outcome was 883 'Yes' against 360 'No', a resounding vote of confidence from the people of Zermatt who were prepared to raise the money to complete a project which had been accepted and was to become a **reality**. A company was set up in May 1977: Standseilbahn Zermatt - Sunnegga AG with the Zermatt municipality holding 59.27% of the share capital.

The building of the underground rail track proved to be a demanding task. All who worked on the project met with great challenges. Costs were ever increasing. In May 1980 a further credit of 8 million Swiss Francs was granted on a unanimous vote. The final figure of the available capital, to cover all costs, stood at 21.5 million Swiss Francs.

On 14 November 1980 the track railway was submitted to a final inspection by the federal authorities. On 21 November, only seven days later, the permit to operate the underground trains was granted.

THE SUNNEGGA BAHN

The tunnel in its entirety is 1,696m long. This includes the 171m of the horizontal tunnel which leads from the entrance hall to the trains.
The 1,525m stretch, i.e. the long uphill tunnel, climbs 689m over that distance, i.e. at an average ratio of '1m up to 2m forward!'
The tunnel's incline is between 36.4% at the departure point and 63.3% at the arrival point.
Platform elevations: lower terminal 1,599m; upper terminal 2,288m.

There are two trains fixed to a cable, on rails with a cog and a pinion in the centre of the track. The effect of gravity on the descending train is used to assist in hauling the ascending train to the top.
The shortest travel time is 3 minutes.
The trains travel at a speed of 10 metres per second.
There is one passing-place.

The Sunnegga Bahn fulfilled all its promise.

SUNRISE ON THE ROTHORN

During the summer season there is a weekly trip to observe the sunrise on the Unter-Rothorn, using the Sunnegga-Express, the Blauherd Gondelbahn and the Rothorn cable car. The round trip ticket includes breakfast at the top.

For further information
Contact the Administration Offices
Sunnegga-Express, Zermatt
Telephone 028 67 22 26

RESTAURANT SUNNEGGA, *Discover a Sunny Place*
Tel: 028 672219 Fax: 028 672286

RESTAURANT ROTHORN, *Discover a Special Cuisine*
Tel: 028 672675

INSPIRATION KLEIN MATTERHORN

T O BUILD THE highest cable car in Europe needed inspiration and a great deal of courage; the technical challenge and extreme climatic conditions could have defeated even the bravest of hearts. Zermatt, in common with other famous Swiss resorts, has a history of great and ambitious schemes. In 1892, a Swiss Federal authority granted the construction licence for an 'aerial tramway' to the summit of the (Great) Matterhorn itself. The deadline for the project was not observed, the licence was revoked and the whole project abandoned - if it had been a serious proposition in the first place! Instead, a few years later, in 1898, the Gornergrat Railway was commissioned and paved the way for Zermatt's remarkable transport infrastructure. The project, which began at the end of the 19th century and developed well into the next century, constantly being updated to this day, was a huge success. The railway provided universal access to the stunning mountain world of the Gornergrat, with views stretching over one third of all the 4,000m European summits. It opened the eyes of the world onto a dream landscape of white summits and flowing glaciers. The commercial success of the Gornergrat Railway encouraged further projects, as well as the development of what are often referred to as 'mechanical aids' to reach areas which in the past had only been accessible to Alpinists and mountain people.

Each development posed, and still poses today, even with all the latest sophisticated technology, its very own challenge. But the cable car 'Klein Matterhorn' is certainly the realisation of one of the great challenges of all times in the history of Alpine transport.

The Klein Matterhorn, altitude 3,833m, was first climbed in 1792 by Horace-Bénédict de Saussure, the famous scientist, whose portrait figures on the current Swiss twenty franc banknote. In Zermatt his memory is honoured by a bronze plaque placed on a large block of granite next to the small chapel at Winkelmatten.

De Saussure climbed the Klein Matterhorn as a scientist. He wrote a detailed geological and mineralogical report. He had already crossed the Theodul Pass three years before, in 1789, accompanied by his son and their guide Marie Coutet of Chamonix.[1] He described the ascent of the Klein Matterhorn as:

'Not without danger, but worthwhile, as an incomparable panorama
unfolds under the eyes of the Alpinist.'

It was this first ascent and those written words which were to open the doors to the beginning of Alpinism. The Theodul region became the meeting place for mountaineers. Much later, its huge potential was recognised as a recreational area, for all year round skiing. It represents eternal snow, situated above the tree-line, outside the restricted zone.[2]

On 5 December 1965 the decision was made to build a cable car up to the top of

---

1. That time he had come to measure the height of the Matterhorn, a feat he achieved with an amazing degree of accuracy.

2. In Switzerland forests are protected by law and must be preserved and maintained (see the chapter 'The Swiss Forest').

the Klein Matterhorn: an aerial ascent from 2,939m to 3,820m. But it took a further eleven years before the construction could begin. Yet, even before the Swiss Company *Von Roll* applied for a construction licence from the relevant Federal Authorities, negotiations were under way between the Swiss Alpine Club and the Swiss Society of Nature, regarding a division of the territorial region into conservation zones and a potential tourist area. Two protection zones were decided upon:

The Monte Rosa region to the west, the Matterhorn region to the east.

The bridging region between the protected zones, namely the region stretching from Schwarzsee over the Theodul Glacier to the Klein Matterhorn was set aside for tourist development. The recognition of two protected areas was not sufficient to silence the voices of protest. Some citizens of Zermatt objected, unsuccessfully, to the development plans by filing a petition to disallow the project with the authorities of the canton of Valais. The Federal Authorities granted the concession to build in 1970, and there was a further appeal against this decision. Inevitably this appeal procedure delayed the project, but the intervening time was not wasted. During that period, four glacier ski-lifts were erected. On 17 December 1973, a historical date for Zermatt and its development as a major tourist resort, the Federal Council rejected the final appeal and granted the construction licence.

THE CONSTRUCTION OF THE CABLE CAR

On 2 August 1976, on the day following the Swiss National Day celebrations, work began on all three sites: on the bottom and top stations, as well as on the three pylons.

The first task had been to assemble the work force, which had to be carefully selected. The working conditions would be very demanding, and only the young and very fit, tough and fearless, were expected to cope with the anticipated difficulties, including low oxygen levels. The altitude of the project was known to reduce the average performance of the work-force by 50 to 70%.

Camaraderie and team spirit were important, as the work-force lived in the camp on the Klein Matterhorn itself, week in, week out. Entertainment was basic: hotly disputed card games and table football provided the fun, and television kept them in touch with the outside world.

Operating the canteen for the 30 to 60 men required many adjustments to conventional catering. At that altitude, pasta takes forty-five minutes before it is cooked 'al dente', potatoes can take up to an hour, pressure cookers do not work either, because the boiling point of water is only 98 degrees at that height above sea level. However, lunch was always served on time!

The forces of nature were also to be reckoned with: wind speeds of up to 100km and more per hour, storms and heavy snowfalls. Thick fog and poor visibility caused unavoidable interruptions to work. Temperatures as low as -40°C stopped many tasks and activities. On the credit side, there were also, as there always are in the mountains, days when up on the Klein Matterhorn the sun shone, and down in the valley the villages were shrouded in mist.

17 May 1977, less than a year after the start of the construction, was a day of celebration. It was the day of the breakthrough of the 176 metre long tunnel which traverses the top of the mountain from the north side, i.e. the Zermatt side, to the south side, i.e. the Breithorn plateau. Once the tunnel was completed, it was possible to begin the construction of the arrival platform for the top station. Protection for the work-force was of paramount importance, as there is a 400m vertical rock face between the station and the glacier below.

Bearing in mind that the top station alone required around 2,000 cubic metres of concrete, it is easy to appreciate the enormity of the enterprise. Until the building site cable-car was erected, the concrete had to be flown in. Without the help of the helicopters, which transported everything from kitchen equipment, compressors, and power supply generators down to tools and building materials, the entire project would have been unthinkable. *The project involved 15,000 helicopter flights to carry 7 million kilogrammes of building materials and 6,000 passenger flights to carry the work-force.*

The first 'concrete flight' took place on 9 June 1977. It was early summer, and yet great care had to be exercised to stop the concrete from freezing during the five minute flight. The concrete was mixed with warm water, to which 2% antifreeze had been added, and was then poured into double walled, insulated containers for the trip to the top station site.

Meanwhile, the construction of the three pylons between October 1976 and July 1978 came across unexpected problems. The designated sites for the erection of the pylons contained moraine rubble trapped in permafrost.

In fact, each construction step presented its own challenge ... the bullwheels, the transmission and electrical motors, all had to be transported in sections.

One of the most interesting aspects of the construction was the cable installation:

35.8km of cable weighing 300 tons was dragged from above Zermatt to Trockener Steg. This represents a journey of 3,600m in distance and 1,000m in height difference. Then the cable had to be re-wound. Needless to say, this took several weeks! Laying the cable was extremely hazardous and even involved flying the helicopters sideways.

By the early summer of 1979 a team of specialists had put in place the high performance drive systems and made them operational. The cable system was all set to start grinding its way up and down the mountain. It was ready to receive the two large cabins, which take up to 100 passengers each. The cabins were transported by road, on lorries as far as Täsch. From there, they were flown by helicopter to the bottom station at Trockener Steg, attached to hanger frames and lifted into position on the thick cable.

It took nearly three years to achieve the realisation of one of the most courageous visions and enterprises in the history of Alpine transport.

AT THE TOP

'*At the Top*' is the title given to a book dedicated to the Klein Matterhorn Challenge.[3] It is a comprehensive record of the construction of the cable car and includes detailed technical information and many spectacular photographs. What is it like at the top? **Spectacular** is probably an understatement. The cable car carries 600 visitors per hour to a height of 3,820m, making it the highest cable car station in Europe - the Gateway to an extensive summer skiing region. The journey is fascinating, and truly beautiful. From Trockener Steg the cable car follows a ridge, rising above the Gandegg Hut, which stands on top of a moraine with a glacier on either side.[4] Then comes the 'ascent' of the north face of the mountain of the Klein Matterhorn itself. The cable car moves up, close to the rocks and ice, providing the thrill of a real mountain climb, but from the comfort of the cabin.[5]

From the top station there is a stunning view over Zermatt nestling in the valley against a backdrop of the Bernese Alps, straight ahead in the distance. Left and right of the valley the mighty 4,000m summits rise, way up into the rarefied atmosphere.

Skiers clatter their way through the tunnel to reach the ski pistes on the Breithorn plateau, seldom pausing to look at the north view. Follow the skiers inside the tunnel to take a lift up to a platform on the summit of Klein Matterhorn.

Breathtaking views await the visitor.

A 360° journey for the eye - a feast over a circular crown of mountains, interlaced with valleys and a network of cols linking the Alpine world into one whole vast

3. The book is available from the ticket office at the bottom station of the Zermatt-Kleinmatterhorn cable car, situated at the end of the village, appropriately in the direction of the Matterhorn.

4. The Theodul Glacier flowing down from the Testa Grigia area to Trockener Steg, and the Unterer Theodul Glacier, which runs down to Furi on the east side.

5. See sections 'The Breithorn' and 'A Summer Ascent of the Breithorn' in the chapter 'Climbing with a Mountain Guide'.

and intriguing web. An overall view, where the Matterhorn, undoubtedly the jewel in the crown, holds the eye, but cannot steal the show ....

Down to the southern exit. This is where the skiers' world begins. In the summer months a ski-lift brings the skiers back to Klein Matterhorn from the Gobba de Gollin, a small summit straight ahead from the cable car station, across the flat glacier of the Breithorn plateau. It rises on Italian soil, and far beyond it, as far as the eye can see, the blue coloured world of the Italian Alps stretches into the distance. White patches mark the Italian 4,000m peaks like Monte Viso and Gran Paradiso. To the west, Mont Blanc stands out, and so does the formidable, black north face of the Grandes Jorasses. Finally, the Matterhorn and its east face, wider than the pointed profile seen from Zermatt, but instantly recognisable ....

The Klein Matterhorn cable car enables everyone to enjoy the experience of high Alpine scenery and to take away with them the memory of a world of great splendour and immense grandeur.[6]

6. Children under the age of four cannot be taken up to Klein Matterhorn, as the altitude is too high. For them, the journey stops at Trockener Steg, where there are good restaurant facilities with extensive views over the ski pistes.

FAVOURITE WALKS

WALKING AND RAMBLING in Zermatt can be as arduous or as undemanding as you choose to make it. The many transport systems available ensure a great variety of *'downhill only'* and *'on the flat'* walks which can ease the office-weary, the idle young and the not so young into the pleasures of walking.

Walking in the Alps is such a totally new experience that it will be different from any walks ever undertaken in the lowlands. The beauty of the landscape, the flora and wildlife, the air so clear and pure, means that taking the first step along the path looks like being the only difficult one .... Others will follow, and lead on to new discoveries around the corner.

Zermatt boasts 388km of walking paths at different altitudes. Here, there is something for everyone, from families with children to the mountaineer, involving all degrees of difficulty. It is not possible within the scope of this book to describe all of the various walks and tours. We have chosen examples of the different categories in chapters **Children in the Mountains (six easy excursion days for everyone)** and **Chapel Walks** and hope that we may whet the reader's appetite by sharing some of our experiences which have undoubtedly enriched our lives.

Walking in the Alps can be a constant progression: starting with easy walks, venturing further away from the village and maybe ending on a 4,000m summit accompanied by one of Zermatt's Mountain Guides who will encourage and teach you all you need and may want to know. We have described several **Climbing tours with a Mountain Guide** to encourage a first ascent, up the Breithorn for instance, a welcoming 4,000m summit. Other tours portray training climbs for some visitors, or unforgettable days for mountaineers with prior experience. These chapters can be read as an invitation to climbing or enjoyed as a chance to dream.

Equally, walks can be made into ever longer day excursions, starting early in the morning to enjoy the freshness and beauty of an Alpine sunrise, followed by a hearty breakfast somewhere on the way. Dotted over the meadows, on the side of mountain roads and along narrow paths are some of the many restaurants Zermatt has to offer. Mouth-watering and sophisticated dishes, simple food and local specialities are always available as Zermatt honours its traditions. These can be seen in many of the restaurant buildings which are housed in old converted wooden farmhouses or in Stadels (barns). They convey an intimate atmosphere in an authentic Alpine setting and are an added asset to the pleasures of walking.

One of the great favourites of the day tours starts up the Trift valley, on the west side of Zermatt, rising to the area known as Hohbalm. At the beginning there are no summits in sight ahead on the path. The first to come into view is the Wellenkuppe (3,903m) with its distinctive rectangular shaped glacier-mound sitting on top like a hat. Then, one after the other, the peaks reveal themselves. At last, after a steep slope above the Trift Alp, around a corner appears the Matterhorn. The path goes on circling grassy mountainside with the Matterhorn constantly facing the walker, coming closer all the time. The steep descent ends above the impressive waterfall which lies directly opposite the north face of the Matterhorn. Then it is a left turn down the Zmutt valley and back to Zermatt. It is a long day's excursion, one of the most beautiful and rewarding trips in the area.[1] A purist's walk, as there are no mechanical aids to shorten the climbs on that side of the valley.

Another 'gold star day's excursion' takes the visitor to the east of the valley. Up from Blauherd to Fluhalp, over the top to Pfulwe and down to Täschalp. This is an excursion which is perhaps easier done in reverse and provides an occasion for a night's stay at the Täsch Hut, as described in our chapter, **A Night in a Mountain Hut**, to ensure an early start. Less demanding is the day excursion from Sunnegga, climbing way up along the west flank of the Zermatt valley to the Col and descending steeply to Täschalp.

Round tours, connecting routes with endless variations, this is the scene which tempts visitors back to Zermatt year after year. Challenges and relaxation are found in a landscape of unique beauty which combines the sharp contrasts of dramatic scenery with tranquillity and peace.

Pure scented air from the forests, rising above the tree-line to open meadows and further to a world of rocks and glaciers: this is a step by step adventure, a progression into the realm of the world's upper reaches.

HAVE A GO!

---

1. The trip should not be undertaken as long as there is still snow in the gullies and/or on the upper paths.

CHILDREN IN THE MOUNTAINS

NO CHILD IS too young for the mountains. The question one may ask is rather: how soon can a young family enjoy a mountain holiday? The answer is: as soon as you like. From the pram < to the backframe < to the buggy < to the independent child.

Independence for a child means freedom, and in today's world this is becoming a rare commodity. The mountains provide the children with a vast, magical playground where many of society's constraints disappear, or at least fade into the background.

But let the children speak for themselves. Here they are:

Anne-Julie	8 years old
Olivier	11 years old
Marc	13 years old

They are going to talk about their summer holidays in the Alps. First, however, we have to break the ice ....

'Shall we play journalists? I am going to ask questions and pretend this is an interview'. It sounds all right, and the children look keen and co-operative.

'Do you like mountains?' A unanimous loud '**Yes**' is the reply.

'Why?' has to be the next question. They look at each other. Silence.

At last, Olivier says 'Well ....'

Then Marc takes the lead. He is the oldest after all, and this is serious business. An interview is not something which happens every day! Marc is an articulate 13-year-old and he delivers what amounts to a speech.

'We live by a lake and see mountains in the distance. They look tempting. We feel like going and exploring rocks and streams, forests and Alps. Besides, there are swimming pools in the mountains. You can get water and everything else you want. Things like fresh air, that *makes you want to run....*'

'I like cable cars and Gondelbahns', says Anne-Julie.

'You only like walking downhill', says Olivier, 'we know that.'

'It was you who wanted to take the train to the top ....'

'Well, it's got new locomotives. You don't see that every day.'

'I like the grasshoppers, the butterflies and all the flowers', Anne-Julie's contribution.

'Flowers, that's for girls. What about the frogs by the stream? They're huge!'

'Do you remember the fish at the green lake? There were thousands of them.'

'That's where we found all those shiny stones. I've still got mine'.

'So have I. The one with holes, just like tiny caves.'

'That's when we met our friends from Zermatt. The boys and their girl cousins. We are going to stay with them next year. I can't wait, we had such a good time. The things we did! The places they showed us!'

'I'm taking my mountain bike' says Marc. 'Tim's got one, and I'm going to cycle to one of those picnic places. I'd rather ride than walk any day.'

'You can't go everywhere on your bike' says Olivier. 'I want to go back to the

green lake.'
'Me too', says Anne-Julie.
'It's too far for you.'
'No, it's not. I can do it. It's not boring, like walking at home.'

An interview? I did not get a word in, once they got started.

EASY WALKS FOR EVERYONE

EXCURSION NUMBER ONE

ZERMATT - SCHWEIGMATTE NEAR FURI

N THE SCHWEIGMATTE day we split up the party. The boys, Marc and Tim, Olivier and David follow the road up to Furi on their mountain bikes.

Parents, Anne-Julie, and Chantale plus Janine, the youngest of the party, still in a buggy, elect to take the Gondelbahn up to Furi.

Everyone, including the girls, is carrying rucksacks full of goodies for the picnic. At the bottom station there is a lift from the ticket office up to the Gondelbahn departure hall. This makes life a lot easier. The cabins of the Gondelbahn take six people at a time, and there are seven of us. We spread ourselves comfortably in three bubbles, as there is never a crowd problem in the summer. That way, we all enjoy the ride and watch the marmots playing in the sunny meadows below us. At the top, another lift takes us down to join the road from Zermatt to Furi. No steps to be negotiated anywhere! We walk back towards Zermatt, past the bridge, where we turn right into a forestry road on the edge of a large meadow. This is the area for winter cross-country skiing. Today, the meadows look like large multi-coloured bouquets of summer flowers. The grass has not yet been cut, and the field is out of bounds. 'No trampling on the grass'. No matter, there is plenty of room for running around and playing hide and seek behind the larches. We walk past a chalet and follow the track towards two large rocks. The area behind is where we are heading for. Fifteen minutes at the most. We are going to light our fire in one of the *designated places*, prepare a feast, and enjoy the day.

The first thing the children do is gather wood and pick out suitable sticks to use as cooking forks. Sausages (the favourites are Cervelat)[1] and chipolatas with chunks of 'Burebrot', farm-loaf, as well as a local rye-bread are on the menu. There is also 'Anne-Julie's special' which consists of toasted bread, covered in soft processed cheese and put back on the fire for a last roasting. Scrumptious, they say! Chocolate and muesli bars, apples (the only fruit which does not squash into a pulp inside the rucksack) make an excellent dessert. Apple juice, water and cold tea quench a huge thirst. In the meantime the grown-ups enjoy a real taste of the Valais 'picnic-style', melting Raclette cheese over the fire and scraping it onto hefty slices of rye bread, with a glass of Fendant, of course!

There are streams to amuse the children, a multitude of rocks, sculptured branches and snake-like sticks of larchwood. Best of all, where the biggest rocks are, is a secret passage. It is known as 'the fox's hole'. There are no real life foxes this time, but the children make up for it, pretending....

The hours fly by - the day ends too quickly.

---

1. Cervelat is a finely minced pork sausage available in all supermarkets and butchers.

EXCURSION NUMBER TWO

ZERMATT - SUNNEGGA - BLAUHERD - GRINDJISEE - GANDT -
OPTION ONE: **GRÜNSEE - UP TO RIFFELALP - DOWN TO ZERMATT BY TRAIN**
OR
OPTION TWO: **GRÜNSEE - PAST THE RESERVOIR - FINDELN - THROUGH THE VILLAGE - PAST THE CHAPEL - DOWN THE MAIN PATH TO WINKELMATTEN**

A day's tour for older children or exceptional 'young walkers'.
This is the day for the four boys and some of the parents.

We catch the Sunnegga-Express, followed by the Gondelbahn to Blauherd. From there it is downhill all the way to Gandt. The Alps are grazed by sheep which look up inquisitively, no doubt hoping for bread. A long stop at the Grindjisee proves to be irresistible. A morning stop for elevenses, a feast of bread and chocolate, not forgetting a large drink, as dehydration soon sets in. The Grinjisee is a lovely little lake fringed by rocks and larches and with a stunning view of the Matterhorn. 'We'll come back here for the day', is the unanimous feeling.

The Grünsee is where we plan to have lunch. From Gandt, it is uphill to the lake, a 30 minute climb, well worth the effort. The waters are green and transparent. Hundreds of small fish come to the edge to fight for the remains of the picnic.

Bärghüs
Findlgletscher

Discover a Cosy Spot Tel: 028 672552 Fax: 028 672553

Bernie and Andrea
A warm welcome at the Olympia Stübli!
Tel: (028) 67 24 07

The adults are reminiscing. They remember spending a night in the Bärghüs Findlgletscher, a mountain hotel by Grünsee. They talk about a late evening walk. It was a very clear night, illuminated by stars and a full moon. They had walked to the snout of the Findeln glacier and watched the moon reflecting off the ice onto the lateral moraines which looked luminous and phosphorescent. It was an unforgettable sight. 'When you're older, this is something we can do again....' Back to reality ....

'Are we going up to Riffelalp to catch the train or shall we walk back through Findeln?' Olivier has a soft spot for trains, so Riffelalp wins the day.

EXCURSION NUMBER THREE

ZERMATT - WINKELMATTEN - HÖHENWEG - ZERMATT

From Winkelmatten a short climb takes Anne-Julie, Chantale, Janine plus parents, across the Gornergrat railway track to the beautiful Höhenweg to Ried.

The path is flat and suitable for the buggy. The walk leads all the way through the forest. We count the well camouflaged dark brown squirrels and listen for the tapping of the woodpeckers. The older girls scramble among the rocks on the side of the path playing hide and seek, with Janine pointing and giving the game away, sitting like a small blond elf in her comfortable buggy. They know that at the end of the path there is 'one of those mountain restaurants' with such goodies as home-made cakes, ice cream and a play area. What better incentive to walk! The parents, on the other hand, might indulge in 'one of those' well-laced coffee specialities!

It is a hot day, and a swim back at the village will be just the thing to round off the day.

EXCURSION NUMBER FOUR

EN FAMILLE TO SUNNEGGA AND THE LEISEE

Another very hot day, just right for testing the water and swimming in a mountain lake.

The older boys and the girls eagerly pack their swim-suits. Janine's arm-bands are safely stowed in the rucksack. The worst thing is carrying the towels ... plus the picnic. Fortunately there is a restaurant at Sunnegga, where we can supplement our frugal lunch.

There is great excitement because we are going to see a marmot colony at play just below Sunnegga. With luck they will come close enough for us to see their whiskers move as their noses sniff the air. In the event we see all we ever hoped to see, and even the water does not feel too cold.

A good day for everybody, with time to read, relax and sunbathe.

After the day's swimming in bracing waters, we go back to Zermatt by the Sunnegga-Bahn but promise ourselves to come back another day and walk the long way round, over Tuftern (also suitable with a buggy) with the mountain bike party leading the way.

EXCURSION NUMBER FIVE

ZERMATT - GORNERGRAT - RIFFELBERG - WINKELMATTEN - ZERMATT

En famille, parents and children alike take the train to Gornergrat. It is one of the new trains with a fast locomotive and large picture windows. The children are fascinated by the sights - rising above the village, the forest, the tunnel, then the meadows - and there is no time for boredom. The playing cards remain in the rucksack!

At the top we walk up to the Kulm Hotel where there is an observatory and weather-station, as well as a kiosk which sells sun-glasses and sun cream; just as well, as we have forgotten some of the essentials....

The panoramic views are some of the best in the world. All of us manage to spot the grey, stone built Monte Rosa Hut on the glacier moraine, sitting below the Monte Rosa massif.

There is a vote, and the children, except for Janine, elect to walk down. We say goodbye until we meet for lunch at the Riffelberg Hotel, half-way down from the top of Gornergrat to Zermatt. Downhill walking with children is quite fast. There is always a temptation to run. Past Rotenboden, the Riffelhorn rises on the edge, brown rock, good climbing rock. Below it, the Riffelsee nestles in a hollow, with the Matterhorn reflected in its waters from way across the valley. This is a perfect spot for a long rest. The older children are intrigued by the climbers they see negotiating a number of different routes on the Riffelhorn.

'I'll tell you what, as a special birthday treat, if you like we'll book a guide and you can try climbing and learn how to do it properly and safely.'

Dreaming of a rock climbing adventure makes the rest of the way to the Riffelberg Hotel seem very short. As a bonus we come across a herd of ibex below the Riffelhorn. We stand very still and observe them, from a distance, as they graze. They become aware of our presence and gradually move away.

After lunch on the terrace of the Riffelberg Hotel, watched over by the Matterhorn, Olivier and Janine, with Marc and Tim in charge, take the train back to Zermatt. Marc and Tim have booked a tennis court, and Olivier has volunteered to keep an eye on Janine in the playground next to the courts. No doubt it will cost us an ice cream or two!

The rest of the party make their way down to a lush grazing Alp and then descend towards the sound of bells, emanating from a herd of Eringer cattle (large inquisitive, dark-brown animals), a breed from the Valais, one of Riffelalp's great attractions.

Safely past the herd, the children take off and run ahead to the terrace of the hotel. No wonder, they have been promised one of the delicious, special ice cream coupes: this has given them the energy to complete the day's walking down to Winkelmatten and back home.

EXCURSION NUMBER SIX

SUNNEGGA - TUFTERN - TÄSCHALP

Janine was going to spend the day at the Kindergarten, but in the end we decided to take her and her inseparable buggy with us on our expedition to Täschalp. We know that she cannot come all the way, but one of the adults has 'things to do' down in the village, and is more than happy with a shorter outing. Once again, we set off and take the Sunnegga Bahn, for the first time with the buggy. We step into the bottom carriage, which will be the nearest to the lift as we reach the top station. Fortunately, thanks to the lift, there is no need to carry a buggy or encourage small children up the long flight of stairs alongside the train.

We set off towards Tuftern from where the path is 'buggy-proof' for a further half hour's walking. At the given point, Janine happily waves goodbye, clutching the yellow bucket she is going to fill with precious stones during a playtime session beside one of the red painted benches, strategically placed in the sun.

The rest of the party walks on. The path alternatively widens and narrows and becomes stony. It has, however, the great advantage of being nearly flat all the way to Täschalp. It is a very relaxing walk, as the path is particularly suitable and safe for children. We come across another family with a very young child sitting inside a backframe, its small face hidden under a floppy white sunhat.

The walk to Täschalp could take as little as 2½ hours. But as there is always something to look at and to stop for, we arrive in Täsch a good three hours later.

Täschalp itself is a beautiful, wide Alp with a mountain stream rushing between rocks and meadows. It is a wonderful natural play area. There are restaurant facilities, open from around mid-June to the end of September, or even into October, weather permitting. A road links Täschalp to the village of Täsch, and it is possible to call a taxi if the walk down to the village proves too much for small legs.

The actual Täsch Hut, which belongs to the Swiss Alpine Club, is in the care of a Zermatter, having passed on from father to son and thus remained in the family. A wide road leads up to the hut from Täschalp, and in our minds a plan is already taking shape .... Why not go and spend a night up there? We could hire a taxi as far as the Alp and walk on from there. It is not too far, and we could experience a night in a mountain hut, watch the sunset and get up early to taste the freshness of a true Alpine morning.

'How far is it to walk up to the Täsch Hut from the Alp?' asks Marc.
'An hour and a half is all it takes' answers David, who knows it well.
'That's not too far. We can manage without a taxi ... perhaps.'
Yes, a night at the Täsch Hut could be our next big adventure.

For further information about Täschalp and the Täsch Hut telephone:

Verkehrsbureau Täsch	028 67 16 89
Täsch Hut (SAC)	028 67 39 13
Guardian of the Täsch Hut	028 67 27 71

NOTE   It is essential to book Swiss Alpine Club huts in advance. In high season a family holiday outing is better done during the week.

When in need of a taxi contact Taxi Fredy from Täsch on 028 67 33 66.

EXCURSION NUMBER SEVEN

ZERMATT - EDELWEISS - TRIFT

This is a day Janine spends in the company of her little friends at the Kindergarten, which will be a real treat for her. We know that she is going to be spoilt as she has a way with adults.... The rest of us set off for the day. There are at least two starting points from the village in the direction of the Trift Valley, on the west side of Zermatt.

1   Past the church, climb for about one hundred yards, on to the paved road. On the right you will spot a signpost, nailed half-way up a house, pointing to Edelweiss, Trift, etc.

2   This is the path which we followed on the day we did this excursion. It starts next to the guide office, on your right as you walk up the main street halfway between the station and the church. The signpost reads like an invitation into

the high mountains (the times allowed are for the uphill climb only):

Edelweiss	1 hour
Trift	2½ hours
Hohbalm	3½ hours
Mettelhorn	5 hours
Rothorn Hut (SAC)	4½ hours

The path called Triftweg rises between old Chalets and Stadels built on stilts and resting on stone wheels to stop the mice getting at the hay. Just a few yards from the Bahnhofstrasse the beautiful gardens, an explosion of colour, of the Hotel Romantica deserve more than a cursory glance. From the path we look back between the houses at the two distinctive jagged rock points of the Täschhorn and the Dom.

It is early morning and the sun is still rising over the summits on the east side of valley as we walk amongst sunbathed meadows. We cross the foaming waters of the Triftbach over a wooden bridge. This is where the actual steep climb to Edelweiss begins: fortunately, most of it is in the shade of a forest of larches. We take it slowly on the wide and easy path and save energy for the 300 metre climb, *en lacet*[2] up to the Edelweiss balcony. From there the view is open, wide, and breathtaking. Right across the valley is the Breithorn and its heavily indented ridge. The Gornergrat lies straight across, the long train track only just visible in the shadow of the hillside. The pylons of the cable car to Stockhorn stand out clearly against the skyline.

2. En lacet = winding.

'What are those?' asks Olivier. 'That's a cable car from Gornergrat to Stockhorn'. 'I thought the trains stopped at Gornergrat'.

'Oh no, you can climb higher and further along the ridge by cable car all the way to Stockhorn. That's where the best 'mogul slope' is for winter skiing and it's steep'.

'I suppose you're an expert at it, Tim. I haven't been skiing for very long. Do you think we could go and have a day on Klein Matterhorn and try out summer skiing?'

'Why not. That's a good idea. Why don't we make it tomorrow's outing'.

'Is that the Riffelhorn where we saw the climbers practising rock climbing techniques?' asked Marc.

'Yes it is, and to the left are the Strahlhorn and the Rimpfischhorn, which they say consist of 'pillow lava'. That's why the rocks look like large, dark humps moulded together. They come from an ancient seabed'.

'You seem to know a lot of things!'

'Well I live here and the teachers at school tell us a lot about the interesting things to be found in the area'.

This is a good place for a long break and refreshments but we have still a long way to go to get to Trift (over 400m height difference). The steepest part of the trip is now behind us and we follow the river all the way up to Trift, beyond the tree line. Trift is an Alpine paradise. A wide plateau before the big climb, gentle and inviting with brooks and streams meandering amongst the meadows. There are flowers and rocks, and the mountains look so fresh that we feel as if we have just discovered an unexplored new world. There are a few cows grazing around a small lake and an unexpected swamp adds to the variety of the landscape. It is a perfect place for our picnic. We take a long rest, admiring the natural beauty of our surroundings and *wishing we could stay here for ever*.

RESTAURANT FINDLERHOF
FRANZ + HEIDI

THE COSY MOUNTAIN RESTAURANT IN FINDELN (2050m)
On the way up : First by the main path from Zermatt
On the way down : 150m beyond the Chapel

In the centre of the walking and skiing area Sunnegga - Rothorn

Franz + Heidi's Findlerhof offers
genuine rustic charm and pleasant ambience

Renowned Cuisine - Stylish menus - Rösti Quiches Walliserteller
Fresh Salads garnished with fish or meat
Italian dishes a speciality -
Antipasti Carpaccio Risotto Pastas Polenta Dolci

Extensive wine list includes
From the Valais - Humagne Rouge Cornalin Syrah Chardonnay
From Italy - Barolo Ubo Tignanello Ornelaia Sassicaia

Bergestaurant Findlerhof bei "Franz + Heidi"
Familie Schwery
CH 3920 Zermatt
Tel : 028 67 25 88 and 67 28 80

BEAUTIFUL CHAPEL WALKS

I N THE AREA around Zermatt stand numerous Chapels, in which divine services are celebrated and prayers are said regularly. In contrast to the Parish Church, no incumbents are attached to the Chapels.

KAPELLE DER HEILIGEN FAMILIE, WINKELMATTEN
(CHAPEL OF THE HOLY FAMILY) CONSTRUCTED 1607

The walk to this Chapel is pleasant and easy. The building is very pretty, and the elegant porch reminds one of similar buildings in neighbouring Italy. The Chapel houses an interesting, very ornate Baroque altar, and is regularly used for marriage ceremonies because of its romantic interior and setting.

There are two rogation processions from Zermatt to Winkelmatten in the spring, when the people pray for God's blessing on the meadows and fields, as well as on their own work during the coming year.

KAPELLE DES HEILIGEN JAKOBUS, FINDELN
(CHAPEL OF SAINT JAMES)

The best time to visit this Chapel would be after a day spent walking around Sunnegga and Rothorn. The Chapel contains a jewel of a very special kind, a late Gothic winged altar, which is thought to have been carved by the famous 'Nelkenmeister', whose works may be found all over western Switzerland. The three figures of the Saints were carved almost two centuries later, but fit in very well with the older triptych. The wings of the altar are folded over the centre panel during Lent, so that the visitor is offered the sight of the Annunciation by the Archangel Gabriel. In reality, the Chapel's true altarpiece is the Matterhorn, which stands in the wings of the sumptuous landscape and forms the backdrop to this sanctuary.

In centuries gone by, when the weather was so bad that the precious grass could not be dried for hay, the villagers would make a pilgrimage to the Chapel of Findeln, to 'get the sun' metaphorically speaking from there.

KAPELLE DER HEILIGEN LUZIA, RIED
(CHAPEL OF SAINT LUCIA) CONSTRUCTED 1693

A walker coming from Findeln en route to Zermatt might wish to make a most pleasant detour by taking the Höhenweg (upper path) through the forest towards Ried. The Chapel in this isolated, widely-scattered hamlet is dedicated to the patron saint of all who suffer in any way with their eyes.

In the olden days the people from Ried are said to have been constantly bothered by malicious spirits. Although the ghosts had been exorcised by the Abbot of St. Maurice, no one expected them to have given up and cleared out so easily. In those early days, on the Friday before Pentecost, the people would therefore go in procession (and not alone) up to the Ried Chapel to pray - and to scan the larches fearfully to assure themselves that no more ghosts were lingering in those giant trees.

CHAPELS IN THE DIRECTION OF THE MATTERHORN

For over a hundred years all Alpinists have left the village of Zermatt in the Matterhorn direction through the 'Ober Dorf', the upper village. This ancient route takes us into another world full of small Chapels and Sanctuaries.

KAPELLE DER GOTTESMUTTER MARIA, BLATTEN
(CHAPEL OF MARY, THE MOTHER OF GOD)

This little Church, standing among sleepy chalets and Stadels, is the destination of many private pilgrimages. Members of the older generation of Zermatt are very content if they are able to visit Our Lady of Blatten at least once a year. They consider it a special grace if they have the physical strength to do so.

Nowadays all the people of Zermatt come here to celebrate every other year, since it was decided in 1986 that the Parish Fête should be held in Blatten bi-annually. This happy day enables personal contact between the busy people of Zermatt, who might otherwise be in danger of not knowing one another any more.

The fête is also a reminder of the important rogation procession, the 'long way round', which used to wind its way from the village centre to the Vesperwald, the forest where the male choir sang Vespers. After a short rest, the cross and banner used to be taken up again and the pilgrims would continue to Moos, where a Capuchin monk was permitted to collect alms. Down to the Chapel in Winkelmatten, where a special blessing was given with the holy arm, an ornate relic. As the procession wound its slow way back to the Parish Church, a special peal of bells would announce to those who had to stay in the village, mothers with

small children and the elderly, that it was time to go to the Church, where they could at least enjoy the final blessing by the clergy in all their glory.

KAPELLE DER HEILIGEN BARBARA, WEILER ZUM SEE (CHAPEL OF SAINT BARBARA) CONSTRUCTED 1963

The hamlet of 'Weiler on the Lake' led the life of a half-orphan for centuries because the little village lacked a focal point. In contrast to the other hamlets around Zermatt, there was no snow-white chapel in Weiler. But the Rudolf Taugwalder Family, who have their family seat here (in the famous Restaurant Zum See), changed all that by having a chapel built in 1963 in memory of their mother Barbara.

The village is always referred to as Zum See, although there is no permanent lake. There is evidence, however, that centuries ago there was a lake where the Chapel now stands. This is corroborated by the fact that one of the names for the area was 'Z Moosji', translated 'rich in moss', i.e. damp. Nowadays only a spring remains in the meadowland.

KAPELLE DER MARIA DER SIEBEN SCHMERZEN, FURI (CHAPEL OF THE VIRGIN OF THE SEVEN SORROWS)

You will find this Chapel at Furi away from ski-lifts and ski-pistes, hidden amongst old Stadels and a mountain restaurant where the family still farms the land. It is the smallest of the sanctuaries around Zermatt. Until recently the Chapel contained only one decorative element, a very impressive Pietà, i.e. a painting which depicts the Virgin Mary holding her dead Son in her lap while a sharp sword pierces her heart. In 1986 four small windows were added to the Chapel, created by a member of the Geneva watchmaker dynasty, Marion Cartier. The windows are small works of art of exceptional beauty.

There is a special annual celebration held in this Chapel the Friday before Holy Week, a day of quiet prayer, when the light of hundreds of candles may be seen shining from the Chapel from afar, well into the night.

DIE KAPELLE MARIA ZUM SCHNEE, AM SCHWARZEN SEE (THE CHAPEL OF THE HOLY MARY OF THE SNOW)

This Chapel is a place of prayer which lies close to the heart of not only the people from Zermatt, but also of many faithful guests. This is not surprising. For over half the year the Chapel is only accessible on skis. It is visited mainly by people with problems in their love-life or marriage.

The Chapel feast is celebrated on the 5th of August and is probably the most important of the religious happenings in the mountains of the Valais. When in years gone by the sun beat down mercilessly on field and meadow, so that the earth became rock-hard and the meadows took on the red hues of a fox, the people of Zermatt would trail in procession to the Schwarzsee 'to fetch the rain'. It is said that the result was immediate and that raindrops as large as five franc pieces[1] would fall before the people reached home. However, there were always those who

1. The Swiss five franc piece is an extra large and thick coin with a historical mystique about it. It was used as a special gift or reward and was referred to as 'Es Fünfliber'.

attributed the success of the well-timed procession to the barometer of the priest or the rheumatic knee of his housekeeper!

DIE KAPELLE DER HEILIGEN KATHARINA, MUTT (ZMUTT)
(THE CHAPEL OF SAINT CATHERINE)
We visit this chapel on our return from Schwarzsee back to Zermatt. The Chapel is adorned by a simple altar. Zmutt is a very attractive hamlet which lies in the path of large avalanches. But, thanks to the wonderful protection of Saint Catherine, the icy snowmass would always stop a few centimetres short of the houses and stables.

DIE KAPELLE DES HEILIGEN BERNARD
(THE CHAPEL OF SAINT BERNARD) CONSTRUCTED 1950
Most readers will make a trip on the Gornergratbahn and find this chapel between Gornergrat (top station) and the Kulm Hotel. The Chapel was consecrated in 1950. It is dedicated to St. Bernard, the Patron Saint of climbers, and St. Theodul, first Bishop of Sion. St. Bernard is represented on the altarpiece. Thousands of candles are lit in this Chapel each year, visible proof that many people pray here, and often.

DIE BRUDER KLAUS KAPELLE, RIFFELBERG
(THE CHAPEL OF THE EREMITE BROTHER SAINT NICOLAS VON DER FLUEH)
The wanderer coming from Gornergrat via Rotenboden along the Riffelsee towards Riffelberg will sooner or later notice a modern Chapel set in the wide sweeping landscape. To his delight he will discover that the contours of the Chapel coincide with those of the mighty Weisshorn outlined behind it.

The small Church was consecrated in 1961 by the then bishop, Arthur Léon Elchinger, native of Alsace. Its patron Saint is Sankt Niklaus von der Flueh, a peacemaker, who lived in the 15th century and was canonized in 1947 by Pope Pius XII. The Chapel is adorned by a jewel which is sure to captivate any friend of the fine arts: the detail from a Gothic altarpiece, created around the year 1400 in Barcelona. After centuries of roundabout travels this work of art was acquired from the Schaeffer Gallery in New York, from where Dr. Hans Schaeffer had it transferred to the Riffelberg Chapel shortly before his death.

DIE HERZ JESU KAPELLE, RIFFELALP
(THE CHAPEL OF THE SACRED HEART OF JESUS)
This Chapel used to belong to the Riffelalp Hotel. The many commemorative plaques remind the visitor of the pioneers of the Zermatt hotel trade, the large Seiler family. Many marriages services are celebrated each year in the Herz Jesu Kapelle. It was built and consecrated three years after the first Riffelalp Hotel opened its doors.

THE ENGLISH CHAPEL ON RIFFELALP
Alexander Seiler started to build the first Hotel at Riffelalp (2,200 metres high) in 1878. It took six summers to complete. At the same time he built the Anglican Trinity Chapel, expecting his main clientele to be British.

THE THEOSAAL, ZERMATT
Theo Imboden who lives in nearby Täsch, an artist working with glass, created this room in 1980, furbishing it with remarkable skill. It serves as a house of God to the Catholic and Reformed communities alike, and children of all ages at local schools attend the obligatory weekly Mass here.

COMMEMORATIVE CROSSES
Over the whole Zermatt area may be found more than 70 wayside crosses. Most of them are simple manifestations of faith, inviting the passer-by to a moment of reflection. But some of them are reminders of mankind's destiny, the cross put up in memory of a dead villager or guest.

Our thanks go to Ivo Kronig, who told us the stories of the Zermatt Chapels. Ivo Kronig: Graduate in Theology and History, Licentiate of the University Fribourg Teacher at the Primar and Orientierungschule Zermatt Since 1991 Chief Librarian of the Zermatt Community Library.

Restaurant Aroleid, Furi (Near the Chapel)
Familie Lauber
Tel. 028 67 26 58

The Aroleid "Käseschnitte" : Melted cheese on bread, soaked in white wine is one of the well known specialities of our mountain restaurant

---

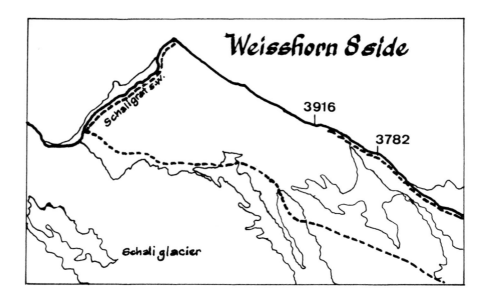

François Gos

SNOWSTORM — SUNSHINE ON SCHWARZSEE

An adventurous first encounter with Zermatt
dedicated to James N, to whom we owe the story.

'**H**ELLO JAMES. WELCOME to Zermatt! It's good to see you here at last.'

'Well, it's nice to be here.'

'It's not quite what you expected I imagine - pouring with rain, instead of glorious sunshine.'

'Oh, I don't mind. I've got a warm jumper and an anorak and - believe it or not, I've seen rain before.'

'Yes, I know, but I'd hoped that having enticed you up to Zermatt and promised you 'the experience of a lifetime', the place would have put on a sunny smile to welcome you with.'

'Well, tomorrow's another day, and I know that I'll enjoy my supper if nothing else.'

'We're booked in for a 'raclette evening'[1] at a café or Stübli – whichever you want to call it. Thought it'd make a change from a businessman's lunch.'

'I only had time for sandwiches today. That's how they treat us young executives now!'

'Wicked times we know. But you're miles away from all that now. Let me take you home first, and then we'll go straight out to supper.'

It was the middle of June, and the weather should have been glorious, the Alpine flora beautiful enough to stir the heart of even the most inveterate city dweller, let alone the mountains .... But even the best laid plans can fall victim to the weather. James's words 'tomorrow's another day' came true. The following morning brought a different scene altogether. We woke up to find ourselves gazing at a winter landscape: the village looked as pretty as a Christmas card. As we sat having breakfast, it stopped snowing but the clouds hung low. They seemed to be clinging to the mountains, hiding the spectacular shapes.

'It's stopped snowing.' I said, stating the obvious but trying to sound cheerful. 'We can go out for a walk if you like.'

'Yes of course, that's what I'm here for. Let's go. We can always dive into one of the mountain restaurants I've heard so much about.'

'Well, we'll do that on the way back anyway. Now I've got a couple of suggestions, and you must choose what you want to do. We can go up a gentle path - to ease you into walking up a mountain ...'

'Wait a minute, I'm not that unfit. I play squash ....'

'Yes I know you're fit - I was only teasing. You'll probably 'outwalk' me. As I

---

1. Raclette: a local speciality - indeed of the whole canton Valais (French terminology) or Wallis (German terminology). Cut a large circular slab of cheese, about 3' deep, in half and put the uncovered rindless face of the cheese under a hot grill. As the cheese melts, scrape it off with a sharp knife on to a plate and serve with small potatoes boiled in their skin. Tiny white pickled onions and gherkins are a good accompaniment and the local white wine, Fendant, or a glass of 'Schnapps', are perfect with it.

was saying, we can walk up to the south facing slopes where the snow'll melt first when and if the sun comes out. On the other hand, we could take a cable car up to Schwarzsee and walk back down to Zermatt.'
'Where's Schwarzsee?'
'Up there, underneath the Matterhorn.' I pointed at the window in the direction of the mountain. 'You won't see it. You probably won't see anything ....'
'Oh let's go there. I haven't been in a cable car for ages and that'll be an experience in itself.'
'Tell me James, why has it taken you so long to come up to Zermatt?'
'It's not Zermatt, it's the mountains. I always thought that you had to be an expert to enjoy them. I'm stuck in an office for hours on end and when I go on holiday I like to feel that I'm off on some kind of adventure. I never thought you could get it here unless you were a mountaineer - which I'm not.'
'That was a long speech for James' I thought to myself and smiled.

★★★★★★★★★★★★★

We rose in the cable car through the mist, towards Schwarzsee and the Matterhorn. As we got there we found a good 6cm of wet, sticky snow. The cloud line seemed to be just above Schwarzsee, and I was surprised to see how much visibility there was below the drifting clouds. There was a strong wind, gusting and tearing at the Swiss flag hoisted up on a tall white mast. We soon put up the hoods of our anoraks and did them up firmly - we looked set for a polar expedition.

The path down to Zermatt follows the winter ski-piste and its outline was only just visible under the blanket of snow. Yet the snow was not thick enough to hide the contours of the land, the rocks and the rivulets of hard caked earth snaking down the slope. They were etched in black against the white background.

Below Schwarzsee we came across the tiny Chapel of 'Heilige Maria Zum Schnee' (Holy Mary of the Snow). Its white walls blended into the whiteness of the light, and the flat expanse of the small lake beside it. I remembered the week before when I had walked to the water's edge and admired the reflection of the Chapel in the perfect stillness of the lake.
'It's not fair' I thought to myself.
'Isn't it lovely!' was the next thing I heard and I turned around to see James busy with his camera.
'You won't get a picture in this light, will you?'
'Yes I will. It'll come out black and white like one of those photos my father used to take.'
'It's true' I thought. 'It is lovely, even today. It looks untouched ... ethereal.'
'It's wonderful, there's no one here at all' James said echoing my thoughts.

I breathed a deep sigh of relief to see that our guest was enjoying himself in spite of the weather: the unseasonal cold, the snow ... indeed, maybe because of it all. He was loving it; he was experiencing the extraordinary thrill of being drawn into an intimate dialogue with nature, a feeling enhanced by the swirling, wispy, soft grey mist.

James put his camera away and we set off again. We were slithering down the path .... Slithering? I looked at James's feet and noticed to my horror that he was wearing some kind of light-weight trainers.

'James!' I exclaimed. 'Are those the only shoes you've got?'

He had the good grace to look embarrassed.

'I didn't think it was worth investing in anything else - just for one day.'

Tumbles, twisted ankles, dislocated shoulders, and all because of a pair of shoes. I could see it all! But then I reassured myself: 'Well, at least he's a good squash player - sure footed and quick thinking and though this *feels* like an adventure trip because of the weather conditions, the slope is not really steep and we're not far from civilisation.'

Shortly afterwards we reached the place where the paths divide: straight on down to Zermatt, or to the left, hugging the side of the mountain, on to Stafelalp. We decided to aim for Stafelalp - the longer way. As we rounded the corner, the westerly gale hit us. We stood there, caught in a fierce gust. We felt the full force of nature unleashed as the driving snow hit our face. We stopped and stood with our backs to the wind. James laughed: 'Haven't been in a blizzard for years. We don't seem to get much snow in London.'

Then, as suddenly as it had come, the storm blew itself out.

Slowly I began to hope ... then I knew almost for sure and thought to myself - 'Yes, by the time we get to Stafelalp, the weather will have cleared and we'll see **it**, the Matterhorn, emerging from the clouds ....'

'The Matterhorn is here, just above you. Maybe you'll see it before you leave,' I said in what I hoped sounded a casual enough tone.

'I hope I do, but it matters less than it did. I've got all this' James waved his arms as if trying to catch hold of everything around him.

Stafelalp Restaurant
Tel: (028) 67 30 62

We made our way down, watching our feet and not saying much - there was no need to make conversation. I kept an eye on my left. Every now and again a slab of mountain would appear in a gap through the clouds. The slabs became larger and at last grew into a full sized silhouette.

'Look James, here it is. Look at it **now!**

There it was, the Matterhorn, still enveloped by the remains of the short-lived summer storm, appearing and disappearing again, back inside swirling clouds.

By the time we reached Stafelalp, the great peak stood out in all its splendour, as white as if it had been sprayed by a giant cannon of icing sugar. We stopped and leaned against the gnarled trunk of the first Arolla pine at the onset of the tree line and admired the spectacle. We felt like pioneers and explorers who have braved the elements and discovered a new country – everything looked so fresh. Later on, we met up with the first tourists. They were happy and smiling in the sunshine. But we 'explorers and pioneers' who had come in from the cold, felt a kind of vague pity for them. Hadn't they missed the best part of the day?

We walked down through meadows where the flowers were shaking off the last of the melting snow and on to the large pine forest which grows on an old moraine. We came across hamlets and sunburnt wooden huts. Birds were singing and marmots whistled their shrill calls of warning across the valley. Zermatt and civilisation came into view.

'Let's go shopping!' said James. 'Where's the best place for boots? I think I'll stay another day. It'd be a pity to leave now the weather's changed and all that.'

'What about your job?' I asked, holding back a note of self satisfaction and a 'I told you you'd like it here ....'

'Oh my job – well, yes, I've got a few days owing to me. I might as well take them now.'

In the shop I heard him ask: 'How much training do you need to get to the top of the Matterhorn?'

'Some training – good conditions – fitness and a Mountain Guide. But there are other mountains to be climbed first, so you can see how you go. You can start with the Mettlehorn for instance and get used to your boots ....'

This was the kind of shopping which takes time. I settled myself into my chair and thought about our trip, which had turned into an adventure.

Yes, it had been a very good day in the mountains.

A NIGHT IN A MOUNTAIN HUT

MOUNTAIN HUTS ARE familiar places to the many climbers who come to Zermatt. Even with the help of modern transport systems, e.g. cable cars which whisk you up a mountain in a matter of minutes, most great ascents are too long to be tackled in one day from the resort itself. The answer for them is: a night in a Mountain Hut, nearer to the chosen summit, in order to have a good head start the following day. It means sleeping at a considerable altitude, in the heart of the mountains, where the grandeur of the surrounding landscape gathers up minds and thoughts to hold them almost spellbound ....

It is fortunately not necessary to be a climber to experience a night in a Mountain Hut.

Access to the huts around Zermatt is sometimes a long walk but does not require the skills of a climber. Everyone who comes to Zermatt and enjoys walking can experience a night 'away from it all', away from the hustle and bustle, from sophisticated civilisation, and enjoy a unique experience - an adventure.

Perhaps the most famous Hut and Mountain Hotel of all the region of Zermatt are the Hörnli Hut and the Belvédère Hotel beside it - at the foot of the Matterhorn. All Mountain Huts, however, have their own special place in the history of Alpine climbing. The majority of visitors to Zermatt who climb, or rather walk, to a Mountain Hut, go up in the morning and descend back to Zermatt the same afternoon. There is, however, **a real alternative: STAY THE NIGHT** - watch the sun go down in a blaze of colours, watch as the sky displays a progression of colours: shades of blue – a streak of turquoise onto pale yellow – golden sky – orange, red – pink and amethyst. The last of the sun's rays dart across from the summits, as if thrown off a diamond. When at last all of the sun has dipped behind the western peaks, light lingers on whilst a whole world, coloured in the shades of distant blue, the white of glaciers, and the greys and browns of earth and rocks darkens, to allow the moon and stars their hours of glory.

In the morning the process begins again, in reverse, with the spectacle of the great awakening and warming up of the grandiose landscape.

When we talk about the silence of the mountains we mean freedom from 'man-made noises'. What we hear up at the Huts is the noise of falling rocks and stones, the distant rumble of the occasional ice falls, sometimes the sound of rushing water. Then there are the birds: mountain choughs - scavengers eyeing titbits of food, the bigger the chunks, the better. They are perhaps the most graceful 'flyers' of the Alps, dancing intricate ballet routines in the thermals. One becomes aware of the twittering and singing of small birds, the shrill, bird-like whistle of the marmots, the sudden sound of dislodged stones as a herd of chamois clambers up a mountainside.

Every Hut has its own atmosphere and its own surprises. The higher Huts stand away from all vegetation but still offer the sight of Alpine flowers surviving, who knows how, on a handful of soil amongst the rocks. Lower altitude Huts may appear a little less dramatic but gain from the 'green' of their surroundings – although all of them are situated above the tree line.

In the early evening the climbers gather in the Huts for supper. They drift in, in smaller and larger groups and some, very few, on their own, solitary and silent figures. To begin with, the conversation seems to take place in muted tones – somehow the atmosphere carries a feeling of anticipation. As the meal progresses, the inside of the hut becomes warm and feels protective. Everyone settles in and pushes along the benches to make room for newcomers. When the first hunger is satisfied and, more important still, some of the huge thirst is quenched (hopefully not just with wine ...) the conversation starts to flow. There is a lot of talk. Memories of previous climbs and adventures (could there be a hint of a fisherman's tale?). The Mountain Guides sit with their guests entertaining them with stories, vying with each other to see who has got the best jokes. By nine o'clock the first serious climbers drift off to bed.

Although the Belvédère Mountain Hotel has one single room and three double rooms, Mountain Huts on the whole are divided into smaller and larger dormitories. There are plenty of blankets (which must be carefully folded up again in the morning) and a pillow for everyone.

The Huts which are listed below all belong to the Swiss Alpine Club, but not all to the same section. As an example: the Weisshorn Hut belongs to the Swiss Alpine Club Section Basle. The guardian of the Hut operates the food and restaurant facilities on a franchise basis, but he or she, when in residence, is in sole charge of the place.

Although the Swiss Alpine Club huts are always open, as they represent amongst other things a refuge from the elements available at all times for a stranded climber, the restaurant facilities are only offered when the guardian is in residence. The beginning of the summer season depends largely on the weather conditions, which vary from year to year. Most of the Huts are open for food from the beginning of July to the end of September. The Weisshorn Hut opens later at around 20 July till the end of September.

An awareness of conditions is always necessary. In snow conditions the access can be slippery and an 'easy' path become treacherous.

On the whole, the month of July is not so busy as August, but advance booking for an overnight stay is a **must** at all times. Climbers have been known to spend an uncomfortable night on hard benches!

In the event of 'no reply' to your telephone call get in touch with the Tourist Office: Tel. (028) 66 11 81 for Zermatt, and Tel. (028) 67 16 77 for the Weisshorn Hut only, which comes under the Tourist Office of Randa, a small village below Zermatt. The Tourist Offices will put you in touch with the guardian of the Hut whenever possible, especially for advance pre-season bookings. Prefix from UK 00 44 28 followed by the last 6 digits.

Schönbiel Hut 2,694m 62 sleeping places Tel: (028) 67 13 54
Route 1 From Zermatt Village - 4 hours
Route 2 Zermatt - Schwarzsee by cable car - Schwarzsee - Stafelalp - 50 minutes
        Stafelalp - Schönbiel Hut - 2 hours
        (This is an almost 'downhill only' route, which includes one short climb
        alongside a spectacular waterfall and a last slope before the Hut.)

Monte Rosa Hut 2,795m 130 sleeping places Tel: (028) 67 21 15
From Rotenboden (last train station before reaching Gornergrat) - 2 hours
Access across the Gorner Glacier (dangerous when covered in new snow)

Rothorn Hut 3,198 m   104 sleeping places Tel: (028) 67 20 43
4 hours from Zermatt via Trift

Täsch Hut 1,701m   70 sleeping places Tel: (028) 67 39 13
1 hour from Täschalp

Hörnli Hut 3,260m   50 sleeping places Tel: (028) 67 27 69
and
Hotel Belvédère 3,260m 120 sleeping places Tel: (028) 67 22 64
2 hours from Schwarzsee

Weisshorn Hut 2,932m   30 sleeping places   Tel: (028) 67 12 62
4½ hours from Randa.   or (028) 67 38 53

In the event of no reply from the Weisshorn Hut numbers listed above or for
further information do not hesitate to contact Familie Pollinger at the Hotel Dom
in Randa (028) 67 35 56. As the descendants of the renowned Mountain Guide
Aloys Pollinger,[1] they are always glad to help and give any information you may
require regarding the Weisshorn Hut, its access and the conditions of the day.

Reaching the Hut is not difficult: it requires good boots and some training, i.e.
don't embark on it on the first day of your holiday!

The guardian of the Mountain Hut always checks his booking list against arrivals.
It is therefore most important to cancel a booking, should it not be possible, for one
reason or another, to reach a Hut. Failure to do so could spark off a costly search
and rescue operation.

A telephone call is all it takes.
Coins needed for public telephones:
10 centimes, 20 centimes and 1 Swiss Franc piece.

Water supply is often a problem at the altitude of Mountain Huts. Bottled water,
together with all other refreshments can be bought from the guardian (not cheap
because of the cost of transport - mainly by helicopter). It is worth bringing an
extra amount of tap water for brushing teeth, etc.

1. Aloys Pollinger (1844 - 1910) originated from Skt Nicklaus. He was one of the great guides of the Golden Age of
Mountaineering and achieved many first ascents, skillfully guiding English climbers. He excelled at rock climbing and
introduced the double-rope abseiling technique.

Respect the environment: no litter and please use the WC facilities provided.

Warm clothing must always be carried as the difference between day and night temperature is greater here than in other areas of the Swiss Alps. Evenings are fresh!

Some of the walks to the Huts are long, and elementary precautions must be observed:

Sun-hat, sun-glasses, and generous application of sun cream.

Good boots are essential.

A stick can be helpful and in the event of snow and/or ice, a piolet and crampons may be required.

For example: A walk up to the Hörnli Hut, following *fresh snow* on the Matterhorn or a *frosty night* may require crampons and/or a stick on the north facing slope. Children must be discouraged from running and if necessary held on a rope until the 'age of reason'.

Adequate quantities of fluid are needed as well as some food. Scissors and plasters are always a good precaution!

A visit to a Mountain Hut is always worth whatever effort is required. It should be considered a real privilege to be able to leave the trappings of civilisation behind and step close to nature, enjoy its overwhelming grandeur and beauty, and absorb the changing atmosphere between daytime splendour and night-time mystery.

THE FUNCTION OF THE ALTIMETER

Barometric Altitude Measurement

THE USE OF a large scale map such as Landeskarte der Schweiz 1: 25 000 No. 1348 for Zermatt, a compass and an altimeter are a must for the security of any mountaineer or off-piste skier. Within the snow–line it can be the only way to establish a location especially in poor visibility when the human eye is of little use!

Altimeters work on the principle of the weight of the column of air above a given point on the earth's surface: The higher this point lies, the lower are the weight of the air column and the air pressure. Altimeters use the same principle as barometers. Instead of the barometer's column of mercury, the aneroid altimeter consists of a small vacuum capsule with an elastic surface which reacts to air pressure and gives a reading via a spring gauge.

Added to the air pressure is the temperature factor. An erroneous reading could occur if air temperature differences are not interpreted correctly. For an altimeter to be as accurate as possible it is important that the dial should be evenly graduated and the divisons set far apart. In the case of the recommended altimeter *THOMMEN* with altitude scale divisions of 10m, a reading error by the user should not exceed $\pm$ 2m. Because of its high degree of accuracy this particular altimeter copes with the high altitudes of the Himalayas and is used by expedition teams.

When using an altimeter it is of great importance to reset it on a daily basis because of the variations in barometric pressure. A precondition for accurate setting is knowledge of the exact height above sea level at the altimeter's location. During a climb, check the altimeter against an up-to-date map or triangulation point at regular intervals and reset if necessary. The altimeter is affected by fluctuations in air pressure. If the reading of a correctly set altimeter exceeds the altitude at a 'check point' it means that a drop in atmospheric pressure has taken place, or vice versa.

In the mountains it is important to know when to turn back in order to survive to climb another day. To be caught in a thunderstorm on a rockface is extremely dangerous. As an example, the sudden fall of barometric pressure in summer signifies that a thunderstorm is in the offing, when a cautious retreat is indicated.

On a lighter note, an altimeter will monitor a climber's progress. With the information obtained from it a formula to measure one's degree of fitness may be applied: Height gained of so many metres, time taken so many hours, plus evaluation of difficulties and contours of a climb. Thus an altimeter may help to assess one's improved fitness during a stay in the mountains: an encouragement to get fit and shake off the pressures of everyday living.

For your orientation.

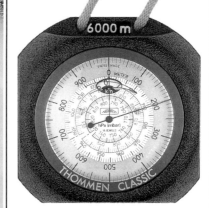

ALTILAND

Watch with altimeter and compass, interchangeable. Self-winding mechanical movement. 0–4500 meters mechanical altimeter with barometric scale. Magnetic compass.

THOMMEN CLASSIC

Mechanical pocket altimeter plus barometer. Extremely robust and shock-resistant. The compact size and the versatility makes the THOMMEN CLASSIC your partner for altitudes up to 9000 meters.

ℛ

REVUE THOMMEN

Fine Swiss Watches Since 1853

CH-2300 La Chaux-de-Fonds
Tel. 039 26 40 22

ALTIMETERS

Revue Thommen AG
CH-4437 Waldenburg
Tel. 061 965 22 22

Available in Zermatt at G. Muther and other optic & sports shops.

CLIMBING WITH A MOUNTAIN GUIDE

WITH THE HELP and professional advice of a Mountain Guide, a fit and eager 'would be mountaineer', even a beginner, can achieve rewarding climbs within the grading section of PD + or 2 + **within a matter of days** and find himself standing on the summit of a 4,000m mountain with a tremendous feeling of achievement.

A Mountain Guide will teach you the basic techniques required for the various climbs. He will soon know exactly what your overall capabilities are and only attempt the climbs he knows you will cope with and enjoy doing. He will also remove uncertainties and give you confidence. A Mountain Guide has infinite knowledge and knows the best routes: route finding is invaluable.

In climbing, as indeed in all sport, there is progression. Each year adds to the knowledge and experience of the mountains, and more testing climbs can be attempted and enjoyed.

Here, the message is: keep fit and you can find yourself standing on top of a summit, up into the dizzy heights and stunning beauties of the Alps with the world at your feet.

But never forget that the beauty of the mountains is to be found at all levels : high up amongst the peaks or down in the valleys. Stunning views are everywhere, whether you look UP at the summits or DOWN from their dizzy heights.

There is truly something and somewhere for everyone.

GRADINGS AS USED IN THE TECHNICAL DESCRIPTION OF CLIMBS
DEVISED BY
U.I.A.A.
UNION INTERNATIONALE DES ASSOCIATIONS D'ALPINISME
INTERNATIONAL UNION OF ALPINIST ASSOCIATIONS

Rock climbs are numerically graded. Mixed climbs (rock and snow) are alphabetically graded.
Both gradings are in six stages:-

Rock Climbs		Rock and Snow Climbs	
Grade 1	corresponds to	F	(Easy)
2	corresponds to	PD	(Moderately difficult)
3	corresponds to	AD	(Fairly difficult)
4	corresponds to	D	(Difficult)
5	corresponds to	TD	(Very difficult)
6	corresponds to	ED	(Extremely difficult)

The alphabetical abbreviations come from the French terminology. In order to show variations within the grading system a plus and minus rating can be added to the basic grading system: + means above and - means below.
The following examples demonstrate how the grading system operates:

(a) Climbs from the starting point of the Rothorn Hut (the right hand side of the valley)

Wellenkuppe   Grade PD
Obergabelhorn   Grade AD

(b) Climbs from the starting point of Fluhalp or Täsch Hut (the left hand side of the valley)

The Rimpfischhorn which is often used as a training mountain   Grade PD
Its north Ridge, however, which represents a traverse from Fluhalp to the Täsch Hut   Grade AD

(c) The Matterhorn

Climbs from the starting point of Hörnli Hut and Belvédère Hotel
following the easiest and most popular route   Rock climb: Grade 2
Above the shoulder and above the Solvay Hut   Rock climb: Grade 3
     Snow and rock mixed areas: AD+

(This is made more accessible by the presence of fixed ropes.)

The grading system takes into account the following three aspects:
1 The technical expertise required.
2 The length of the climb: the physical endurance and degree of personal fitness expected.
3 The possibility of natural dangers.

NB. The pacing of personal energy levels must be taken into account.
Be realistic about climbing ability and endurance level.
Always take as much note of the time required to make the DESCENT as you do of the time of the ASCENT.

METEOROLOGY AND CONDITIONS

Note the CONDITIONS on a daily basis. Conditions are everything.

They include:
Weather forecasts, LOCAL weather forecasts for day and night time, with special emphasis on temperature.

In warm and dry weather the mountains are friendly and accessible with something and somewhere for everyone.

Excess heat can affect high altitude areas and cause thawing, resulting in rock falls and snow slides, etc. Wet, icy, or snowy rocks, slopes and even simple mountain paths can become treacherous. Specialist equipment is required to deal with the conditions.

Rain in the village can turn to snow on the higher slopes.

THE BREITHORN

The Breithorn, altitude 4,164m, was first climbed on 13 August 1813, 21 years after the first ascent of the Klein Matterhorn. Those were early days in the history of mountaineering and looking at old photographs and pieces of equipment (especially the boots!) which are preserved in the Alpine Museum at Zermatt, one wonders how anyone reached the summit, let alone lived to tell the tale. Modern climbing equipment has made the mountains much more accessible, and in good conditions the ascent of the Breithorn (graded F: easy) presents no problems. The Breithorn, a large and imposing mountain, is the easiest 4,000m summit to climb - easy and yet exciting. A contradiction in terms? Because of its size, or rather its huge volume, climbing the Breithorn is a powerful experience, to be remembered always. No one who has climbed the Breithorn on a good day will ever forget the exhilarating feeling of freedom he or she experienced on reaching the summit with its generous wide surface to stand on. With the world seemingly at your feet, it is a true and perfect escape from civilisation and everyday preoccupations - in short, it is an adventure.

One of the most extraordinary and rewarding elements of the Breithorn is that it can be climbed by so many people. **After just a few days' walking and rambling (in short: training) there is no reason why a fit but complete amateur cannot experience the thrills and the beauty the Breithorn has to offer**. The only proviso being: you must be accompanied by a qualified Mountain Guide.

A climb up the Breithorn includes several basic aspects of climbing techniques such as walking in a party roped together across a glacier (the Breithorn plateau), putting on crampons, jumping a crevasse. These techniques present a new experience for a first time 'climber' and enhance the sense of adventure.

The Breithorn is aesthetically a very beautiful mountain with its large dome curving gently against the skyline like an almost perfect white bow. Thus it is perhaps not surprising that in 1909 the French government purchased a painting by the well known Swiss painter Albert Gos[1] who painted many Alpine scenes in Zermatt, both of the mountains and the Stadels.[2] The painting was destined for the 'Musée du Luxembourg' and it was the first time that a 4,000m summit was the subject of a painting chosen to join the well-known state collection: a tribute to the great painter and to the mountain which inspired him. Indeed, the mountain which has invited so many people to make a **first ascent**.

A SUMMER ASCENT OF THE BREITHORN (4,164m)

The conditions for today's climb are perfect. The weather is warm, sunny, and the wind still. You can see this from the village. The snow- and ice-covered dome of the Breithorn stands out white and clear against the blue sky. There is no feathery cloud rising from its summit to indicate wind and whipped up snow.

1. See the chapter: 'The Artist's View of Zermatt'.

2. Stable/barn

A day like this is a climber's dream.

We catch the first cable car to Trockener Steg, where we change for Klein Matterhorn. There are at least two dozen climbers in the same cabin - not surprising when conditions are so good - and there will be more 'Alpinists' following on the next cable cars ... latecomers. We, however, have a serious plan. We want to be the first party of climbers to stand on the summit. Well organised as we are, there will be no time wasted at the top of the cable car ride on adjusting boots and rucksacks and putting on sun cream.[1] This was seen to whilst waiting for the cable car at Furi.

But for now, we are enjoying the ride. However many times you take the cable car up to Klein Matterhorn it is always a fascinating experience. There is so much to see: the Gandegg Hut with its flag wrapped round the flagpole - another good sign regarding the wind. Then the ride over the ridge above the Unterer Theodul glacier which disappears down towards the Gorner glacier. Above and straight ahead of us, the almost vertical north facing wall of the Klein Matterhorn which the cable car is going to rise up against. On our left, the north and north west sides of the Breithorn loom larger as we get closer to them.

The wide face of the Breithorn which looks down on Zermatt presents a completely different aspect from the south-facing side we are going to tackle. What we are looking at now, from the cable car, is the domain of expert climbers: exacting, with exciting and delicate routes, including an ice climb on the north face of the central summit (4,159m) graded TD.[2] Because of its great variety of routes and its long extended ridge (2.5km), the Breithorn is many a local climber's favourite mountain.

Between us and the Breithorn lies the spectacular Klein Matterhorn glacier. It must be one of the most crevassed glaciers in the area: crevasses followed by a series of short flat plateaux, constantly eroded, are covered in icy rubble. They are potential death traps, as ice falls are unpredictable. It is beautiful and awe-inspiring even from the safe distance of the cable car. We play games and try to work out a route over the dramatic ice fall - we fail. The whole glacier looks as if an earthquake had shaken its foundations and left it looking like a heap of slabs leaning together at crazy angles.

At the top, first out of the cable car .... We are going to be the first team to stand on the summit of the Breithorn today. A long corridor traverses the top of the Klein Matterhorn and takes us onto a large south-facing plateau.

Directly opposite, the ice dome of the Gobba di Rollin (3,902m) rises gently at the edge of a white expanse. As far as the eye can see there are chains of mountains: the Italian Alps.

Over to the west: Testa Grigia and the Italian cable car station.

Behind it, far away in the distance: Mont Blanc.

Nearer to us the omnipresent Matterhorn exposes its sunbathed east side.

Rucksacks on the ground, the climbers are getting ready to rope up. Our guide uncoils the rope with his usual careful, measured gestures - no haste. We are rearing to go, like horses let out of the stable. 'This is not really the way to approach a

1. A high factor protection sun cream is strongly recommended.
2. TD (very difficult) corresponds to grade 5 in rock climbing. See beginning of chapter.

mountain climb'. These thoughts are written all over the face of our Mountain Guide and echoed by wise words: 'A little calm won't hurt. You'll need your energy and stamina to get up to the top and be fit enough to enjoy the experience.' He is right, of course. Although the south-facing climb up the Breithorn is relatively short, we shall climb well above 4,000m, a magical level of altitude in the Alps.

Ready to go, roped together, rucksacks comfortable, boots well adjusted – we set off, in the lead, a party of four including our guide. We are all friends sharing a walking holiday in the Alps. The three of us have been walking for five days now, longer distances each day, and are fit and ready to conquer the mountain. This is going to be our first real climb with a guide.

At the start our party keeps to the ski piste straight ahead. Now we turn our backs on 'civilisation' and progress eastward, in a long bow across the vast, empty plateau. One half expects to hear the sounds of an Eskimo sledge with its pack of dogs. The landscape has a true polar atmosphere at this time of the morning. The snowfield looks innocent enough but is treacherous in parts, hiding deep crevasses, and we must keep to the track.

Slowly but surely we curve round and are now climbing north. The south face of the Breithorn is facing us, white robed with a band of rocks near the top. At the foot of the mountain, just before crossing a wide crevasse, we put on our crampons. This is a new experience, and we have practised putting them on the night before. Our guide checks to see that they are safely strapped on and allows us a short break to drink some fluids and put on another layer of sun cream. It is getting hot, and we have been climbing gently but steadily towards our mountain. We are the first of the groups. The others are quite a long way back.

'Good progress' says the guide. 'Now be careful how you walk with the crampons. Keep your feet apart so that they don't catch.' On we go, carefully, one after the other up to the crevasse. One jump, and we are over it. Although there is always a crevasse in that area, some years it is so narrow that it is hardly noticeable.

There follows a long traverse to the west before turning the corner and climbing almost straight up, to the top. The last stage is steep and we walk heads bent, watching our feet. The crampons give us a wonderful feeling of security as they dig into the slope. Concentrating so hard, it comes as a surprise when we emerge at the top and raise our eyes. The summit is wide and slightly convex which gives the impression of standing on the surface of a globe: in other words, on top of the world. The feeling is indescribable, words too difficult to find. But standing up there, first looking across to the Matterhorn, then down at the tiny village of Zermatt, raising our eyes and focusing on the Bernese Alps in the distance, beyond the Zermatt valley, over to the Monte Rosa and its adjoining peaks – then turning around to look at a seemingly endless sea of blue tinted Italian Alps – turning further west towards the French Alps and back to the Matterhorn – we know why people climb mountains, know why some feel drawn to attempt the impossible.

The Breithorn, on a good day and in good conditions, is the most welcoming 4,000m mountain. On this glorious, wind free day we savour the moment. It was well worth being first on the top! It is time to pass around the traditional wine to celebrate a successful ascent. The Fendant has been kept ice cold in a military flask inside the guide's rucksack. It tastes better than anything we could dream of. A fleeting thought of the special bottles of 'Fendant Réserve' served from shining ice buckets in the small restaurants dotted over the mountains and down in the village crystallises the contrasts one can experience on holiday in the Alps: sophistication and simplicity, tranquillity and adventure.

No doubt we shall enjoy a good meal tonight, but at this very moment in time nothing could taste better than our frugal picnic here on top of our first 4,000m summit.

Approximate ascent time: 1h 30min to 2h
Approximate descent time: 1h 30min

Equipment: Strong boots
                         Ice axe – Piolet
                         Crampons
                         Rope
                         Map/Compass/Altimeter optional

Important items: Sun-hat and warm hat or cap
                         Dark sun-glasses with good UV filter
                         Gloves

THE PIOLET (ICE AXE)

The piolet is about 1m long, depending on the height of its owner. Point downwards it is used as a stick to ram into soft snow or mud to hold the climber's weight. The other end is used to cut steps in the ice with the axe head to create a foothold.

ROUTES TO THE BREITHORN

ROUTE A

The most popular route up the Breithorn and probably one of the most frequented route up the 4,000m summit. It is described in some detail in 'A Summer Ascent of the Breithorn' (earlier in this chapter).

Route: ZERMATT
      TROCKENER STEG
        KLEIN MATTERHORN
          BREITHORN PLATEAU
          BREITHORN

Cable car as far as Klein Matterhorn.
Time of ascent: 1h to 1h 30min.

ROUTE B1 ZERMATT
      TROCKENER STEG
        GANDEGG HUT
            TESTA GRIGIA (Italian cable car station)
          BREITHORN PLATEAU
          BREITHORN

Cable car as far as Trockener Steg.
Trockener Steg to Gandegg Hut: a mere 30 minute walk following a path on the moraine, straight ahead on the left of the glacier/ski slope facing Trockener Steg cable car station.
Overnight stay at the Gandegg Hut (altitude 3,029m). The hut is privately owned, and has approximately 35 sleeping places. Advance booking is strongly recommended. Mobile telephone number: (077) 28 39 96; other telephone number (028) 67 21 96.
Open from about 20 June to 20 September, but it is advisable to check the dates. This ascent requires a very early start.
Before the cable car section Trockener Steg to Klein Matterhorn was open, the Mountain Guides from Zermatt took their clients up to the Gandegg Hut and stayed overnight before starting the ascent of the Breithorn. Now that the final section of the cable car is in operation, it has transformed the climb of the Breithorn into a 'one day tour'. But for the purist and very fit mountaineer the 'Gandegg Hut' option remains.

Short description of the route:
Follow well marked path on top of the moraine, gently climbing straight ahead, direction south. The path eventually edges down to the glacier (Oberer Theodul Gletscher). **ROPE UP** and cross the glacier, rising steadily and moving right over to the ski piste, direction south east. In summer and in the absence of fresh snow the crevasses are **usually** visible. Should there be a fall of fresh snow to a

depth of 20cm or over, a glacier crossing can become dangerous, and the new snow must be allowed time to settle. This can happen quickly if the cold weather conditions change back to hot and sunny days. At all times follow the recommendations of the guide office and of the guardian and staff of the Gandegg Hut.

This route by-passes the Theodul Hut and the Theodul Pass itself. Instead, it curves slightly to the left, following the ski piste all the way up to Testa Grigia (the Italian cable car station). From there, the route follows a zigzag pattern: left, right, and left again, up to the Breithorn Plateau.

At the point where the Klein Matterhorn cable car station is on the left and the dome of the Gobba di Rollin on the right, Route **B1**) joins up with Route A as described in 'A Summer Ascent of the Breithorn' from: 'Now we turn our backs on civilisation'. The same applies to this part of Route **B1**. Up to this point the glacier is peopled with skiers and ski-lifts. There are refuge facilities both at the Theodul Hut and at Testa Grigia. And up to this point a Mountain Guide is not necessary **for a visitor with prior mountaineering experience** provided proper equipment is used, i.e. good boots and a **rope**, sun-glasses, sun-hat, and high protection sun cream (for face, neck, and ears) and lip cream. Adequate clothing is important: on a hot day, cover your arms, or protect them with sun cream.

Approximate ascent times: Gandegg Hut – Testa Grigia 1h 30min
                                Testa Grigia – Breithorn Plateau 1h 30min
                                Breithorn Plateau – Breithorn 1h to 1h 30min
Total: Between 4h and 5h depending on conditions and
                                fitness!

ROUTE B2   ZERMATT
TROCKENER STEG
THEODUL HUT
TESTA GRIGIA (Italian cable car station)
BREITHORN PLATEAU
BREITHORN

Cable car as far as Trockener Steg.
Trockener Steg to Theodul Hut via Gandegg Hut: 1h 30min
Route as described in **B1**, except that on reaching the Theodul Pass (3,301m) you climb up to the Pass and on to the Theodul Hut (3,317m).
The Theodul Pass and the Theodul Hut are on the far right of the ski piste – where one ski lift ends and another begins to take the summer skiers back up to Testa Grigia. The Theodul Hut, a white washed building, blends well into the landscape of ice and rocks and is therefore not always easily spotted.
Overnight stay at the Theodul Hut, the property of the Italian Alpine Club: 67 sleeping places, but it is always well used so advance booking is strongly recommended.
Tel: (0039) 166 494 900 from Switzerland, (0039) 166 494 900 from the UK.
The Hut is open from about 20 June to 20 September, but it is advisable to check the dates.

It is important to have an early start for next stage: Theodul Hut to Testa Grigia (Italian cable car station) to Breithorn Plateau to Breithorn.
The Route is described in **B1**. The main difference lies in the division of the ascent times; Route **B2** takes 30min more on the first day and 30min less on the second day.

None of the routes mentioned in the Breithorn Section is a 'one man walk'. It is always advisable to be **roped** on a glacier, even on a ski piste. Skis act as 'bridges' on possible cracks in the ice, **boots do not**. Provided every precaution, as mentioned in the book, is taken and additional advice sought at the guide office in Zermatt and/or the Gandegg Hut, the section Gandegg Hut to Theodul Hut in particular, with a possible extension to the Testa Grigia complex, provides an excellent short trip and an exciting experience of the glacier world. But if in doubt, or in the case of a beginner's first encounter with the land of ice and rock, why not take a guide? A Mountain Guide will pass on his specialist knowledge, teach you the art of 'roping up' and make your day relaxing and enjoyable by taking over the responsibility for your safety.

Telephone number of the Mountain Guides' office Zermatt (Bergführerverein Zermatt)

67 34 56 from Zermatt, 00 41 28 67 34 56 from the UK.
Fax number of above: 67 21 55 from Zermatt, 00 41 67 21 55 from the UK.

The North Face of The Breithorn: Alpine guide books list in the region of eleven routes and/or variations on the north face of the Breithorn apart from the well-known traverse from east to west graded AD with pitches 111/111+ and termed 'delicate'. All the other climbs on the north face are for experts only and their description can be found, among others, in:
    The Swiss Alpine Club Book *Hochtouren im Wallis, Vom Trient zum Nufenenpass* by Hermann Biner, President of the Zermatt Guide Association.
    The British Alpine Club Guide Book entitled *Pennine Alps Central*, compiled and edited by Robin G. Collomb. It has two companion volumes covering the East and West Pennine Alps. The books are produced and sold for the Alpine Club London by West Col Productions, Goring, Reading, Berks.

THE GANDEGG HUT
Altitude 3,029m

The Gandegg Hut was first built in 1885. At that time, the Burger Gemeinde sold the site above Trockener Steg, which was non-arable and consisted of glacier rubble on top of the moraine. It was sold to Peter Ludwig Perren and his partner Viktor Furrer. The Hut and land are still owned by the same families, now in the fourth generation. It is the only privately owned Hut on such terrain.
    In the summer, the Gandegg Hut is run on the lines of a mountain hut with sleeping accommodation for about thirty five people.

Reservation in high season is strongly recommended.

Telephone number from the UK 00 41 28 67 21 96, from Zermatt 67 21 96.

In case there is no reply use the Mobile telephone Natel: 077 28 39 96 from Zermatt

The Gandegg Hut advertises itself as open during the winter season, on a daytime basis only. Here, even the fastest 'piste bashers' can get a taste of the pioneering days of mountaineering.

FOLLOW UP TOURS FROM THE KLEIN MATTERHORN CABLE CAR STATION

After a first climb of the Breithorn, the ascent of neighbouring Pollux (4,092m) can be a good continuation and progression in mountaineering terms, as it involves some rock climbing.

Moving towards Liskamm (4,527m), the Cabane Margherita (at 4,554m the highest mountain Hut in the Alps), and the Monte Rosa Massif (4,634m), the summit following Pollux is Castor (4,228m), a snow mountain. The distance from the Klein Matterhorn cable car station to Castor is further still than to Pollux, and therefore the climb up to the summit of Castor is longer. An option for the descent from Castor is to go and spend the night at the Sella Hut in Italy before returning to Zermatt.

CIMA DI JAZZI (3,803m)

THE HIGHEST PEAK ON THE FRONTIER RIDGE BETWEEN THE STRAHLHORN AND MONTE ROSA

This is an excellent spring tour on skis and summer tour on foot.

The most popular route is

ZERMATT - GORNERGRAT (First morning train) - CABLE CAR TO STOCKHORN STATION (3,405m)

The height difference between Stockhorn station and Cima di Jazzi is not great. After rising over 100m to the Stockhorn summit (3,532m) following the Ridge, there is, however, a descent to the Stockhorn Pass (3,394m) which inevitably prolongs the tour.

From the pass the route goes east climbing to a height of about 3,650m, where the direction changes to north, to be followed by a climb via the north-facing slope to the summit. There are particularly beautiful views to the east from the wide, flat expanse at the top.

The Cima di Jazzi, which looks like a harmless snow mountain, an inviting, broad sugar loaf, is in reality a glacier which hides many dangerous crevasses and must therefore never be under-estimated. In the event of a sudden weather change or fog, route finding becomes extremely difficult.

In warm and sunny conditions, the popular ascent of the Cima di Jazzi is always rewarding. It can be a great introduction to Alpine spring ski-touring (for good skiers), as well as to summer climbing. The rise is gentle, and only the last slope shows any significant steepness. The return route follows the ascent line.

Approximate ascent time Stockhorn cable car station to summit: 3 hours.

Recommended equipment:		
	Rope	Altimeter
	Strong boots/Crampons	Compass
	Ice axe/Piolet	Map

Respect the recommended distance between roped up climbers, i.e. a 'long rope'.

PFULWE TO UNTERROTHORN TRAVERSE

ZERMATT
  SUNNEGGA
    BLAUHERD
      STELLISEE
        FLUHALP
          ZERLAUENEN
        PFULWE
            SCHWARZGRAT
           SATTEL
             FLUEHORN
            SATTEL
               CONTINUATION OF
                 SCHWARZGRAT
                   UNTERROTHORN

Recommended equipment:	
	Climbing Boots
	Map
	Altimeter/Compass
	Rope
	Climbing Stick (for descent to Fluhalp)

Check the running times of Sunnegga Express, Blauherd Gondelbahn and Unterrothorn cable car before starting out.

The day starts at a gentle pace. Most days in Zermatt start this way. Sun on the Matterhorn. The sound of church bells. Sleepy looking houses. Empty village streets. A few speeding mountain bikes and early risers hurrying to work.

Climbers gather at the train and cable car stations, rucksacks, sticks and ice axes resting on the ground, whilst they wait for the first 'take off'. There is always an air of excitement and anticipation surrounding the climbers early in the morning.

We catch the first Sunnegga Express train. In no time we are taken at high speed through a steep tunnel inside the mountain up to Sunnegga where we step into the sunshine to face a full view of the Matterhorn – breathtaking! From there on, we use bubble cars to reach Blauherd, the next station up. We could have walked but prefer to save our strength for the big climb.

A short distance above Blauherd a signpost points to the right, to Fluhalp. The air is fresh and crisp at it always is, even on the hottest summer day. The path circles the mountain and a few metres around the corner an entirely new panorama unfolds in front of our eyes.

We are walking facing the sun rising above the Adlerpass (3,789m), the Strahlhorn (4,190m), and the Adlerhorn (3,988m), its distinctive shape pointing into the sky like a snow clad finger. As we walk on, the rather squat shape of the Rimpfischhorn (4,198.9m) comes into view, its face darkened by vertical stripes of black rock.[3] The Matterhorn is behind us and we are all too frequently tempted to stop and gaze at the tall elegant peak, its east face bathed in warm sunlight – pale gold.

Further on, a signpost on our left indicates 'Stellisee' and a narrow path takes us straight up to a small lake teeming with tiny fish. There is not a breath of wind. An entire glorious panorama of mountains is reflected in the still waters of the lake. The shapes of the Strahlhorn and of the Adlerhorn appear first as we approach the shores of the lake. The Klein Matterhorn area from the direction of Italy comes into view, followed by the long ridge from Gornergrat to Stockhorn. Cable cars connect the two mountains and the cable car cabins come and go on the surface of the lake as they move along the ridge.

As we round the top end of the lake we see reflected in the water from right across the valley a whole chain of mountains.

From left to right: three peaks stand out:

The Zinalrothorn (4,221.2m), a famous rock mountain, probably the most beautiful rock climb of the Zermatt area.

The Obergabelhorn (4,062.9m), a large pyramid mountain, lower than the Zinalrothorn, but from here taller looking.

The Wellenkuppe (3,903m), generally known as the 'satellite' of the Obergabelhorn. The Wellenkuppe has a special shape which always catches the eye: a rock face with its point hidden inside a white rectangular shape of snow and ice. The 'geometrical' figure looks as if it has been deposited by a giant hand on to the top of the mountain, as a kind of afterthought.

At last to the left of the chain of mountains, on its own, is the Matterhorn, reflected full length into the waters of the Stellisee – a sight of unbelievable beauty. When a faint breeze disturbs the water the sharp reflection becomes blurred and

---

3. Behind all these mountains, through the Adlerpass which translated means 'the Eagle Pass', you will find the Britannia Hut (3,030m) built in 1912 thanks to a subscription from the association of British Members of the Swiss Alpine Club (hence its name). The way to the Britannia Hut is long and there are many treacherous crevasses on the glaciers. In clear weather, however, and good conditions - as well as with the help of a Mountain Guide who knows where the crevasses are - the crossing can be achieved without too much difficulty. The passage from Zermatt to the Britannia Hut is the last but one section of the classic 'Haute Route', the 'Alpine Highway' which stretches all the way from Chamonix (France) to Saas Fee.

mysterious as if the mountain is about to vanish.

As well as mountains, clumps of plants and small rocks bathe their image in the water of the lake. Shapes, lines: a photographer's paradise and a painter's inspiration. Why proceed and climb at all? A day's meditation is tempting. But further up there will be more - other views, dramatic sights - and rocks to be conquered, smooth rocks, warm to the hands on this sunny day.

As we leave the Stellisee we turn around once more and see the upper half of the Matterhorn singled out and perfectly framed inside a wide V, beween two large rocks. We pass Fluhalp and come across two wooden huts, the wood darkened by years of strong sun. Another small lake sparkles next to the narrow, well-worn path: the path to Pfulwe (3,155m). It soon gets steep and we start to climb up in earnest. We leave behind much of the vegetation and move towards the scree. At the height of 2,920m[4] we leave the path and climb up slightly to the left. We continue, always bearing left. Just below us an ibex and her young offspring run across loose rubble and rocks, sure-footed and fast. At last, we reach a point where we can climb onto the ridge. We are standing at the Schwarzgrat, and this is where we rope up. Route finding is a very good reason for climbing with a Mountain Guide and once again it proves to be invaluable. How could we have found the best access to the ridge without his expert knowledge?

We follow the ridge by climbing over rock turrets or circling them when we can. It is good rock, sometimes dark brown and coppery in colour or sometimes silver grey with patches of vivid orange lichen. Occasionally we have to look out for loose stones. This is the 'real thing', real climbing: what satisfaction when we

4. Use an altimeter.

find the 'perfect' handhold! Our guide tells us that we are climbing grade 2 - 3. We move quite slowly and savour the moment. The views on both sides of the ridge are spectacular: on the one side the valley leading to Ottavan, the hamlet on the Täschalp with all its surrounding peaks and on the other side, a wide open view across the Findeln Glacier to the mountains beyond. Suddenly, we come across one of those 'miracles' of magnificence the mountain world has to offer: a window in the rocks, a perfect porthole which frames the Allalinhorn (4,027.4m).[5] Fortunately, at this point the ledge is wide enough to enable us to stop comfortably and take the camera out of the rucksack. As an extra bonus, next to the porthole, the Rimpfischhorn is in full view and poses between two large jagged rocks.

As we reach the end of the ridge we arrive at a saddle (Sattel) and easy terrain. From that point it is possible to descend down to Fluhalp. The scree is very loose, and one must keep high, just below the solid rocks, in a south westerly direction. We lose height gradually and reach the grassy area safely before moving slightly over to the left in order to avoid a rock band.

The classic route, however, continues from the saddle up to the Fluehorn (3,225m). We step over easy blocks of rocks in a gentle ascent to the top. The same terrain takes you down to the next saddle and on to the last climb of the 'Schwarzgrat'. This is the most interesting climbing area of the whole expedition. It is a little more difficult than the first part but it is also the most satisfying.

At point 3230 of the map: Landkarte 1 - 25,000 (Zermatt-Gornergrat area) we leave the ridge in the direction of the Unterrothorn and the end of our expedition. From there, a cable car takes us down to Blauherd.

THE FURGGGRAT

In Italian: Cresta della Forca

The Furgggrat follows the ridge between the Theodul Pass and the east face of the Matterhorn. The tour is best undertaken from east to west, facing the Matterhorn all the way. To reach the departure point of the tour there are two possibilities:

1 **Trockener Steg (by cable car)**
    Gandegg Hut
        Edge of Theodul Glacier, from there ROPED UP to
           Theodul Hut
                Furgggrat
2 **Klein Matterhorn (by cable car). Descent ROPED UP to**
    Testa Grigia and on down to the
        Theodul Hut
           Furgggrat

5. The Allalinhorn is considered to be one of the easiest 4,000m mountains. It consists mainly of snow and glacier (which varies from year to year) with a cap of black rock at the top.

In both cases a 7.00h departure is the norm. The climb up to the ridge begins behind the Theodul Hut. From there on, the walk follows the frontier line between Italy and Switzerland. There are conically shaped frontier stones all along the ridge. Multicoloured rocks of all shapes, within the snow-line, offer a feast of variety to the eyes.

From the foot of the Theodulhorn the climb follows the left hand ridge in easy rock climbing. On top of the Theodulhorn is a very distinctive, totally calcified rock which looks as if it must have originally lain under water.

The view is magnificent and all embracing: down, to Breuil or Cervinia. To the south, the Italian Alps, Gran Paradiso, and Monte Viso. Back east, to the Breithorn, which hides Castor and Pollux, on to Lyskam, Monte Rosa, Adlerhorn, and Strahlhorn with Gornergrat below. On to the Rimpfischhorn, the Alphubel, Allalin, and the jagged points of the Mischabel Group further down the Zermatt Valley, the Matter Tal.

Straight across, in the distance, are the Bernese Alps. Then, to the west, past the Matterhorn, is the Dent d'Hérens on its left, and the Dent Blanche on its right. Then follow the Zinalrothorn, Obergabelhorn, Wellenkuppe, the mighty and daunting Weisshorn, and closer to, the Mettelhorn which, situated on the right of Trift, is one of the best training mountains in the area.

We leave the Theodulhorn to the right, over snow and most interesting calcium silicate rocks. The area looks like a field of calcium, grey white in colour. An easy descent of approximately 120m leads to the Furggsattel where a ski-lift, which operates in the winter season from Trockener Steg, ends up. From the Sattel, a snow climb takes us up to the Furgghorn. The Furgghorn provides an overall view of the ridge and of the Furgggletscher all the way down to Hirli.

From here, a beautiful white snow ridge, stretching straight ahead, leads to the Furggen Station where a tiny cable car used to ascend from the Italian side.

The eyes drop down into Italy, to the artificial lake: Lago Goillet, and below to the cable car station of Plan Maison, seen from up here just as a small white square amongst the meadows. A few snow steps and small towers, i.e. 'Kletterei' (easy climbing), as our Zermatt guide calls it, before a last snowfield brings us onto the roof of the cable car station.

Standing on the left of the station is an orientation table, showing all the surrounding peaks. In the middle of the roof, two benches invite us to rest. We tuck into our sandwiches, munch a dried sausage, drink sweet lemon tea and finish off with dried fruit. A real feast! Then we pass round the wine in the traditional military gourd to sip a toast to the remarkable views. We see three of the Matterhorn ridges: on the left the imposing Italian ridge, La Cresta Leone. In the middle, the steeply rising Furgggrat and on the right, dotted with many towers, the Hörnli Ridge under the shoulder of the Matterhorn, and the Solvay Hut, a small brown hut at an altitude of 4,003m. We also notice at the right base of the Matterhorn great activity at the Hörnli Hut.

On the left, at the lower Glacier 'del Cervino', we spot the refuge Orionde at 2,802m, to the right of a small lake. A deep couloir marks the Colle del Leone, a dangerous and difficult pass, only of historical interest, which lies between the Matterhorn and the Testa del Leone (Lion's Head). On the first part of the Italian

Ridge we also spot the Rifugio di Savoia 3,835m, with the nearby hut: Il Rifugio Jean-Antoine Carrel, opened in 1969.

The view from here seems to be particularly clear and beautiful over the Obergabelhorngrat. Then, the entire chain from the Obergabelhorn to the Weisshorn rises, mighty and splendid, etched against the blue of the sky. Looking back, further away, now to the east, the Breithorn and Monte Rosa massifs look peaceful and sparkle in the sunshine. This is a perfect resting place in which to regain strength and vitality.

The descent of about 140m is on snow and rocks and over several small towers. These are the key places of the tour which provide slightly more difficult climbing, but still on the easy side. The descent goes to the right to start with, in the direction of the Furggjoch. It takes us down to 2,972m and requires 'Mountain Guide technical skills', both for the climbing and the route finding. At the above mentioned altitude the route goes right into the face, over a rock band, onto the base of the Furgg Glacier below, negotiating more rocky obstacles. This part of the climb is on a short rope.

We increase the rope and distance between climbers to negotiate 70 to 80m on the glacier. Some crevasses are too wide to jump. In conditions which provide a thick enough snow cover, crampons can sometimes be dispensed with. They are otherwise indispensable. A small hollow precedes the clear ice zone. In springtime it fills up with water. In late summer you will find deep gullies which the water has shaped or channelled during the thawing processes of the summer months. Where the water has dug into the ice, it reveals wonderful shades of blue in rounded, meandering rivers: some reach depths of 10 to 20m into the glaciers, beyond what the eye can see.

Towards the end of the glacier the water goes underneath the surface to reappear in the milky waters of the glacier river.

This expedition is one of the classic tours with a guide. It is not classed as difficult if the conditions are right, and the climber's equipment is adapted to the degrees of difficulty. Without expert route finding it can become a difficult traverse, especially after the Furggen cable car station. The traverse takes between 3½ to 4 hours and is excellent training practice for tackling the 'big summits'.

Recommended equipment: Strong boots/Crampons Altimeter
Ice axe/Piolet   Map
Rope   (Binoculars for a good
study/inspection of the
Matterhorn)

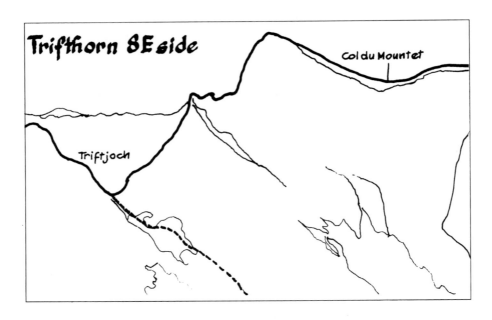

Trifthorn SE side

Col du Mountet

Triftjoch

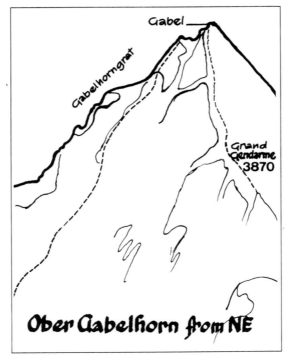

Gabel

Gabelhorngrat

Grand
Gendarme
3870

Ober Gabelhorn from NE

ROCK CLIMBING WITH A GUIDE

ZERMATT
  ROTENBODEN (last station before Gornergrat)
   RIFFELHORN
   RIFFELBERG
   ZERMATT

The Riffelhorn is Zermatt's rockclimbers' Paradise. It rises between Roten Boden and Riffelberg, high above the Gorner glacier. It is not a large mountain when compared to other Alpine giants, but its distinctive shape stands out clearly from the surrounding landscape. It consists of good climbing, dark coloured Serpentine rock (very slippery when wet), providing routes graded from 2 to 5. Hermann Biner in his recently published book[6] lists **twelve different routes**.

The Riffelhorn is where the hopeful Matterhorn climbers come to train. It is a place which has been the starting point, the catalyst, for many life-long love affairs with rock climbing. Like every other mountain it expects to be treated with respect. The Riffelhorn is no play area!

For beginners: book a Mountain Guide and have a go at rock climbing. A guide will soon assess your potential and select a suitable route up to the top.

The top of the mountain is like a long, wide, and generous back with beautiful views that can be enjoyed in comfort before tackling the descent using one of the twelve routes.

For a dramatic addition to your photograph album this is the place to pose!

---

6. *Hochtouren im Wallis, Vom Trient zum Nufenenpass*, published by the Swiss Alpine Club, available in German and from 1995 onwards in French translation. English translation under consideration.

YOUR MOUNTAIN GUIDE

T O BE A MOUNTAIN GUIDE is to belong to one of the world's noblest professions. It is from the combination of vigorous training and natural aptitude, with a deep feeling for the mountain world, that the personality of a Mountain Guide emerges.

The tradition of mountain guiding in Zermatt is more than a century old. It has come a long way since the early pioneering days, mainly because revolutionary equipment has opened up previously inaccessible terrain. But the basic qualities which are the number one pre-requisite for a Mountain Guide are the same today as they were all those years ago in the Golden Age of Alpinism:

> Physical Fitness   Commitment
> Mountaineering Experience   Team Spirit
> The Ability to Make Decisions
> Constant Awareness of Security, Needs and Requirements,
> Helpfulness, in other words, Unselfish Behaviour at all Times

Those are the qualities which separate the mountaineer, the individualist, from a Mountain Guide who assumes the responsibility for other people's lives. On a personal note we should like to add one more basic requirement, namely: Courage.

Every would-be guide is subjected to a strict period of training, followed by a set of final examinations under the supervision of two experts. To begin with, each candidate attends a series of courses which aim at assessing his or her Alpine technique and which include a general introduction to guiding techniques. Knowledge of a foreign language is a prerequisite. This is how the initial programme runs:

> One week is spent on the in-depth study of avalanches.
> Two weeks are devoted to coping with all aspects of winter conditions.
> Two and a half weeks' instruction points out the essentials of summer climbing,
> i.e. technical know-how in rock and ice climbs, as well as guiding techniques.

At the end of the general teaching of theory and on successful completion of the examination, the candidate is accepted as an 'Aspirant Guide'. He or she then embarks on a two year practical training period. During that time, an Aspirant Guide may lead a tour under the supervision of a qualified Mountain Guide. The theory which had been acquired is thus put into practice and the knowledge transformed into experience.

In the course of the second year an Aspirant Guide may start to sit exams which count towards the final qualifying examinations. These examinations, leading to the much coveted Diploma and proudly worn badges, are divided into summer and winter sections. Both summer and winter examinations are extremely thorough in testing every aspect of mountaineering, including basic knowledge of the following:

Taking Charge of a Tour   Route Choice and Route Finding
Walking and Climbing Rhythm   Recognition and Appreciation of Dangers
Use of maps, compass, altimeter, combined with a natural feel for orientation

The winter section takes place over a two week period, in which every aspect of winter Alpinism is scrutinised. Included are:

Skiing technique and ability   The use of a rope in a skiing party
Walking and climbing amongst snow covered rocks with or without crampons
The causes and effects of avalanches (which can also occur in the summer in different overall climatic conditions!)

The summer section of the qualifying examinations, referred to as 'Sporting Climbing', places great emphasis on rock and ice climbing techniques and ability. It also includes a section testing climbs from Grade 6 onwards, where agility and balance are of paramount importance.

The importance of securing and handling the rope in rock and ice climbs is stressed by the large part it plays in the final assessment. Related to this are rescue techniques in rock and ice climbs, crevasses, etc. The expert judges also take note of the individual's response to the difficulties he or she may encounter during a climb. In layman's language: 'How do you get yourself out of a delicate situation?'.

Last but not least, all candidates have to complete and pass a theory examination to show that they possess a good knowledge of:

Geology, Glaciology, Ecology   All aspects of Alpine Dangers
Avalanches   Snow composition and crystallisation
Guiding Techniques   Equipment
Fauna and Flora   Alpine History
First Aid   Means of Orientation
Law   Guide Organisations

Because of a Mountain Guide's lengthy and thorough training, his presence will always be a mountaineer's best insurance policy. Why take the chance and venture out alone?

Climbing with a Mountain Guide also brings the benefits of deeper knowledge and of shared experiences in the extraordinary and moving world of the mountains, shared experiences which in turn can result in lasting friendships. Once a guest has established a good contact with a guide, they usually continue climbing together, even in other areas, or abroad. As a Mountain Guide becomes familiar with the individual's abilities and preferences, it becomes easier for him to find the right tours to ensure maximum satisfaction.

All guides are professionally independent, and financial transactions between Mountain Guide and guest take place on a personal basis according to a set level of tariffs, which varies according to the tour.

Extras are: the cost of hut accommodation and food and certain modes of transport.

REMEMBER: All climbers need to be insured, including for helicopter transport (e.g. Air Zermatt, 028 67 34 87).

How to book a Mountain Guide:

Guests of Zermatt, climbers and mountaineers, as well as beginners and would-be mountaineers, can find a guide either through the Zermatt Guide Office, or by making private arrangements. The Guide Office is open daily, from early July to Mid-September and from March to the end of April.

Tel from UK: 00 41 28 67 34 56 or in writing to the Zermatt Guide Office.
Tel from Zermatt: 028 67 34 56 or 028 67 11 81

The Zermatt guides are masters of their profession and experienced in mountain rescue. At the time of printing, both the technical leaders of the Mountain Guides of the Valais and the Swiss Mountain Rescue are from Zermatt, thus following in the footsteps of a glorious past. They risk their lives in rescue missions to help or retrieve climbers. Recklessness or carelessness should have no place in the mountains.

The guides of Zermatt go beyond their frontiers. They have climbed and are still involved in climbing the Himalayas. The latest project involves the climbing of the 'Four Matterhorns': The Zmutt Grat of the Matterhorn in Zermatt and the other three respectively in Nepal, Peru, and Canada.

The Guide Office organises daily guided excursions as follows:

Glacier excursions, e.g.
Klein Matterhorn - Gobba di Rollin (3,902m) - Testa Grigia - Trockener Steg.
Excursions to the Gorner glacier.
Visits to glacier lakes.
Excursions to the Monte Rosa Hut.
Beginner's rock climbing techniques.
Basic or advanced climbing courses on the Riffelhorn, including 'Sporting Climbing'.
Ice climbing for beginners.
Ascents of two easy 4,000 peaks in neighbouring Saas Fee.
A helicopter flight to the Alphubeljoch, followed by the ascent of the Alphubel (4,206m).
In high season, daily climbs of the Breithorn (4,164m), Pollux (4,092m), Castor (4,228m) and the half traverse of the Breithorn Ridge.

THE HISTORY OF THE THEODUL PASS

T HE THEODUL PASS is an obvious crossing point between Italy, more precisely the Val d'Aosta region and the Rhône Valley in Switzerland. It straddles glaciers flowing on the one side down to Zermatt and on the other side to Breuil or Cervinia, as the resort is mostly called today. At the top it consists of a wide expanse of snow and ice with gentle descents in all directions on the Swiss side, and easy descents on the Italian side, particularly so below the Theodul Hut, bearing westwards towards the Matterhorn. Because of the ice cover, the Theodul Pass has never been without danger. There have always been many crevasses which must be reckoned with. Even in the High Middle Ages, from about 1400 AD until 1500 AD, when the climate was particularly warm and the glaciers retreated, it is assumed that the Theodul Pass was still covered in ice. Between 1500 AD and 1600 AD the climate changed and the glaciers surged forward, making the crossing much more dangerous. We find the first reference to a casualty on the Theodul Glacier in the writings of Pfarrer Ruden (1870), the vicar of Zermatt, who noted that in the year 1584 a certain Anton Fux died on the Theodul Glacier.

We do not know with certainty when a pass or a crossing such as the Theodul was used for the first time but there is sufficient evidence by the number and the dates of the many Roman coins found in and on the glacier to assume that the pass was used in Roman times. Historians have also linked the name of 'Mont Cervin', the French for Matterhorn, to the presence in the western part of the Southern Alps of the Roman general, Servius Galba who was meant to have wintered in the region then called Octodurum,[1] where from the year 57 BC until 56 BC he was the Commander of the XII Legion. His task was to open and control the mountain passes, especially the Grand Saint Bernard Pass. It is presumed, but cannot be proven, that he came and saw the great 'Obelisk' to which he allegedly gave his name. This corresponds with the earliest recorded names of the mountain as being Mos Silvius, Servio or Silvio and later on Servino.

The origins of the naming of the Pass 'Theodul Pass' steps forward into the Christian era, and is told in the form of an entertaining and spicy legend. It concerns St. Théodule who was Bishop of Sion from 381 - 391 AD. He was a saintly man of great ability who could be relied upon to outwit the devil himself.

The story goes that the Pope who reigned in Rome at that time decided to give a large brass bell to the Bishop of Sion. The gift was generous, but the cost of transporting it all the way from Rome to the Rhône Valley was much greater than the value of the gift itself, and the money to pay for the journey was not available. The bishop might have had to worry about it for a long time had it not been for Satan, always on the look-out to capture a new soul. The soul of a bishop was worth a great deal to him, and he hastened to make what he saw as an irresistible

---

1. Octodurum, today Martigny, the city where a road up the Rhône Valley branches away from the direct route to the south towards the Grand St. Bernard Pass and tunnel. From Martigny there is also access by mountain road to France and Chamonix.

proposal: 'I'll take you to Rome to fetch the bell and we'll bring it back together. The only stipulation is that if we complete the journey before dawn your soul shall belong to me'. The bishop agreed and the deal was sealed.

In no time the devil flew the bishop to Rome where they collected the bell. On the way back, the devil set out with the bell and with the bishop clinging firmly to it. They flew at speed into the Valais over the Theodul Pass which later took on the bishop's name. The devil and his precious cargo reached Sion well before dawn. The devil was about to leap over the walls of the city, ready to claim the much prized soul, when Bishop Théodule shouted out loud from inside the bell:

Coq chante!	Sing cockerel!
Que tu chantes!	Go on, sing!
Ou que jamais plus tu ne chantes!	Lest you shall never sing again!

All the cockerels of Sion woke up immediately on hearing the voice of their bishop and burst into a huge cacophony of song. When the devil heard this he was seized with rage and dropped the bell, which sank several feet into the ground. He bounded away from the city of Sion to go and nurse his wounded pride. It is from this day onwards that cockerels have sung so early in the morning.[2]

The first official record of the Theodul Pass appears in the year 1538 in a work compiled by Tschudi who is recognised as the first cartographer of the Alps. It does not mention the Matterhorn and refers to the pass as 'the glacier'. It took a further two hundred years before Horace-Bénédict de Saussure, a man of exceptional intelligence and culture, a scientist with a keen eye for detail, beauty, and art, came to recognise the uniqueness of the Matterhorn.[3]

Horace-Bénédict de Saussure climbed the Theodul Pass for the first time in 1789. He returned three years later and spent three days up there. On his second journey de Saussure, familiar with the demanding climatic conditions which can prevail at that altitude, brought with him a makeshift roof which he fitted onto the old fortress.[4]

Fortress? Yes, a fortress had been standing on the Theodul Pass - as perhaps a monument to man's folly - for one hundred years already. As a result of the revocation of the Edict of Nantes by the French King Louis XIV, protestant and religious minorities such as the Walsens left their homes and fled France and Savoy to seek refuge in Switzerland, Germany, Holland, and England. They followed arduous, difficult and sometimes almost impassable routes over the mountains: the Theodul Pass was one of them. As a result of this, the soldiers of Victor Amadeus II, Duke of Savoy, King of Sicily and Sardinia, with the help of the local inhabitants of the valley designed and built a fortress - a bastion on the Theodul Pass. It was intended to stop the refugees from **returning** to their homes in northern Italy: to keep them out of their homeland forever and thereby stop them spreading their

2. Extract from *Les Veillées des Mayens* by L. Courtlion, Geneva, and quoted by Edward Whymper in *A Guide to Zermatt*.

3. See chapter 'Inspiration Klein Matterhorn'.

4. De Saussure's makeshift hut stood where the Theodul Hut stands today. It is situated below the modern Testa Grigia skiing complex, close to the Matterhorn, on the right-hand side of the Theodul Glacier. It is a whitewashed building, perched on a rock escarpment and not always easy to spot. The col itself is quite narrow a dip between the Theodulhorn and a glacier-covered line of rocks.

religion. The defence wall was named 'Garda du Monservin'. Today, the Swiss/Italian border runs alongside the ridge of the southern Alps following the watershed, south to Italy, north to Switzerland. There is no visible man-made wall to separate the two countries.

When de Saussure first crossed over the Theodul Pass and went down to Zermatt, he found nowhere to stay because at that time tourism concentrated primarily on the south side of the Matterhorn: that is, the Italian side. But after he published his writings, in which he portrayed his experiences of the region and presented the unbelievable beauties of this Alpine world to the scientists and travellers of the day, people's interest was awakened and they began to visit the Valais.

At the beginning of September 1800, a certain Mr. George Cade embarked on an Alpine Tour. He and his party crossed the Grand Saint Bernard, continued up the Val Tournanche, crossed the Theodul Pass, and arrived at Zermatt: thus becoming the first British tourists to climb the Theodul Pass. Mr. Cade was well received by the local priest and they spent an interesting and agreeable evening together, locked in deep conversation, with the priest describing the French invasion of the 'Valley of St. Nicholas', known today as the Visp Valley.

In his diaries Mr. Cade refers to barter trading which was carried out via the Theodul Pass. It appears that these commercial exchanges took place mainly at the top of the pass. The people from the Valais brought iron up to the top and received wine and rice in return. When you see the pass today it seems incredible that it could have been used as a trading post.

The first half of the nineteenth century saw the very beginning of tourism in Zermatt. Tourism in the country as a whole was developing, and a first guide book entitled *The Traveller's Guide Through Switzerland* by Mr. J. G. Ebel was published and translated into English in 1818, in which Zermatt is mentioned, albeit briefly. In 1838 Murray's *Handbook for Travellers in Switzerland and the Alps of Savoy and Piedmont* was published. It includes several pages describing the Saas and Zermatt valleys. Accommodation in Zermatt was still the vicar's house which was praised for its cleanliness and comfort. The guide book already speaks of an 'influx' of scientists, mineralogists, botanists, and entomologists.

Up on the Theodul Pass in 1849, sixty years after de Saussure put up his shelter against the fortification wall, a nephew of Jean-Jacques Meynet, one of the scientist's great admirers, went up to the pass to restore and rebuild de Saussure's hut and make it into a refuge. He was Jean-Pierre Meynet, known as Minette. He married Anna Katharina Willisch from Zermatt. They made a remarkable couple. Anna Katharina knew how to make the travellers welcome and comfortable, and Minette was a man of stature with an intelligent, original and sensitive mind. Together they built the refuge (today's Theodul Hut) using the rocks from the old bastion, and named the resulting 'house' Hotel Steinbock.[5] Minette and his wife, by 1852, could accommodate several tourists at any one time in their Hotel Steinbock, carrying the provisions needed from Breuil. Each trip took about four hours. Minette never tired of the magnificent landscape and, as a true idealist, he

5. At that time the Steinbocks (ibex) were very rare in the region, so much so that hunting them was forbidden by a special decree signed in Turin. No doubt we owe the survival of the species to the foresight of the local authorities.

shared his love of the mountains with his guests. By then he was getting on in years, but still kept his imposing gait and personality. He was a legend in his own time.

One day, after 1852, Jean-Pierre Meynet vanished, never to be seen again. Some said that he perished in an accident, others that he wandered off into the world to spread the word and inform others about the beauties and secrets of the Theodul Pass. As to what happened to his wife - history does not say. Before Jean-Pierre Meynet left his valley he sold his house to his nephew. The new owner finished the building of the house by adding a permanent roof, and passed it on to his brother Jean-Baptiste. He in turn kept the old tradition of hospitality alive and well. He, too, was an exceptional man who had served in the Napoleonic army and as a result spoke excellent French.

History says that it was impossible for Jean-Baptiste, as for his forebears, to live from the proceeds of tourism alone. Smuggling helped out with the family finances. Murray writes in his handbook, published in 1838, that the Napoleonic blockade of all the continental harbours against English goods was broken by the successful smuggling over the Theodul Pass.

Unfortunately the tradition of passing down the Steinbock Hotel within the Meynet family came to an end when another local family proved that it had rights to the land the 'Hotel' stood on. The buildings went over to the Pession family.

The second half of the 19th century saw the conquest of all the great peaks, which led to Alpinism, open to all who cared to indulge in it, to get close to nature and conquer as well as admire the grandiose mountain world. Jean-Pierre Meynet with his Hotel Steinbock on the Theodul Pass was a true pioneer in providing high altitude accommodation which facilitated the conquest of the mighty summits. Everywhere in the Alps mountain huts were built and Alpinists organised themselves into clubs. The first of them was the Alpine Club (the British Alpine Club) founded in 1857. Other nations followed suit and 1869 saw the foundation of the Italian Alpine Club to whom the Hotel Steinbock, now an Alpine Club hut, renamed the Theodul Hut, belongs today.

Much loved and much used, the Theodul Hut is still the true bastion of the Theodul Pass.

FROM THE DEPTHS OF THE MIDDLE AGES, HISTORY PRESERVED IN ICE

THE REMAINS OF A SOLDIER, WHO ALMOST CERTAINLY USED THE THEODUL PASS AS A CROSSING POINT ON HIS JOURNEY FROM THE PRINCIPALITY OF LOMBARDY TO THE RHÔNE VALLEY AROUND 400 YEARS AGO.

I T IS ASSUMED that the soldier was on his way back from south of the Alps, as almost all the coins which were found in the vicinity of the human and clothing remains came from the Principalities of Lombardy, Milan, Savoy, and Mantova. The remainders, three only out of the thirty five coins which were found after the first major search, originated from the Bishop's Seat of Sion (Switzerland).

It was, however, a small dagger and a mere few coins which caught the eye of Mrs. Annemarie Julen-Lehner during a ski descent from Klein Matterhorn. The artefacts were found on the eastern side of the Upper Theodul Glacier, around 2.5km below the Theodul Pass itself, slightly west of the Gandegg Hut.

In the autumn of 1985 a further search of the area took place and revealed a wealth of historical remains. These were strewn over 10 square metres, lying loose on the ice or on the adjoining moraine. Beside the thirty five coins already mentioned, the searchers found pieces of shoe leather and material ranging from small to larger patches, some measuring as much as half a metre in width or length. Most of the material consisted of roughly woven cloth: dark brown, almost black in colour, and edged in gold. A few pieces of pleated silk with bound edges were also found.

At the same place, large numbers of small bone fragments lay on the surface of the ice. The only human bone which could be identified was that of a thigh bone, together with a broken knee section. The bone material had turned into spongy, soft collagen, totally devoid of calcium. This presents clear proof of the age of the remains and indicates that they may well have been released by the glacier once before, during a warmer climatic period, such as in the 17th century. They were then covered again by ice, as the glaciers grew and advanced to reach their dramatic maximum size in recent times around the year 1850.

A year following the first search, in the autumn of 1986, the area was visited again. The glacier had melted away, losing two to three metres of ice, and uncovered more of the moraine. Additional artifacts were found: ninety more coins were discovered, *including two large silver pieces* from the principality of Milan. The 'pièce de résistance', however, was a splendid épée: a riding sword, 125cm long, its blade severed but otherwise well preserved. The handle is made of wood and the basket of iron bands. At the top end of the narrow blade is a copper inlay depicting the sign of the wolf, i.e. the mark of a German weapon.

A 40cm long dagger with a deflecting blade and its accompanying knife were also found. A partially preserved pistol was buried in the sand and rubble of the moraine, complete with firestone and trigger. Last, but not least, the remains of a human skull were found. Tufts of reddish brown hair lay near the skull and on the surrounding ice.

It is almost certain that the soldier, whose remains lay hidden in the ice of the glacier for so long, met his death through an accident, probably by falling down into a crevasse.

Below this particular glacier area, several hundred metres lower, horseshoes as well as horse or mule bones were found. There is not sufficient evidence, however, to connect the two findings.

Since 1989 only a few coins have been found, and it appears that the area has finally revealed and given away all its secrets.

An interesting footnote can be added, that when a metal detector was used to try and find further remains, it proved to be most unsatisfactory. Much of the stone rubble, consisting of serpentine rock, contains magnets which give out stronger signals than metals.

The glaciers preserve and eventually release a multitude of historical evidence. Hence they are an unpredictable and important source of knowledge for archaeologists and historians.

The weapons and other metal relics have been restored by the Landesmuseum in Zürich. The clothing remains are cared for by the Abegg Foundation. Ultimately all the findings will be housed in the Alpine Museum at Zermatt. Zermatt is to have a new museum, in about three years from the time of going to print. It will be situated in the centre of the village, in a substantial wooden clad building, about twice as large as the present Chalet Museum. The main objective, besides better security, is to provide more room to display the existing exhibits, especially the geological and glaciological sections.

The increase in space will make museum visits - above all on rainy days, when large numbers of visiting guests come to view Zermatt's historical heritage - more comfortable and therefore even more enjoyable.

Something to look forward to ....

We thank Mrs. Annemarie Julen-Lehner and Dr. Peter Lehner
for their help in compiling the article.

Het hotel du Mont-Rose te Zermatt.

Hotel Alex
A Family De Luxe Hotel

THE HOTEL ALEX is a constantly evolving Alpine fairy-tale. It was made possible by the coming together of two people, who combine to achieve what has today become a legend in the history of Hotel Keeping in the Alps.

The Zermatt tradition is represented by Alexander Perren, a fourth generation descendant of Peter Taugwalder, the guide who climbed the Matterhorn with Edward Whymper on the first ascent of the summit. Himself a Mountain Guide, steeped in the mountaineering tradition of Zermatt, he was dealt a cruel blow in an accident on the Obergabelhorn. This prevented him from pursuing his chosen career. It must be some consolation to him that his grateful guests are aware that they have benefited from having the unimpaired attention and dedication of his talents as a Hotelier. As a result the Alex Hotel has become the jewel we know.

He has been admirably seconded and inspired by Gisela, his artistic wife, whose passion for collecting antiques and curios is reflected throughout the Hotel, as is her sensitive and spiritual personality. It was she who found the oldest known painting of Zermatt, in her native country of Austria.

Choosing the interesting and unusual daily menu with the help of long-standing and attentive staff is one of her favourite tasks. This may be the origin of the menu collection decorating the walls of the Stübli. The cuisine is healthy and wholesome. It is always possible to taste a local speciality, as well as more sophisticated dishes.

Above all, the Hotel building itself is remarkable in its individuality of design. The bedrooms are masterpieces of luxury, comfort and artistic decorations, including painted ceilings. They represent various phases in the development of the Hotel. In order to keep up the high standards of furnishings, only a few rooms and suites are refurbished, or rather re-created, at any one time. Thus, every period is represented by its own style.

The winter Garden is a new addition. Stained glass 'paintings' decorate the upper part and sides of the windows rather like a garland. They seem to absorb the tangible glass, and after a while the feeling of sitting outside, in a 'Garden of Four Seasons', becomes very real.

The sports facilities are excellent. There again, the touch of the artistic hand of Gisela Perren comes through, and the swimming pool is an experience in itself. An indoor Tennis Court as well as Squash Court, luxurious Sauna and Fitness Rooms provide everything anyone could wish to have, to feel 'on top of the world'.

The nightlife is buzzing, but one may always find a quiet corner without feeling shut out of the action. This is because the 'living area' is a large circle, which revolves around the bar, with smaller, open sided-rooms leading off it. Pink soft furnishings blend with the carved Arolla pine ceiling and walls to create a mellow and romantic atmosphere.

The Hotel Alex is everyone's Hotel. It takes care of every generation's needs and wishes. That alone can explain the great achievements and success of this remarkable Hotel, where hospitality and courtesy are the natural way of life. God willing, it will pass on to the very competent and hard-working next generation of Exceptional Hoteliers.

Tel. (028) 67 17 26 Fax (028) 67 19 43

The Schloss Hotel Tenne

Part of our Family
Offers a Warm and Personal Welcome
Following the Best Traditions of Hotel Keeping

Tel. (028) 67 18 01 Fax (028) 67 18 03

Rosa Canina - The Wild Rose

« Auf den Gipfeln der Berge ist man dem Schöpfer näher »
Ulrich Inderbinen
geboren am 3.12.1900

M
FOR
MAJESTIC
IMPOSING
DOMINATING
BREATHTAKING
AWE INSPIRING
ETHEREAL
ETCHED OR ELUSIVE
ELEGANTLY POISED
WILD AND ROMANTIC
MASKED IN WHITE
OR STRIPPED OF SNOW
DAPPLED IN LIGHT AND SHADOW
PINK GREY AND BLUE GOLDEN
ABLAZE   ALONE AND ALOOF
THIS IS THE MATTERHORN
ATTRACTING AND HOLDING
THE EYE   ALLURING AND DEFYING
THE BRAVE AND FOOLISH HEARTS TO
THE ULTIMATE SYMBOL OF MOUNTAIN
SPLENDOUR AND CHALLENGE

THE MATTERHORN, LE CERVIN, IL CERVINO

A PORTRAIT

THE OLDEST TOPOGRAPHICAL reference to the Matterhorn is found on a map published in 1545 by Sebastian Münster. There the Matterhorn is referred to as Mons Silvius, Augstal Berg. It is more than a century later that we find it first mentioned on an Italian map as M. Servino.

In 1768, however, an extract from the map of the Canton of Valais by G. Walser reads:

Matter Horn alias Mons Silvius Germ.
Augst Thal Berg.

On the same map we find the familiar name of Zmut (spelt here with one 't'), then locally known as Mutt, an independent hamlet (until 1791) with the ☿ symbol beside the name, indicating the presence of a fully consecrated chapel.

Zum See, Auf den Blatten, Findel, Winkelmatt, Ried, Tuftern and Aroleit Wasser are also names which appear on this ancient map and which are still in use today.

In 1840 A. Cuvillier from Geneva gives us the French name of Le Mont Cervin.

As late as 1841 we come across a reference by Alexandre Calame, Swiss painter and master of etchings, still spelling the name with an S, i.e. Le Mont Servin, a relic from the original Latin terminology of Mons Silvius.

THE HISTORY OF THE FIRST ATTEMPTS TO CLIMB THE MATTERHORN AND THE FINAL AND TRAGIC VICTORY OVER THE ELUSIVE SUMMIT, A VICTORY WHICH REPRESENTED THE ULTIMATE PRIZE OF THE GOLDEN AGE OF ALPINISM

Zermatt, 14 July 1865

The Dent d'Hérens (4,171.4m), which stands next to the Matterhorn (4,477.8m), on the west side at the southern end of the Zmutt valley, is considered to be the most difficult summit in the region because of route finding. Its north face consists of a 1,300m high cascade of ice, a most spectacular sight.[1] It was first conquered from the south-west face and west arête on 12 August 1863 (by W.E. Hall, F.C. Grove, R.S. Macdonald, and M. Woodmass with three guides: Melchior Anderegg – who was to lead Lucy Walker, the first woman to climb to the summit of the Matterhorn – and P. Perren and J.P. Cachat).

The Täschhorn, the Dent Blanche, and the Weisshorn are regarded as the next most difficult mountains of the area. The Täschhorn rises tall, a pointed, jagged peak, south of the Dom and close beside it, to the east of the village of Randa below Zermatt. It was climbed from Randa for the first time on 30 July 1862 (by the Rev. J. Llewellyn Davies and J.H. Hayward with two guides from Zermatt, Johann and Stephan Zumtaugwald, and Peter Summermatten from Randa).

If the Matterhorn is not the most difficult summit, why was it the last to be conquered? For by August 1865 (apart from the Meije in France) only the Matterhorn remained as the last of the major 4,000m summits: the ultimate prize.

Even if the Matterhorn is by far **not** the most difficult 4,000m mountain of the Alps it is the most imposing of all summits standing, as it does, quite alone, in separate splendour, detached from all the other chains of mountains. Because of its isolation, no face and no arête is protected from the winds. Its warm south side and cold north face create their own microclimate which results in sudden swirling mists and treacherous storms which can rage around part of the mountain, whilst immediate surroundings may be basking in warm sunshine.

Seen from Zermatt, the north face of the Matterhorn looks so daunting that for a long time it was presumed that the mountain could not be climbed at all from

---

1. Excellent views of the Dent d'Hérens may be enjoyed from the Zmutt to Schönbiehl Hut path and of course from the hut itself. The main difficulties of the climb are because of snow or ice, so that in perfect conditions the climb suddenly becomes 'perfectly easy' in terms of advanced Alpinism.

that side. Instead, the first attempts to reach the summit took place from the Italian side. There, the rock looks more accessible and seems to offer better foot and hand holds, in spite of the cuirass of rock, a large fortress rising above the green pastures of Breuil.

In fact, the Italian side contains many treacherous passages. It is the east arête from Zermatt, named the Hörnli Ridge, which is the easiest and most accessible route of all. This is the route which Edward Whymper followed on the first ascent of the Matterhorn and it is the popular route used today by the great majority of climbers. The Hörnli ridge, however, back in July 1865, did not look as it does today. Then, the ridge was littered with loose rocks and rubble which have now largely been cleared by generations of climbers passing by. Whymper and his party had to climb mainly on the face of the mountain rather than on the ridge. Let us not, however, anticipate the great day of the conquest. Before the ultimate victory, many attempts were made to reach the summit, not least by Whymper himself, all from the Italian side. On his fourth attempt (in the year 1864) Whymper narrowly escaped death on his way down after reaching the height of 4,080m on the south-west ridge of the Matterhorn (397.5m below the summit). This accident did not prevent him from making a fifth attempt with J.A. Carrel (his ultimate rival in the race to the top), all in the same year.

Edward Whymper

Extract from his book *Scrambles amongst the Alps in the Years 1860 - 69*

MAP OF SOUTH SIDE OF MATTERHORN

A   indicates the position of the Great Tower;

B   the place where we now saw something that looked like a flag.

C   the 'cravate' (the strongly-marked streak of snow referred to on p.91 which we just failed to arrive at on the 26th);

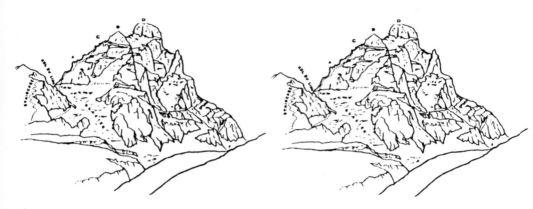

*Behind the point **B** a nearly level ridge leads up to the foot of the final peak. It was just now said, we considered that if the point **C** could be passed, success was certain. Tyndall was at **B** very early in the morning, and I did not doubt that he would reach the summit, although it yet remained problematical whether he would be able to stand on the very highest point. The summit was evidently formed of a long ridge, on which there were two points nearly equally elevated - so equally that one could not say which was the highest - and between the two there seemed to be a deep notch, marked **D** on the outline, which might defeat one at the very last moment.*

One of the most famous attempts which so nearly succeeded is the one Whymper refers to in the key to his map: in 1862 Professor Tyndall[2] climbed with two guides, Bennen and Walter and two of the Carrel brothers (one of whom was J.A. Carrel) who came along as porters. The party set off, again from the Italian side, and reached what is today known as Pic Tyndall at the height of 4,145m, 332.5m below the summit. There is no apparent reason why Tyndall did not proceed to the true summit which was so temptingly close. With hindsight, it seems that the real reason was the result of a rivalry between Bennen, the guide, and Carrel who, although the strongest and ablest climber in the guiding party, was on this occasion

2. John Tyndall, physicist and glaciologist, born in 1820 in Kilkenny, Ireland; died 1892 in London.

only a porter. When Tyndall asked Carrel for his opinion about crossing from the first summit to the second, as the Matterhorn presents itself from the Italian side,[3] Carrel replied: 'Ask your guides'. The guides were not keen on continuing the ascent, and the party turned back. In the end it can be said that justice prevailed, as Professor Tyndall, three years later in 1868 was the first Alpinist to climb up the Matterhorn from Breuil (the Italian route) descending to Zermatt via the Hörnli ridge - a remarkable achievement[4] and the first 'round tour' of the Matterhorn.

By the summer of 1865 Whymper had decided on an attempt to reach the Matterhorn via the east ridge, i.e. the Hörnli ridge, and the attempt was to be made with J.A. Carrel, the guide from Valtournanche. Meanwhile, however, the Italian Alpine Club was born, founded by the Minister of State Quintino Sella and Professor Felice Giordano. These two important gentlemen decided, perhaps not without honourable feelings, that the ascent of the Matterhorn, or the Cervino, as it is called in Italian, would be a splendid beginning for the newly created club. They approached J.A. Carrel who agreed to go along with his fellow countrymen. He withheld this information from Whymper (probably scared of dire consequences) and did not inform him of his change of heart.

On learning that Carrell had already started the ascent (on 11 July) with his Italian sponsors Whymper was at first overcome by anger. On reflection, however, he realised that the weather conditions were not favourable to the Italians and might give him a second chance to conquer the Matterhorn, but from the side not hitherto attempted - from Zermatt. As luck would have it, Whymper met Lord Francis Douglas in Breuil who spoke to him about a Mountain Guide named Peter Taugwalder. This Zermatter was convinced that it was possible to conquer the summit from the east side, from Zermatt via what is known today as the Hörnli ridge. Lord Douglas, too, wished to rise to the challenge of the mountain and decided to team up with Whymper's expedition. They left Breuil together on 12 July and hurried over the Theodul Pass to Zermatt, where they engaged Peter Taugwalder as their guide. As they arrived at the Hotel Monte Rosa they found Michel Croz, Whymper's old companion and chief guide from Chamonix, sitting on the wall in front of the hotel. He too had come to Zermatt, with the intention of acting as guide to the Revd. Charles Hudson on his attempt to climb the Matterhorn.

That evening (12 July) Whymper, Douglas, Croz and Hudson met in the dining-room of the Hotel Monte Rosa where they agreed to combine forces for the following day's enterprises. Hudson's friend, the 19-year-old student Douglas Hadow, would go along with them, despite his lack of mountaineering experience.

July 1865 had already begun as a glorious month in the history of mountaineering.

Lord Douglas had impressed Whymper by a first ascent of the ice and snow-capped Wellenkuppe (3,903m)[5] on *5 July 1865* with the guides P. Taugwalder and P. Inäbnit. This ascent took place only *one day* before the conquest of the

---

3. The two summits are separated by a leap across (an *enjambement*) or by a vertiginous breach, depending on the individual's perception of the mountain scene.

4. Tyndall's guide was Joseph Maquignaz - another great name amongst famous Mountain Guides.

5. Known at the Satellite of the Obergabelhorn.

neighbouring mighty Obergabelhorn (4062.9m) by A.W. Moore and H. Walker with J. Anderegg (Brother of Melchior). July 1865 was to fulfil its early promise when at last, on 13 July, it was the turn of the Matterhorn. The atmosphere in the village of Zermatt must have been tense, electric and exciting with no adequate words to capture the feelings of the men preparing to conquer the unconquerable, at a time when so many great climbs had been successfully completed. The same feeling of anticipation and the smell of victory must have filled the hearts of those in Valtournanche and in the Alp of Breuil (which is known as Cervinia today) on the Italian side, when Carrel set off with his important caravan, including the Minister of State. He was, however, burdened by an excess of material which slowed him down: this delay proved fatal as Whymper, on the other side of the mountain, hurried on with his preparations.

Thus the final race for the conquest of the Matterhorn took place between J.A. Carrel from Valtournanche and Edward Whymper from England. Carrel had been born in sight of the great mountain; Whymper had come on the scene in 1862, first as an artist sent over to portray the Alps for the British public, and then as one whose destiny became ensnared forever by a fatal attraction, by the power of the mountain.

Whymper's final team consisted of himself, the Revd. Charles Hudson, D.R. Hadow, and Francis Douglas with Michel Croz and the Taugwalders (father and son) as guides. They set off from Zermatt on 13 July to follow the Hörnli Ridge and reached the summit at 1.40pm on 14 July 1865, three days ahead of Carrel and Bich. Whymper's team was perhaps rather a heavy team, consisting as it did of seven climbers in all. As they reached the summit, Michel Croz and Whymper unroped and raced up side by side and both arrived at the same time on the summit, exuberant and undoubtedly real friends, united in their great moment of victory. They hoisted the flag which was seen by the Italian climbers who knew then that they had been robbed of victory. The tragedy which followed during the descent is only too well-known.[6]

At a delicate passage Hadow falls on top of Croz who in turn is thrown over. Both take with them Lord Douglas and Hudson. Then the rope breaks between Hudson and Taugwalder senior. Thus, Whymper's life and those of the Taugwalders are saved, but all three carried the burden of the terrible tragedy to the end of their lives.

Whymper never again engaged on a difficult climb such as the then unconquered north faces of the Alps.[7] He continued climbing but far away: the main peaks of the Andes to start with, then the Canadian Rockies, accompanied each time by none other than J.A. Carrel.

The tragedy on the Matterhorn cast a deep shadow over the whole world of Alpinism. The entire concept of risk-taking in order to conquer mountains and

6. A visit to the Alpine Museum in Zermatt, where the story is told as well as anyone can ever relate it, is enlightening and worthwhile.

7. The north face of the Matterhorn was conquered on 1 August (Swiss National Day) 1931 in one of the most remarkable ascents ever to be undertaken.

Two young men, Franz and Toni Schmid, left from Munich on their bicycles and made camp at the foot of the great wall. They studied the face in detail and set off on a climb which was to last 32 hours and end up in a snow-storm. Thanks to their masterly techniques, they successfully reached their objective and achieved the first ascent of the awe-inspiring, grandiose north face of the Matterhorn.

achieve glory came under scrutiny. It signified in a way the end of the golden age of climbing, but not the end of mountaineering. To that there is no end. As long as mankind gazes up at those elusive and magnificent peaks there will always be those who will be drawn by something deep inside them to reach the summits, and thereby experience their own kind of elevation.

CRAFTSMANSHIP IN THE MOUNTAINS

Hand crafted piolets have been the hallmark of this family business for the past three generations. Konstanz and Gottfried Willisch are today's keepers of the old tradition. They make, shape and fit together every part of the ice axe. Step by step, the process is carefully and patiently executed. Each piolet represents a personal achievement. The axe is made of stainless steel, and the handle from selected ash wood.
Both can be engraved.
Born close to the Matterhorn and the magnificent chains of Alpine peaks, Konstanz and Gottfried Willisch know that a piolet is more than a tool:

A piolet is a climber's companion, at times a life saver.

The piolets are sent all over the world, representing Swiss quality at its best: Precision work and reliability. It is not surprising to learn that a Willisch Pickel (each one is clearly marked) has been found as far away as the Himalayas.

The Willisch locksmith and piolet manufacturing business is housed in an up to date building at the entrance to Täsch, the last village before Zermatt.

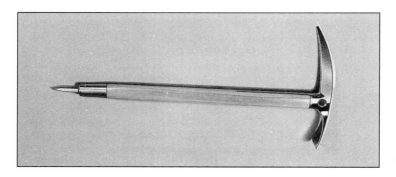

Gebr. Willisch

KONSTANZ UND GOTTFRIED WILLISCH
CH 3921 TÄSCH
Telephone: 028 67 11 67   FAX: 028 67 67 32

Matterhorn

Dach 11
Fixe Seile 10
Ob. roter Turm 9
Schulter 8
Unt. roter Turm 7

6 Solvay-Notbiwak
5 Gebiss
4 Alte Hütte
3 Eseltritte
2 Steinschlag
1 Auf dem Grat

4003

341

Hörnlihütte-
Belvedere

THE MATTERHORN TODAY

The Matterhorn today is the most climbed mountain in the world. It is not unknown (on a good day) for as many as two hundred people to reach the summit, and to have to queue to stand on the top even though it can accommodate as many as forty people at a time.

The mountain has attracted countless feats of courage, as well as eccentricities and records of all kinds. Dogs, monkeys, and even a bear have made it to the top,[8] and so have children (in spite of the suspected possibility of lasting damage to their health).

To celebrate the 125th anniversary of the first ascent of the Matterhorn, the legendary Zermatt guide Ulrich Inderbinnen climbed the mountain at the age of 90 – a remarkable achievement by a remarkable man, revered by all in Zermatt and beyond.[9]

Inevitably, the Matterhorn has more than its share of tragedies. These can be said to have four main causes:

Poor equipment. Would-be Alpinists with little experience, on hearing about the numbers who climb the Matterhorn, are led to believe that it is an easy climb which does not require much preparation. They arrive expecting to be able to reach the top wearing perhaps only a pair of trainers, when in fact strong boots and crampons above the Solvay Hut (and sometimes most of the way up) are essential.

A very sad anecdote springs to mind. A young girl who was working at the Hörnli Hut spent an entire evening trying to dissuade a young climber from venturing up the mountain the following day – his only footwear was a pair of trainers. She failed in her efforts. He set off on his climb and was killed, just as she had felt would happen. To this day she is haunted by his face, by the evening spent together and by the fact that her warnings went unheeded. It raises the same old question: how far can anyone interfere in other people's lives and decisions?

Route finding. Although the north-east ridge, i.e. the Hörnli ridge, is not very steep (until beyond the Solvay Hut) and clearly visible from a distance, the picture changes when the climber is actually 'on the ridge' as it were. There are few points which stand out and it is easy to follow a false trail, such as going into a chimney which leads nowhere. Time is then lost in retracing one's steps, and exhaustion quickly sets in. The climb, it must be remembered, at a steady pace, lasts an average of five hours to the summit and five hours down. Sufficient reserves of energy must be preserved for the descent, which is when most accidents take place.

Rock falls. The third reason for accidents is falling rocks, mainly caused by other climbers climbing *off* course. The rock falls are a real danger, mainly on the face of the mountain. This is the reason why the Mountain Guides mainly choose to stay on the ridge itself. It may take longer and is sometimes tedious, but it is safer.

---

8. Source: Alpine Club guidebook entitled *Pennine Alps Central*, compiled and edited by Robin G. Collomb. It has two companion volumes covering the East and West Pennine Alps. The books are produced and sold for the Alpine Club London by West Col Productions Goring, Reading, Berks.

9. Born in 1900, Ulrich Inderbinnen is still an active guide today. In the early summer of 1994 he carried the flag and led the guides of Zermatt in the Corpus Christi procession through the village.

Conditions. The fourth reason is sudden weather changes. Finding the correct way in swirling mist is no easy task. Besides, even the most up-to-date clothing cannot completely shield a climber from a sudden storm, from the fury of the gusts of wind, and sometimes from the lightning which strikes the mountain in violent thunderstorms.

The Matterhorn is a dangerous mountain for anyone who is not an experienced mountaineer. The safest way to climb it is to go with a Mountain Guide. The guides, true mountaineers, born at the foot of the great summit, understand its idiosyncrasies and varying moods and are best equipped to meet its many challenges.

A mountain like no other, the Matterhorn holds a mystery and fascination which attracts the admiration and devotion of many.

It has been painted and photographed countless times, with a well-known photographer spending a night on the summit to capture the sunset and sunrise, sights of incomparable beauty.

These pictures enable those who will never climb the Matterhorn to share in the magic at the top. At the same time modern technology has lifted man up in the air, and a helicopter flight around the Matterhorn is a unique experience.

The Matterhorn, however, is a wonderful sight to behold from the floor of the valley and may be discovered from all angles, and from viewpoints on countless walks and excursions around Zermatt and neighbouring ascents.

It must be, indeed it is, one of the great wonders of the world.

THE SOLVAY HUT
Altitude 4,003m

1915 saw the start of the building of the first hut on the 'classic route' to the Matterhorn, the Hörnli ridge. This was made possible by a generous gift from the Belgian chemist Ernest Solvay. In 1966 a new hut shell was erected on the site, smaller than the original one. The wishes of the benefactor were quite clear: the hut was only to be used in an emergency.

This is no longer always the case, and a great number of climbers have been using the hut as free lodgings. The upkeep of a hut at that height and in that position is demanding and costly. At the time of writing the hut has fallen into a bad state of repair. It has therefore been decided, after in-depth consultations with the relevant factions in Zermatt (i.e. the SAC section and a representative of the guide's organisation), that the present hut should be demolished and replaced. One option is that of a Bivouac which will provide adequate safety in storm conditions without the attractions of a mountain hut. The second option is that a replacement hut be built on the lines of the existing one.

The Solvay Hut is the only refuge which is the sole property of the SAC, Swiss Alpine Club, rather than the property of one of its Alpine Club sections.

Part of this information appeared in the Monthly Bulletin of the SAC,
No. 9, September 1994, Year 70.

·

LA GRANDE DIXENCE
HYDRO-ELECTRICAL SCHEME

INTRODUCTION: THE EARLY DAYS
OF ELECTRICITY

EVEN BEFORE TRAINS replaced the narrow and sometimes perilous paths, suitable for horses, mules, and sedan chairs (for those who could not ride or walk the distance) – as well as the wider tracks of certain sections of the way where horse-and-coach were used – up to 12,000 visitors a year came to Zermatt. Tourism inevitably made demands on the local population, demands which created changes and resulted in modernisation. One of the biggest steps forward was the introduction of electricity.

Zermatt built its own power station: the first Alpine village to do so, and 1894 was the year when the first street lamps were switched on. The Railway Authorities followed suit. On 24 November 1897 the first three-phase electrical track of the Gornergrat railway had its inaugural trial run.

Zermatt's first power station, which is still in operation today, was the Triftbach power station situated near the Gemeinde Haus (Council House) about 100m up the hill from the Church Square. The power station operating the Gornergrat Railway was built in the Findeln Gorge, in the vicinity of the magnificent 50m high Findelnbach railway bridge, above the area of Winkelmatten. This particular power station is no longer in operation and has been replaced by Zermatt's second power station, located in the region called Wiesti, across the river about level with Zermatt's railway station.

To begin with the local inhabitants did not connect their houses to the 'wonder light'. Only very few of them could afford the price of electricity. Those were the early days of tourism....

Zermatt soon attracted a great number of visitors. The stunning scenery, its history of climbing, and above all the overwhelming sight of the Matterhorn rising above the village, standing alone, separated from all other peaks, basking in isolated splendour, proved to be an irresistible attraction. By 1938 Zermatt had recorded 69,400 visitors and by 1950 the numbers had grown to 158,800. Zermatt was a fast growing tourist resort, and the trend was reflected throughout the region and the canton of Valais. Overall economic growth and industrialisation in the Rhône Valley required an efficient and reliable energy supply using local resources, namely the natural power of water.

Zermatt had shown the way, and now more ambitious schemes came under consideration.

The original idea of using melt-water, freely available, from the Alpine glaciers to operate power stations was first thought of in 1945 by the Federal Catchment Board in Berne. The idea was transformed into a viable project through the efforts and vision of the 'Société Anonyme de l'Energie de l'Ouest Suisse' (EOS) in Lausanne. It gave birth to one of the greatest hydro-electric schemes in the world:

LA GRANDE DIXENCE

La Grande Dixence project is an amazing example of man's success in harnessing the forces of nature. Millions of cubic metres of melt-water from the glaciers and Alpine peaks which would otherwise be wasted are transformed into electricity. Great vision, courage and tenacity were needed to achieve the project, a masterpiece of engineering, planning, and construction.

La Grande Dixence is constructed on the principle of large scale inter-basin transfer of water, through a network of gravity feeder tunnels, into an artificial lake: and from there to two power stations.

The scheme covers a wide geographical catchment area - a total area of 357 square kilometres of which 180 square kilometres are covered by glaciers. It spreads across from the Visp Valley and Zermatt in the east to the Val de Bagne in the west (otherwise renowned for its Raclette cheese which is claimed to be the best in the world, and for the well-known resort of Verbier).

The water catchment points follow the Alpine chains of some of the highest mountains. They start at both sides of the Visp valley, gathering the waters from the mighty Weisshorn (4,505.5m) on the west and from the Mischabel Group on the east which includes the Dom (4,545m), the highest mountain in Switzerland that stands exclusively on Swiss soil. The two catchment sides join up between the Dent Blanche (4,357m) and the Matterhorn (4,478m) at the point where the two mountains face each other. From there, the water catchment points move west and north-west of the Dent Blanche to the valley of Ferpècle, then over to the Pigne d'Arolla (3,796m) above the village and mountain resort of Arolla, to the Mont Blanc de Cheilon (3,870m) which rises above the Lac des Dix in the Val d'Hérémence - a vast artificial lake and the heart of the Grande Dixence hydro-electric scheme.[1]

The site for the construction of the Lac des Dix was chosen because the valley already held a gravity dam - much smaller than the existing one - which was linked to the power station of Chandolin, a link which has remained.

At first, the project looked into the possibility of raising the original dam wall to take the extra water, but research showed that it was not viable. Total security, economic analysis and other considerations required a new structure, namely: the placing of 5.93 million cubic metres of concrete to build a dam wall 285m high - the highest in the world - to hold the 400 million cubic metres of water which the

---

1. Many of the names of celebrated peaks mentioned above will not only be familiar to climbers but also to addicts and amateurs of spring ski touring, as they follow the path of the famous Haute Route - the Chamonix to Saas Fee Alpine crossing.

The 'Little High Level Route' which is the normal route for guided groups cuts out a technically demanding section by traversing from Verbier to the Cabane des Dix (a mountain hut which is the property of the Swiss Alpine Club) via the top end of the Lac des Dix. The Cabane des Dix stands below the stunning north face of the Mont Blanc de Cheilon and above the Lac des Dix. There is a direct summer approach to the Hut following the banks of the lake.

region provides. The building of the dam began in 1950 and was completed in 1961 (four to six years ahead of schedule).

From the Lac des Dix the water gravitates through a tunnel underneath the Rosa Blanche (3,336m) to the first underground power station at Fionnay and from there to the Rhône valley into the second underground power station of Nendaz situated at Biendron, not far from the village of Riddes. From there the waters flow into the river Rhône on their way to the Mediterranean Sea, having produced 840 megawatts of electricity.

The investment which financed the whole project rose to the value of 1,600 million Swiss Francs. What made the project even more remarkable, beside the best 'route finding' for the construction of the water feeder tunnels was:
(a) The inaccessibility of the terrain.
(b) The lack of readily available construction materials.
(c) The climatic conditions which restricted the building process to the summer season (from late May into October).

As the hydro-electric scheme of La Grande Dixence begins in the Visp Valley and in Zermatt (together they supply 60% of the water which flows into the Lac Des Dix), Zermatt is an ideal place for those who wish to see the complex workings of the project.

ZERMATT AND LA GRANDE DIXENCE HYDRO-ELECTRIC SCHEME

Zermatt already had its own power stations and electricity supply before the birth of the La Grande Dixence project. Furthermore, down the valley at Mattsand and Ackersand, a third hydro-electric scheme and power station belonging to the chemical factory Lonza in Visp/Viège was fully operational. There was, however, a huge surplus of water available, an enormous, untapped source of energy and revenue. It was not possible to capture the wealth of water by flooding the area of Zermatt. The alternative was to establish catchment points, drill feeder tunnels and lead the waters, whenever possible by gravity, directly into one artificial lake, i.e. the Lac des Dix; the same system and idea being applicable to the second basin within the scheme: the basin of the upper part of the Val d'Hérens including the Arolla and Ferpècle valleys.

In Zermatt we see two main types of water catchment:
(a)   The waters which flow directly into the feeder tunnels to the Lac des Dix. Added to those are the waters from the Findeln Glacier at an altitude of approximately 2,310m, waters which flow down to Zermatt and are syphoned directly into the feeder tunnel.
(b)   The waters from the Gorner Glacier, as from the Schali and Bis, which are pumped into the 70m deep Zmutt lake, built above the pumping station at Zmutt; and the waters from the Zmutt Glacier which are pumped into the network of reservoirs of Stafel.

Altogether the region produces a total of 260 million cubic metres of water a year.

Of this total, only 60 million cubic metres end up in the Lac des Dix. The remainder is used for:

(1)   'Restitution' or 'compensation' water for the Randa-Ackersand hydro-electric scheme. This obligation guarantees a continuous flow of water in the riverbeds of Zermatt and down the Visp Valley. La Grande Dixence opens its valves on a daily basis from six o'clock in the morning until six o'clock at night.

(2)   Compensation water during the summer period (15 June to 15 September, approximately high summer).

(3)   The washing of sand-removing devices in the sediment holding tanks in the tunnels.

This third point is a most important part of the whole operation as large amounts of sediment would cause enormous damage to the hydro-electric plants. As the water comes off the glaciers it carries with it rocks, pebbles, and sand and may pick up branches and even tree trunks on the way. Rocks, pebbles, and large pieces of flotsam are trapped by grilles, but sand and sedimentation needs special treatment. The level of sedimentation in the water varies. Broadly speaking it is heavier in the spring after the 'resting period' of the glaciers, when water stops flowing in the winter months and rubble accumulates to be released at the onset of thawing (in the middle of May approximately). There is, however, always a certain amount of 'suspended sedimentation' floating through the melt-waters of a glacier. The amount varies from year to year and many factors contribute to this complex 'transportation' of eroded mountain materials. It is not simply related to single events such as summer rain storms or, in the case of the Gorner Glacier, to the yearly emptying of the ice-dammed Gornersee.

Such events cause a period of rising flow which can cause sudden injections of large amounts of sediments into the glacier melt-waters, if these penetrate an area of the glacier subsoil which happens to be rich in sediments. These areas consist of channels which have not been hitherto cleaned out of debris, or of the rock base of the glacier itself.

When the filtration tanks at the beginning of the feeder tunnels are full, they automatically empty themselves, causing unexpected rises in the water levels of the river beds of the area. This explains the many notices which warn tourists not to rest and picnic in the immediate proximity of most rivers. Thus, the waters are best admired from a respectful distance, in any case their powerful roar makes conversation difficult if not impossible. Luckily there is never a shortage of beautiful and comfortable picnic spots.

Although the hydro-electric schemes have to some extent altered the Alpine scenery, they have also added new spectacular sights to the already breath taking landscape. Great care has been taken to blend the various installations in with nature. The pumping-station at Zmutt, above the village of Zermatt, almost at the foot of the Matterhorn, nestles deep into the V of the Zmutt valley. The artificial Zmutt lake and its dam, built above the pumping-station, can be dramatically beautiful, as when the winter ice melts and breaks up to float on stunning blue or green water (which sometimes turns to milky grey, the colour of the water as it flows out of the glacier). One of the most remarkable releases of catchment water can be seen on the way to Trift, where a foaming white tongue of water surges through a concrete window. It is 'restitution water', all the way from the Weisshorn and destined to feed the Visp valley. The quantities of water which crash down the mountain look enormous but they represent only a small part of the catchment of the Weisshorn. The remainder flows directly into the Lac des Dix.

The hydro-electric scheme of La Grande Dixence does not produce any electricity in Zermatt itself. It has to purchase its power to operate the pumping stations from the Randa power station at Ackersand. Likewise, it buys its huge water supply from each individual parish which has a claim to it.

Two maps mounted on large boards at Stafel and at the pumping station of Zmutt enable visitors to study the concept of the operation and the waters' journey through the Alps, a journey which can be 100km long.

As is so often the case, there is a close collaboration here in Zermatt between Britain and Switzerland. The students of the Geography Department of Manchester University, led by Dr. D.N. Collins, have been actively measuring and monitoring – amongst other things – the sedimentation levels of the waters of the Findeln and Gorner glaciers in conjunction with La Grande Dixence operation, and in particular with the help of the Director of the pumping station at Zmutt.

Our thanks go to Dr. D.N. Collins, Mr. Amédé Kronig of La Grande Dixence Zermatt and Dr. Pierre Maître, Grande Dixence Sion, for their help in writing this article.

It is possible to visit the Lac des Dix and the mechanical workings of the gravity dam. A cable car takes you up to the 'crown' of the dam from where one can walk to and along the lake.

The Lac des Dix is a 50 min. drive from Sion, at the end of the road Hérèmence-Pralong.

Opening times: twice daily at 11.00h and 15.00h from July till October.

For further enquiries concerning a visit telephone: (027) 21 43 11 or fax (027) 21 43 82.

It is generally advisable to check dates and times of opening, as these may vary.

Bibliography:
'La Grande Dixence Hydro-Electric Scheme Switzerland' by C.C. Park.
'Climatic and Glaciological Influences on Suspended Sediment Transport from an Alpine Glacier' by D.N. Collins.

THE FLORA

ZERMATT AND ITS surrounding world is one large garden, from the village up to the base of the summits and beyond, where flowers are found in protected nooks and crannies. They survive on minute quantities of soil, as courageous examples of life against all odds.[1] Alpine flowers and plants appear like true miracles of nature. Their brilliant colours illuminate the darkest rocks and transform the green of the meadows into a many coloured vast tapestry.

The colours start in the fields long before the houses bring out their bright flower decorations and the rich and immaculate kitchen gardens mature into succulent displays of green vegetables of all kinds framed by flowerbeds.[2]

Spring in the mountains arrives suffering many a setback, but no sooner does the snow retreat than the grass patches burst into flower. White replaces white as winter melts into spring and meadows are covered in white crocus interspersed with a few purple-coloured varieties.

Later, in April and/or May, depending, shocking pink primulas nestle in the cracks of the large rocks on the road to Furi and beyond to Stafelalp. To see them, all you need to do is raise your eyes and scan the rocks. There they are, apparently looking down at the path with piercing, intense little white eyes.

On the opposite side of the valley the sloping meadows between the Zmutt river and Zmutt village and above are rich in deep azure blue spring gentians, as well as small yellow star shaped flowers, with much of the available space of the lush green carpet sprinkled with shy, tiny white terminal clusters of flowers. The story goes that gentians grow in large clusters because sheep do not eat them unless they require 'a nibble or so for medicinal purposes'.

Spring releases large quantities of water from the melting snows, irrigating the fields and the edge of the paths where dozens of furry yellow blooms attract the bees in the warm sunshine.[3]

Underneath the larches, pale blue and pink anemones (hepatica) grow through the matted pale copper needles of the forest to carpet the ground. The earth is warming and releasing trapped fragrances. To breathe in a lung full of scented Alpine air is one of life's great experiences. As spring gives way to summer in the lower regions around Zermatt, it bursts into bloom higher up, creeping up the mountains, racing behind the retreating snows under the ever increasing heat of the sun. Soldanellas appear, one of the most touching early high altitude spring

---

1. Edward Whymper, on one of his solo attempts to climb the Matterhorn, noted a little white flower that he 'knew not and was unable to reach' at an altitude of just below 13,000ft. Extract from *Scrambles Amongst the Alps in the Years 1860 - 69*.

2. The climate in Zermatt is mild and enables a large variety of vegetables to grow right up to Furi or Findeln: lettuces, onions, leeks, white and red carrots, peas, cabbage, spinach, potatoes, parsley, chives, etc, and even courgettes, tomatoes, and beans (in good summers).

3. There is a considerable number of beehives in Zermatt. In the golden age of Alpinism the strong flavoured, delicious honey would be served at the breakfast table of the Monte Rosa Hotel. Alas, with the great number of tourists nowadays, the local honey is kept for private consumption.

flowers, a purple bell, delicately fringed to catch the flutters of the wind.

June, July: the grass is high and cranes bills and the small yellow ping pong balls of trollius are much in evidence.

Higher up and in the wooded areas, the saxifrages are coming into their own: the countless tamed garden varieties can be recognised almost everywhere, together with anemones, dianthus (tiny, bright pink and pale carnations), violas, campanulas – too many varieties to mention here – and amongst them some rare plants for the eyes of the connoisseur and admiring amateur gardener alike.

Large blue gentians above the Gorner Gorge on the lightly wooded areas of the west side of the valley grow amongst the rhododendrons, the famous 'Alpenrose' of Switzerland, with their small deep rosy, crimson flowers, nestling in shiny green oval leaves, their underneath covered in rust coloured scales which glow in golden brown tones.

Later, in the high meadows between Sunnegga and Täsch or in the vicinity of the Grindjisee someone might be lucky and see an Edelweiss to complete the traditional Alpine bouquet of

Gentian, Alpenrose and Edelweiss.

When the grass is mature, usually at the beginning of July, it is hay making time. The grass cutting is all important for the preservation of the great spectacle of an Alpine meadow in full bloom. Without it, the grass would take over and the 'garden' disappear, for the natural garden is the result of careful husbandry: in the spring, the meadows are cleared of branches and stones left behind from the winter. In June, the flowering begins, followed by hay making. There is a second mowing at the end of August/beginning of September mainly in areas which have been watered or irrigated. The sheep follow as they come down from the mountain and finish off the grazing. On the higher slopes mauve autumn gentians flower in large quantities while in the lower meadows the autumn crocus displays its large, pinkish mauve petals.

Autumn intensifies the colours of the landscape. The bilberry and whortleberry leaves burn bright red. The larches grow into showers of gold and copper coloured needles. The rosehips, the berberis, and the bright orange clusters of mountain ash berries all unite to enhance a final display of reds, yellows, copper, gold, against the enduring browns of bark and the permanent green of the Arolla pines.

Our thanks go to Madame Jacqueline Lauber of Furi,
who kindly shared with us the benefit of her experience in mountain farming.

THE FAUNA

THE ALPINE FAUNA is well represented in Zermatt: for instance one can at times see large herds of chamois galloping across the terrain, or quietly munching grass and surveying the scene. On snow, chamois are well camouflaged and look like just another dark rock until eventually they make a movement which betrays their presence. A good place to see them is in the region between Furi and Furgg or up the Zmutt valley. They live at different heights depending on the time of the year.

The Gornergrat region from the top down past the Riffelhorn harbours herds of ibex, whose large curved horns give them a great air of distinction. During the day they disappear down the steep slopes between the top station of Gornergrat and Gorner ridge down to the glacier. Their sandy coloured fur blends in well with the eroded soil of the slopes. Towards the evening they often come up the slopes for a taste of human civilisation.

The birdlife is varied and seasonal, governed as everywhere else by migration. One constant presence is that of the choughs, the most graceful of Alpine flyers. It is fascinating to watch them glide in perfect balance or dance and play in the thermals, then perch themselves on the edge of the terrasses of the Gornergrat, for instance, to ask for - or demand - food. They become very tame and can be persuaded to eat from the hand.

Occasionally the discerning eye will spot the royal eagle, hunting away from its habitat up the Zmutt valley or from the rocks above Edelweiss on the way up the Trift valley.

Most popular of all are the marmots. These small furry animals, as cuddly as koala bears, live in large colonies everywhere on the Alps. Close to Zermatt, they thrive in the meadows up the Zmutt valley or underneath the Zermatt to Furi Gondelbahn. Each marmot colony posts one marmot on guard at all times, whose shrill whistles alert the others to the arrival of a stranger. The whistle is very much like that of a bird and can easily be mistaken as such by the untrained ear.

The marmots hibernate. As they pop out of their holes in the spring, sometimes burrowing out of the snow after their long winter sleep, they look thin and scraggy but quickly recover and fatten up, feasting on succulent herbs. Their offspring spend endless hours playing, wrestling with each other like young puppies, much to the delight of the visitors.

Pine martins, snow partridges, foxes, hares and deer all inhabit the Alpine scene, not forgetting the red squirrels which, despite their name, have dark brown coats.

Anyone interested in the wild life of the Alps will be rewarded by at least one sighting!

As for the marmots: they are impossible to miss.

★ Hotel ★
★
Jägerhof Zermatt
Fam.
Victor Perren

CH-3920 Zermatt.
Tel. Nr. 028 / 673714
Fax. Nr. 028 / 674545

The warmth of our homely surroundings matches the warmth of our welcome into our family run comfortable and sportive hotel.

"The Hunter's Lodge"

We are situated within easy reach of all the transport systems on the edge of the village centre.

EXTRACT FROM 'THE MARMOTS OF ZERMATT' BY EMU

THE CROSSING OF THE GLACIER

Koby lifted his head towards the sky, sniffed loudly and announced that the following day was going to be even hotter than the day before.

'This means that we have to start very early in the morning to get to the glacier before the sun gets too hot' he declared. 'We shall be crossing crevasses by walking over snow bridges, and if the snow melts, those bridges will collapse under our weight.'

'That means that we'd fall right in the middle of a crevasse!.' Papa Alfons exclaimed.

Koby ignored the interruption and went on as if he had not heard him,

'It'll take about two hours climbing before we even get as far as the glacier. We'll get up very early, well before it gets light, have breakfast in the dark and start off just as dawn breaks. The mountains, coloured pink and orange by the first sun rays, will seem to be on fire.'

Then, as if suddenly remembering Papa Alfons, he turned towards him and added, 'You'll enjoy seeing this!'

'Well, at least it's something to look forward to,' Papa Alfons thought to himself. But as far as the crossing of the glacier was concerned, this was another matter. He had heard about marmots and even humans falling deep into the heart of the glacier, never to be seen again. And now, here was Koby, talking about the collapse of snow bridges. To put it frankly, he was more than a little scared.

'There's no need for you to worry about walking on the glacier,' Koby said, as he noticed the anxious frown on Papa Alfons' face. 'First of all, you'll be in good company with us. We're used to exploring glaciers and we understand them. Secondly, more important still, we'll all be roped together. If one of us falls in, the others will hold on to him or her. It's quite easy.'

'Did you say that we'll be roped?' Papa Alfons asked.

'Yes indeed! Come and see our equipment' Koby replied.

Papa Alfons followed Koby to one of the outlying burrows which turned out to be a real Aladdin's cave. There were bits and pieces of long and short ropes ....

The marmots rested a while to recover from the efforts of the climb and ... nibbled a few green blades of grass, played a little, as much as they could with the rope tied round their middle, and feeling refreshed they set off again.

Tessa went first. She put a hesitant paw on the ice to test its texture. It was not as slippery as it looked. The ice felt quite rough. It was covered with millions of small grains of ice. It felt like sandpaper. Tessa realised that she would have to tread lightly and softly to avoid cuts and grazes on the sole of her paws. She went very carefully, concentrating all the time. Her eyes scanned the ice ahead of her, to make sure that she chose the flattest route. Even so, the going was slow, as the marmots had to make several detours to avoid large gaping crevasses. Once, they heard a loud thud and saw a wide snow bridge, weakened by the sun, suddenly collapse and crash into a deep hole below. It was an awesome sight, and they stopped for a few minutes to catch their breath and regain their composure.

Enquiries regarding the manuscript may be
addressed to the publisher of this book.

François Gos

160

THE FOREST OF ZERMATT

T HE FOREST IS one of Zermatt's most precious jewels. The main part covers the east side of the valley. The opposite slopes are much less wooded: the reasons being that the terrain is drier, steeper and more prone to avalanches.

Here the great majority of trees are larches, which indicates a pioneer forest, as at this altitude larches are the first to establish a foothold when a forest is in the making. The larch has many advantages compared to other conifers. It needs less moisture and, because it loses its needles (deciduous) is less affected by pollution. Other types, e.g. the Arolla pine (a famous local species) replace their needles in six year cycles and have to endure all year exposure.

The forest between the village of Zermatt and Edelweiss (1,961m) and beyond, is well established. The larches above the station, however, have been planted within living memory, on land which was previously cultivated and produced crops, such as rye for the local bread. Avalanche metal barriers, placed above the tree-line, have to some extent stopped the snows from sliding and destroying everything in their wake. This has enabled the new forest to get established. Nowadays, wherever avalanche barriers need to be erected within wooded areas, they are constructed in wood, thus using the material which is available on site.

The main forest of Zermatt, however, grows on the east side of the valley. A wide, luscious band winds its way up from Täsch to Sunnegga, to Riffelalp below the Gornergrat and across the valley of the Gorner glacier to Furgg, across to Hermetje, below Schwarzsee and along to and above Stafelalp below the wide, imposing north face of the Matterhorn. There, the forest gives way to the treeless zones of recent moraines and rock-faces and to high Alpine meadows where an Arolla pine, or a few larches here and there, struggle to survive. The history of their fight against the elements seems to be reproduced in the gnarled trunks and branches of the century-old Arolla pines. This tree resembles a Scots pine, but its cluster of needles consists of five and not two 'leaves', a factor which gives the Arolla pine a thicker crown.

Many of the forest areas are inaccessible and hard to care for. As a result, many of the trees are old, especially the Arolla pines. Within the forest they take up much room and light and hinder regeneration. To the visitor's eyes, however, the older they are, the more beautiful they become, twisted in dramatic shapes on the edge of the paths, perched on rocks with thick roots clutching to get a grip and spreading in search of food. Beside these giants, a young sapling looks fragile and vulnerable.

If the larches lose their needles in winter time, they make up for it with their bark. Chunks of thick, layered bark in warm shades of brown, soft grey and pink, colour the forest, to blend perfectly with the evergreen Arolla pines. In spring, the first buds of the larches spread a hue of soft green and a delicate aroma over the mountainside. In the autumn, the mountains are drenched in copper and gold until the larches fade and become champagne coloured, in the month of November, before shedding their needles.

Walking in the forests of Zermatt is an experience. During June/July, pink flowering rhododendrons, the azalea like 'Alpenrosen', carpet large areas of the forests and clearings.

Besides the large trees there are numerous other species which can easily be seen between Zermatt and Furi, for instance, red elderberry and dozens of mountain ash: a feast of red and orange in the autumn. There are wild cherry trees and whitebeam.

The light and airy forest, on the way to Zmutt, following the main, wide path or one of two other routes consisting of narrow paths cut out of the steep mountain side, presents itself like a huge garden area. It is a mixed woodland of larches, Arolla pine, and wild raspberries; juniper and Alpine Thuja which prevent erosion as well as provide a thick, bluey green ground cover; and berberis and wild roses which produce deep coloured fruit. The rocks - large massive rocks - and lichen covered rubble complete the picture.

The forest of Zermatt belongs to the Burger Gemeinde and forms one of the four areas which since 1984 make up the forestry zone of the Upper Matter Tal, i.e. the Zermatt valley: Skt. Niklaus, Randa, Täsch, and Zermatt. The head forester, based in Randa, is responsible for the management of the whole area. Although geographically close, the forests vary greatly, as do their functions. In Skt. Niklaus, for instance, you can find almost every species of indigenous tree. In the Zermatt area, there are no spruce, no ash trees (only mountain ash), no hazelnuts, no Berghorn. Recently, the forest of Skt. Niklaus was destroyed by a storm. It took 25 foresters to clear up the forest and replant it at a cost of 12 million Swiss francs, paid for by the Swiss Federal Authorities and the canton of Valais. Swiss forests are protected by law and have to be replaced.

In Zermatt, the forest has two main functions: it protects the environment and is a major attraction for the tourist industry. Zermatt is fortunate in having a very high tree-line to decorate its lower slopes. This is due to its southerly location - in line with Locarno in the Italian part of Switzerland - and to the climate as a whole. Trees grow during daylight hours. In the Zermatt area, with high daytime temperatures and relatively cool nights, the average temperature is lower than in Central Switzerland, for example, where the forests stop at a height of 1,800m. For the growth of a forest, daytime temperatures are what counts, together with rainfall. On balance, in Zermatt, there is enough of both to enable trees to grow 'in line' up to 2,300m[1] and sparsely up to 2,800m: this enriches the air with extra oxygen and provides an added bonus of beauty, a feast for the eyes.

The world of Zermatt without its forest is unthinkable. It provides a great variety of walks, shelter for wildlife and last, but not least, a wonderful foreground to the mountain scenery, enhancing the contrast between the greens of the village and first mountain slopes and the white and greys of more distant summits basking in the intense blue of an Alpine sky.

Our thanks go to Leo Jörger, Revierförster, Randa.

---

1. The tree-line in the Mattertal, i.e. the Zermatt valley, is probably the highest in Europe.

SGS cares about the Environment

SGS professionals protect the natural environment by performing ecological base -line studies, environmental assessments, inorganic/ organic laboratory analyses, as well as air, water and land resources management, monitoring and rehabilitation services.

SGS also offers a comprehensive set of environmental auditing and management systems services covering : technical environmental issues, legislative compliance and health & safety, in addition to providing specialized risk assessment services and sustainable forest management practices.

Finally, SGS extends its expertise to supply a full range of environmental services that address areas concerned with : waste management pollution control, environmental certification, infrastructure development and plant & property-related environmental investigations.

SGS Environmental Services are part of the SGS Group which employs 31.000 people in 140 countries and is a world leader in inspection, testing, consultancy and certification services.

SGS
Environmental Services
Place des Alpes 1
P.O.Box 2152
CH-1211 Geneva 1
Tel. : (41-22) 739.91.11
Fax : (41-22) 738.84.72

Société Générale de Surveillance S.A.

Expertise everyday, everywhere

THE SWISS FOREST

O VER A QUARTER of Switzerland is covered by forest. It represents a large percentage of the overall surface area of the country, especially when you take into account the non-arable areas: the world of rocks, glaciers, and eternal snow in the high Alpine regions.

The Swiss woodlands are of great importance to the country's ecological system, to the well-being of the population, and last but not least, to the economy. It is a sobering thought that many mountain areas would not be habitable, were it not for the forests. Thus, in a mountainous country like Switzerland, the role of the forest takes on an extra dimension.

The forest fulfils three basic functions:

a)   It is a natural protection against erosion and creates its own microclimate, reducing temperature extremes.
b)   It plays an important social and environmental role.
c)   It is a source of renewable, self-regenerating raw material of great economic value in rural areas.

Forests prevent erosion by checking avalanches, landslides and rockfalls, and they also act as wind breaks. They regulate water and conserve it: i.e. water in a wooded area remains much longer 'in situ'. This is an additional factor of importance as far as the Zermatt area is concerned, since it has a low rainfall, in line with the Mattertal: the valley as a whole has the lowest rainfall of all the Alpine regions of Switzerland.

As a climatic regulator, forests absorb CO_2 and in return release oxygen, thereby reducing pollution (hence the expression lungs of the earth). To give an example: *only one* 100-year-old beech tree transforms, *on one sunny day*, 18kg of carbon into 13kg of oxygen, which is the equivalent of the daily needs of 10 people.[1] Furthermore, when wood is used as a combustion material, the quantity of CO_2 which it releases into the atmosphere is equal to that absorbed by a tree during its life cycle.

Wood is, ecologically speaking, perfectly balanced.

As a social and environmental asset, the forests provide endless pleasure and relaxation for the local population and visitors alike. They harbour a wealth of plants and flowers, wild berries and delicate fungi, moss and lichen-covered rock, shaded streams: nature's treasures, here for everyone to enjoy. According to Swiss law, forests and meadows are open access to the public, and anyone may pick berries and fungi (in quantities appropriate to personal use), except in areas which are cultivated,[2] or inside protected zones.

Finally, in its economic role, the forest provides winter employment for a large

1. Source: Hermann Blumer, Engineer EPFZ.
2. Cultivated areas include the meadows before mowing takes place.

number of people. It produces a valuable, self-regenerating material, all of which can be recycled.

THE PRESERVATION OF THE FOREST

On the whole, our society is now becoming aware of the consequences of over-exploitation and destruction of some of the world's great forests. Excesses of the past are also well documented, and much has been learned from past mistakes.

In Switzerland, past deforestation had catastrophic consequences. In the second half of the 19th century, there were devastating avalanches and extensive floods which caused widespread destruction. These events brought about a recognition of the importance of the forest. It resulted in the introduction of a Federal Law in 1906 (revised) which states:

'The existing forest surface must be retained. Each surface clearing requires reforestation. Trees must not be cut down in excess of the growth factor, in order to safeguard the permanence of the forest.'

In layman's terms this means: the forest as a whole represents a capital and one year's growth is the equivalent of the interest on the capital. The rule is: use the interest and retain the capital.

The last proviso reads:

'Protection measures and forestry roads, as well as forest regeneration are to be subsidised.'

The results of this law can be seen today, nearly one hundred years later. Forests have been reborn. The woodland surface of Switzerland (and of Europe in general) has increased, especially in areas which are no longer cultivated. This represents a remarkable achievement: a regeneration of one of Switzerland's greatest national assets.

Various factors, however, have intervened to produce under-usage of the forests' economic potential which is resulting in an ageing woodland. As far as forests are concerned, the growth factor, i.e. the interests on the capital, must be collected. It cannot be left in place and allowed to accumulate, as the accumulation becomes destructive. The interests, i.e. the wood harvest must be used to create work and add value extra to its original source. It is therefore of great importance to look at the forests as no longer in need of protection, but of **management**. Forest management is a skilled and specialist profession which aims to achieve the correct balance between economic realities and the long term needs of the forest.

To maintain a healthy, permanent forest means cutting down the mature trees to make way for saplings which need light and space in order to prosper. To enforce this philosophy the new forest law of 1992, which has not yet been approved by all the cantons, states that 'not only the surface but also the quality of the forest has to be maintained'.

SWISS WOOD CERTIFICATION

Forest care was until the late 1950s practically self-sufficient. Income matched the expenditure required to keep a healthy woodland. Today, this is no longer the case, and the 'wood harvest' needs to increase in the region of 2.5 million cubic metres of wood per year to achieve an economic balance. There is an urgent need to encourage the use of wood.

To achieve this, the consumer must be better informed and reassured that the wood from a well managed, permanent forest is there, not only to be used, but that it **needs** to be used.

It is true to say that Swiss forests are permanent forests and in that sense, using Swiss wood means: preserving the environment. This concept gave birth, four years ago, to the 'Swiss Wood Label', which corresponds to a certificate of origin. The wood certification programme, a pioneering project, has been introduced on a voluntary basis, and so far half the quantity of wood processed in local sawmills carries the Swiss wood label, i.e. the wood comes from a permanent forest.

Manufactured products may also carry the Swiss wood label provided it can be shown that all the regulations in force have been strictly observed and adhered to.

The rules for allocation of the valued and much prized Swiss label are strict, carefully monitored and safeguarded. As in other branches of industry, a Swiss label represents precision, reliability, and quality control.

PROFESSIONAL DEVELOPMENTS

Beside the programme of wood certification, the emphasis is on training, education and research, both in the area of forestation and in new techniques to make better and more sophisticated use of the wood. Research showed that architects, interior designers, and engineers needed more information regarding the full potential of wood.

Computer programmes and modern technology are producing exciting designs and opening new avenues. Cutting and shaping, executed with the help of computers, makes it possible to use wood where previously only plastic mouldings or metal parts were precise enough to do the job.

1952 saw the opening of the 'École Suisse du Bois' (The Swiss School of Wood) in Bienne, at the foot of the Jura mountains in western Switzerland. It is a school for 'wood engineers' who specialise in wooden constructions and other related objects.

There are two Schools of Forestry, one in Lyss (west Switzerland) and the other in Maienfeld (east Switzerland). This is where the foresters who manage and care for the forest of today, to ensure its healthy future, are trained. Forestry engineers attend the well known ETH (Eidgenössische Technische Hochschule) at Zürich.

Our thanks for his help and invaluable advice go to Monsieur Marc-André Houmard, Conseiller National Honoraire, President of the Swiss Wood Committee, Promoter and Director of the 'École Suisse du Bois' (also known as 'Monsieur Bois').

We would also like to acknowledge
Mr. Urs Huber's Publication of the 09.11.94
Ref. Mr. Urs Huber, Geschäftsführer für das Komitee Schweizerholz.

Further information including details for certification requirements on manufactured goods may be obtained from
Komitee Schweizerholz, Lignum, Postfach 176, 3000 Bern 16 Switzerland
Tel. 00 41 31 43 27 27 fax 00 41 31 43 41 22
or from
Mr. M.A. Houmard, Grand Rue 22, 2735 Mallerey Switzerland
Tel. 00 41 32 92 17 20 fax 00 41 32 92 11 25

A TASTE OF CHEESE

CHEESE-MAKING IN Switzerland is a traditional craft executed with the utmost care to produce a high quality product. Relatively small parcels of mountain and hill meadows provide the largest regions of dairy farming. Meadows and pastures, carefully tended, watered and manured in the course of centuries past, have become an integral part of the natural scenic beauty of Switzerland. Other pastures in upper and lower Alpine mountain areas (as well as in the Jura mountain chain between western Switzerland and France) bear the name of **ALP**. Altogether there are 10,000 Alps of all sizes representing ¼ of Switzerland's land area. **ALP** is an almost mystical word representing a way of life bringing to mind distant or not so distant childhood memories of Johanna Spyri's book *Heidi*. Today the Alp represents a living aspect of an old tradition, for Alps and their purpose are with us and here to stay, however demanding their environment and finely balanced their economic survival.

The Alp feeds its cattle with a wealth of plants and the cattle in turn produce the unique milk which creates the succulent cheeses which we are privileged to enjoy. The production of cheese starts within moments of milking the cows – cows which have been grazing in freedom all over mountain pastures, sometimes only footsteps away from the world of glacier moraines.

The Alp belongs to the parish community, and the cattle of many local farmers spend the summer months grazing together under the care of the herdsman or of a farming family. These are the people who are responsible for the milking and cheese-making. To visit an Alp where cheese is being made, using a huge copper-lined vat simmering over an open fire, is a unique experience. An Alp, with a few exceptions, such as in the Jura region, is uninhabited during the winter months. Its season is short and depends on the year's climatic conditions. Broadly speaking it is grazed from the middle of June until the middle or end of September.

One of the great sights rural Switzerland has to offer is the cattle leaving the village and ascending the Alp. The herd gathers in the villages and takes off, led by the queen, the mightiest beast of the herd, who wears the largest bell of all. Every cattle neck is adorned by a bell, and the noise made by this colourful procession is enormous. Cow bells, barking dogs and yodelling herdsmen combine with reverberating echoes to create an inimitable Alpine symphony. The descent from the Alp (from mid-September to the first days in October) provides the same colourful spectacle.[1]

The careful and sometimes painstaking form of dairy farming in Switzerland produces 3.8 million metric tons of milk. Of this 1.5 million metric tons are made into 130,000 metric tons of cheese. Not only do cultivated meadows produce highly nutritious food, but the close-cropped grass, be it through scything or grazing, helps to prevent avalanches and land slides, as amongst other things remaining long strands of dry grass act as a slippery base under winter snow. Without farming, the pastures above the tree-line would suffer from extreme

1. Further information concerning these events may be obtained from local or national Swiss Tourist Offices.

erosion which would also have a devastating effect on the rich network of mountain paths. The slopes below the tree-line would turn into primeval forest in a country where woodland exceeds the pasture area by 2,000 square kilometres.

The survival of hill and mountain farming is therefore of the utmost importance despite the overall European problem of over-production. It is and remains the policy of the Swiss government to subsidise dairy farmers, with extra subsidies available for mountain areas where production costs are naturally higher. These subsidies must be considered as a compensation for difficult farming, which also serves as the cheapest way by far of preserving the green Alpine regions. Furthermore, a milk quota system introduced as far back as 1977 has encouraged a shift of dairy farming from the possible arable farmland areas to exclusive grassland zones which is where this type of farming is most needed.

Apart from the summer cheese production on the Alp, traditional cheeses are made in village dairies, and not in distant factories. In Switzerland one speaks of manual cheese production as opposed to manufactured cheese. This means that the milk, which is a vulnerable natural product, is always used straight after milking. This guarantees top quality cheese produced under strict hygiene controls.[2] In 1990 there were 1,277 village dairies operating in the summer months and 1,061 in the winter.[3] The greatest number of dairies (co-operative dairies run mainly by a self-employed cheesemaker-cum-milk purchaser, and sometimes by a salaried dairy manager) were built in the last century. Many of them are now being rebuilt and updated. The modern dairy, however, has not lost its original atmosphere. It is mostly a family run business with a factory shop on the premises. There, farmers and consumers meet up together with the cheese-makers. It provides a great meeting place for the exchange of news and gossip and plays a very important social role in the life of every village.

Zermatt, too, has its **Alp**, namely at Stafel (on the Furi-Stafelalp road), on the south side of the Zmutt valley towards the foot of the Matterhorn. Its easy access in no way deters from the real atmosphere of a traditional Alp. It enables, however, whole families - pushchairs included - to walk there and enjoy the lovely surroundings and the sight of the busy acitivities of Alpine dairy farming.

How to get there
You can either walk all the way from Zermatt, via Furi or Zmutt, or save your energy by taking the Gondelbhan up to Furi and proceed on foot.

THE CHEESES

There are over two hundred different speciality cheeses produced in Switzerland, therefore the Swiss cheeses available abroad do not represent all the available delicacies one can taste in their homeland.

2. All cheeses have been regularly checked for listeria since 1988.

3. Source: Swiss Cheese Union Inc.

Basically, the cheeses are categorised as follows:

Semi-hard cheeses (using raw milk)	Hard cheeses	Extra-hard cheeses
Take some months to mature	Take several months to over 1 year to mature	Take up to 3 years to mature
Tilsiter (Royalp) Appenzeller	Emmental Gruyère	Sbrinz

The unique characteristics of the harder Swiss cheeses are due to the use of raw milk. This is entirely safe as any bacteria present in the milk are destroyed in the production process. Checks are carried out during the first weeks of ripening.

Semi-hard cheeses (using pasteurised milk)	Soft cheeses	Fresh cheeses
Take some months to mature	Take some weeks to mature	Have no maturing period
Tilsiter (Royalp)	Camembert	Quark/curd cheese Fresh and cottage cheese

SBRINZ

Made in Central Switzerland, Sbrinz is probably one of the oldest cheeses in Switzerland, dating back to pre-Roman times. It represents 3.5% of Swiss cheese production. Being extra hard and crumbly in texture, this strong aromatic cheese, high in mineral content, takes up to three years to mature into a sheer delicacy for the connoisseur.

EMMENTAL

By far the largest production is that of the Emmental cheese which accounts for 43.6% of Swiss cheese production. Emmental is a cheese unlike any other - a top performer, holding numerous records and instantly recognisable. It claims the largest cheese wheel and can weigh in at 130kg with an average weight of 80kg (176lbs). It has the lowest salt content and by far the largest holes.

Ever since it originated in the 13th century, the holes of the Emmental cheese have been the subject of much guesswork. The famous holes are in fact caused by a further fermentation process which other cheeses do not undergo and which in turn also gives the cheese its distinctive nutty flavour. To achieve the uniform distribution of holes throughout the cheese is a skilled process - a producer's secret.

The cheese originated between Lucerne and Berne, in the Alps above the valley of the river Emme, hence its name Emmental (Tal means valley in German). The Alps of the region are not high mountains and the relative proximity of the hill pastures mean that today, Emmental cheese is only made down in the valley itself, in the local village dairies.

GRUYÈRE

Gruyère cheese is produced in the western part of Switzerland and bears the name of the Count de Gruyère from the medieval town of Gruyère in the canton of Fribourg. It is the second most popular cheese, representing 16.8% of the total Swiss production.

Gruyère is produced on 60 Alp farms and in village dairies. The manufacturing process is similar to that of the Emmental cheese but both the taste and texture are entirely different. Unlike the Emmental cheese the rind is kept constantly damp to produce a faster maturing time, and furthermore the cheese is stored about two months longer than Emmental. Its holes are few and small. Gruyère plays the most important part in the making of the famous Swiss cheese fondue of which there is a basic recipe (and variations) to be found in this book.

Its taste? It is sharp, honest, entirely satisfying, with its lingering aroma of rich pastures. (Mild and stronger varieties are both available). It cooks admirably well.

RACLETTE

The next most famous 'cooking cheese' of Switzerland is the Valais Raclette cheese. To call it cooking cheese should not in any way limit its general appeal, as it is a near perfect all round product. Cooking cheese is the terminology we use in reference to the famous 'Raclette'[4] where the wheel of the Raclette cheese (6kg in weight) is cut in half, melted over an open fire, and scraped on to a plate, and then served with boiled potatoes in their skins and pickled onions and gherkins. Every plateful represents a small single portion, and hot competition ensues to see how many raclettes anyone in the party can manage to eat. Raclette is a very sociable form of eating and the dish has increased in popularity to such an extent that the numerous village dairies and Alpine farms are no longer in a position to satisfy the demand for their product. As a result of this, Raclette cheese is produced throughout Switzerland using mainly pasteurised milk.

The traditional recipe for the Raclette cheese originating in the canton of Valais is based, however, on the use of raw milk, as is the case for the other hard cheeses.

4. 'Raclette' from the French racler, meaning to scrape.

This method produces a high quality product which is not only enjoyed in its early stages of maturity but which can be kept and hardened to a tighter texture or even to 'extra hard'. At that point it can only be cut with a special grater, into large thin slices which curl into tubes rather like brandy snaps. It is then called Hobel cheese and tastes delicious served with a glass of white wine as an apéritif or at any other time of the day. No excuse is needed to indulge ....

Zermatt is a well known international resort, but at heart, despite its sophistication, it is still a true picturesque village hidden at the end of a valley in the canton of Valais. Eating Raclette is a traditional way of life and as one thing leads to another, its people, the Zermatters, have adopted the fondue which originated beyond their valley with equal enthusiasm. Raclette, fondue, croûte au fromage (in French) or Käseschnitte (in German) (which means cheese on toast with a difference, or a simple portion of thinly sliced dark bread and cheese): these are the omnipresent flavours of Zermatt and of the Valais, besides many more local specialities to whet your appetite.

How to recognise Swiss cheese abroad

All Swiss cheese destined for export is clearly marked with the 'Switzerland' label stamped in rows across the wheel of cheese alternating with rows of the Alpine horn blower symbol. These symbols are the mark of a unique product, and a guarantee of excellence.

In Switzerland itself, however, only imported cheese (often carrying a misleading Swiss name) has to be clearly identified to clarify its country of origin. All other cheese sold in Switzerland will therefore be of Swiss origin.

We wish to thank 'Cheeses from Switzerland Ltd.' for their help and support in writing this chapter and refer our readers to them for further information:

Cheeses from Switzerland Ltd.
2, Haslemere Way
Banbury Oxon OX16 8TY
Great Britain

Switzerland Cheese Association
of Canada Ltd.
116 Albert Street
Suite 1002
Ottawa Ontario K1P 5G3
Canada

Switzerland Cheese Association
704 Executive Boulevard
Valley Cottage
N.Y. 10989, USA

Swiss Cheese Union Inc.
Monbijoustrasse 345
Postfach 8225
CH-3001 Bern Switzerland

173

WINES OF THE VALAIS

ZERMATT IS SITUATED in the Valais region where over 40% of Swiss wines are produced. The Valais is an interesting wine growing region for the connoisseur in that it contains unique grapes such as Amigne, Humagne Blanc and Cornalin. The Valais vineyards are mostly situated on south facing terraces in between Martigny and Loèche. There are numerous picturesque terraced vineyards scattered along the valley; some are etched out of precarious parts of the mountainside. The climate in this region is particularly suitable for wine growing, with warm winds and high levels of sunshine. The vines flourish at 750 metres, well above the normal 600m in France. Some wine is produced in the Haut Valais, the valley leading up to Zermatt. It is at Visperteminen (1,100m) that the highest vineyard of the Valais, one of the highest in Europe, is to be found. It produces the Glacier wine Heida, a dry, fruity white wine from the Savagnin blanc grape.[1]

Over the last two decades considerable progress has been made in developing some very fine, unique wines which were divided in 1993 into three classifications: Appellation of Controlled Origin ('AOC'), Appellation of Origin and Simple Table Wine.

WINES IN ZERMATT

There are numerous shops and hostelries from where wine and Schnapps can be purchased. **One of the main attractions of Zermatt is the extensive web of restaurants, both in and around the village**. A wonderfully indulgent day can be had walking for 30 to 35 minutes up to one of the hamlets, such as Findeln or Zumsee, and passing a few hours, or even a whole afternoon, at a restaurant. The mountain air and scenery can be very conducive to exuberant over-indulgence, but then there can be few more beautiful places in which to have a hangover. One word of advice: remember to take a corkscrew on your picnic!

In addition to wine and eau de vie there are other local specialities to be enjoyed. In particular, many restaurants and Stüblis will have their own variations of Glühwein and concoctions of coffees and teas mixed with something evil - quite delicious. Glühwein is generally a stock mixture of nutmeg, mint, cinnamon and lemon strained into red wine.

One thing is certain. There is no shortage of places to eat and drink, ranging from the exclusive and sophisticated to the simple and rustic.

WHITE WINES OF THE VALAIS

The white grapes used in the region are: Chasselas, Sylvaner, Amigne, Arvine, Humagne Blanc, Rèze, Marsanne Blanche, Muscat, Pinot Gris, Chardonnay and

---

1. Vineyards are precious and the first tasks in the spring take place to the sounds and encouragement of the fifes and drums, a foretaste of the jollifications of the wine harvest festivals.

Paien. Some of the better known wines are:

Amigne The Amigne grape was introduced to the Valais by the Romans at the beginning of Christendom. A rich and soft, slightly sweet wine, popular as an apéritif or dessert wine.

Gletscher Wine (Glacier Wine) The wine is matured at a high altitude and is a mixture of more than one year's vintage. A quite unique taste.

Chardonnay A marvellous dry, fruity, tasteful wine that is particularly suited to seafood or white meat.

Malvoisie Pinot Gris or Tokay presents a rich and aromatic dessert wine which is normally drunk with the sumptuous fruit desserts offered by many of the eating houses in and around Zermatt.

Johannisberg Particularly popular with fish.

Fendant This is the most renowned of all the white wines in the Valais, and there are many specialities and variations offered. The wine is popular at all times and places, whether it be from a mountaineer's flask or within the refined atmosphere of an exclusive restaurant. Fendant is made from the Chasselas grape, widely known as a dessert grape and also used in wine production in the Alsace and Pouilly-sur-Loire in France.

Rèze An excellent accompaniment to some of the traditional cheese dishes.

Other specialities are Arvine, Petit Arvine, Humagne Blanc, Muscat, Ermitage and Aligoté.

Amigne, Arvine, white Humagne and Rèze are indigenous *vines* which are *unique* to the canton of Valais, symbols of a long tradition of viticulture.

ROSÉ WINES OF THE VALAIS

Dôle Blanche The grapes Pinot Noir and Gamay are used to make this onion-skin coloured wine which has been produced in the Valais since about 1920. Dôle Blanche is only put through the wine press once, thus retaining a light colour.

Oeil de Perdrix Made from the Pinot Noir grape. A light, medium dry fruity wine.

RED WINES OF THE VALAIS

The red grapes used in the region are: Pinot Noir, Gamay, Humagne Rouge, Cornalin, Syrah, Diolinoir, and Durize.

Dôle Possibly the most famous of the Valais wines, and certainly the most widespread. Dôle is usually made up of about 80% Pinot Noir and 20% Gamay. Taken from the vines early, with a long fermentation period, the grapes are then processed through a soft wine press. During the second fermentation the carbonate is removed. Dôle reaches its full ripeness after a couple of years.

Goron Widely drunk with meat dishes.

Pinot Noir Quickly harvested so that complex aromas are not lost. The full bodied and interesting bouquet develops slowly over a few years.

Gamay Popular with cheese.

Other specialities are: Humagne Rouge and Cornalin, full and rounded character wines which improve with ageing.

Of course these wines are at their best when tasted on home territory.

SCHNAPPS

Switzerland has as many types of Schnapps as Scotland has whisky. Some of the better known ones are: Kirsch (cherry), Pflümli (plum), Kernobst (pear and apple), Abricotine (apricot), to name but a few. Possibly the most famous is William's, made from the pear.

In 1896 Urban Germanier planted the first vineyards on his family's land. His production was small, and trade just extended to friends and local restaurants. This was insufficient to support a family of five and, while he found work elsewhere, his sons took over and expanded the operation. Their wine became popular. By 1940 the brothers decided to allocate some of their land to the cultivation of pear trees. They planted Christus William Birne which came from England and thrived in the microclimate of the Valais. The ensuing development of Schnapps from these pears happened quite by accident. In 1945, a tremendous thunderstorm stripped the trees of all their ripening fruit. So as not to lose the harvest, Francis Germanier decided to let the pears ripen and ferment. A wonder occurred – the distillation of the pears! Jean Dettwyler, president of the Lausanne State Council at the time, tried the 'Gottestrank', the drink of the gods, and was so impressed he decided to market the product. Thus 'Bon Père William' became a trademark in the Schnapps industry. Today, 100 million kilos of pears a year are used in the production of Bon Père William.

The question is often asked as to how it is possible to grow the **pears in a bottle**, i.e. how does the large, ripe fruit get inside the distinctive bottle? The traveller crossing the pear growing regions in May and June will notice bottles on the trees. The pear trees flower in May, the tiny fruits grow quickly, and the farmers have to keep a careful watch to catch the right moment to invert bottles over selected swelling pears. The bottles are designed to protect the fruit from unexpected frost, too much sun, and disease while the pears grow to normal size in them. In the middle of August the pears are harvested.

THE ARTIST'S VIEW OF ZERMATT

INTRODUCTION

From Edward Whymper's *Scrambles amongst the Alps 1860 - 69*
(Author's Preface to the Fifth Edition London, June 1890)

T
HE ABLEST PENS have failed, and I think must always fail, to give a true idea
of the grandeur of the Alps. The most minute descriptions of the greatest writers do
nothing more than convey impressions that are entirely erroneous - the reader
conjures up visions, it may be magnificent ones, but they are infinitely inferior to the reality.
I have dealt sparingly in description, and have employed illustrations freely, in the hope that
the pencil may perhaps succeed where the pen must inevitably have failed.

From John Ruskin's *Modern Painters Vol. IV.* **(1856)**

Twenty-five years before the first ascent of the Matterhorn, the great mountain is
painted and described, as well as photographed for the first time, by the eminent
Victorian John Ruskin (1819 - 1900), who in his writings on 'Modern Painters' also
includes splendid descriptions of the beauties of the Alps. He remains, no doubt like
many more admirers of his times, an articulate and dedicated **enemy** of Alpinism.
For him:

> *The Alps are never so beautiful as when viewed from below.*

His drawings and watercolour sketches capture admirably the poetry and dramatic
beauty of the Alpine landscape. But neither Ruskin's opinion nor the fear and
superstition of many could stand in the way of the ultimate conquest of the
Matterhorn and the creation of the myths surrounding it.

ZERMATT'S PAINTERS

Every artist who comes to Zermatt cannot fail but be moved by the beauty of the
surroundings. The mountains present a spectacular backcloth to the enchantment
of fairytale meadows, flowers, forests and wooden houses (the immensely paintable
Stadels). Rocks of all shapes and all shades of grey – green – silver – bronze – white
sparkle in the sunshine and glisten in the rain, the glossy surfaces washed into a new
intensity.

Gorges and foaming water, sheer rocks with gnarled trees perched at perilous
angles create a dramatic scene which contrasts with the gently undulating meadows.
Another stark contrast lies in the shadows against the strong light and the brilliance

of a cloudless day, as captured in this diary extract:

The morning was frosty after a cold night. The water on the shallow lakes had frozen in parts. Star shaped ice flakes glittered in the morning sun. Such clarity I had never seen. But always, on our left, as we walked down towards Zermatt, was a dark pointed shadow across the hollow of the valley of Zmutt - the shadow of the Matterhorn.

Each season has its own shadows just as it has its own colours, its intensity and softness of tone. These provide the artist with an experience to be transposed into a vision, culminating in a creation of his own.

Mountains are elusive subjects. It is easy to concentrate on their shape and destroy the poetry, and vice versa. Thus amongst the painters of Zermatt Albert Gos must rank as one of the greatest, for he achieved a perfect artistic balance of the two.

ALBERT GOS (1852 - 1942) was born in Geneva and is often remembered as 'le peintre du Cervin'. He was not only an exceptionally talented painter but an all round artist. His first love was music and although painting took over, the former accompanied him throughout his life. He carried his violin with him wherever he took his canvas and paints. The deep inspiration for his art came throughout his life from his love of the Alps. His passion for the mountains was born in the Bernese Oberland, more precisely near the famous Öschinen See above Kandersteg. In 1874 he discovered the valley of Zermatt and neighbouring Zinal and Arolla and never ceased coming back. He explored it in depth on over forty different visits. 'A landscape has an inner life just as we have a soul' he wrote, and this is what he always strove to capture on canvas throughout his career. It is said of Albert Gos: 'In his paintings, the tones harmonise as in a musical composition'. Frequently, after completing a painting, Albert Gos would take up his violin and 'play' his creation to try and express any remaining feelings which he had been unable to put into visual form.

Albert Gos, who was a friend of Whymper, undoubtedly contributed to the creation of the Matterhorn myth. He often painted at Blatten,[1] a picturesque hamlet on the way from Zermatt to Furi. There, his memory and that of his talented family are honoured in a plaque bearing their names, appropriately nailed on to a large rock:

Albert Gos	(1852-1942)	painter
François Gos	(1880-1975)	painter
Charles Gos	(1885-1949)	writer
Emil Gos	(1888-1969)	photographer

At the turn of the 19th century, Albert Gos was much appreciated in Switzerland but subsequently, as is often the case, lost his popularity at home. The rest of Europe, the United States, and Canada opened their doors to him and his great talent. He staged many successful exhibitions. Nowadays, his paintings are sought

1. It was in Blatten that Albert Gos discovered an empty chalet whose owners had either 'died or gone to America'. He bought the contents and created an Alpine retreat in his Geneva flat. This is where he received his many friends and admirers, from Mountain Guides to Whymper to Lord Leighton, the then President of the Academy, and many more.

after and many amateurs art collectors in Zermatt itself have added his works to their collection.

FRANÇOIS GOS (1880 - 1975)

The art critic E. Combe writes in an article dedicated to the artist: 'Son of a well known artist, François Gos could only make his mark by being different and by allowing a strong personality to come through'.

It must have been that much more difficult for him because he, too, as a keen Alpinist loved the mountains and felt irresistibly drawn to them.

But François Gos had a very distinctive and bold style of painting all of his own, boldness which expressed itself amongst other things in sculptures. He contributed to the statue of Amersfoort, a work executed by Belgian troops interned in Holland, where he himself lived for several years. At that time in his life he also created lithographs in stone on the theme of Salome. These can be seen today in the Rijks Museum of Amsterdam.

As a painter François Gos brought the subject of his works into the foreground of his paintings, in clear lines, renouncing distant subtle and ethereal atmospheric background in favour of an unequivocal artistic statement.

His Matterhorn paintings are sculptured. Shape and tangibility create the atmosphere, and capture the power of his subject matter, a summit which dominates its surroundings, without losing the element of mystery which always surrounds the Matterhorn.

We gratefully acknowledge the help of Pierre-Alain Crettenand, Art Historian from Sion (Valais) in writing about Albert and François Gos.

EMIL AUFDENBLATTEN

One of Zermatt's major painters, Emil Aufdenblatten pursued his studies in Rome, where he acquired a very sound technique for his craft, expressed in attractive paintings, some of them atmospherically rather sombre. The painter's most productive period spanned 15 to 18 years from 1930 with his best works in the 1930s. This epoch was rounded off with another 5 years of excellent work, but after 1945 his career went into a decline. He became more and more isolated and took to drink as his hopes of recognition as a great artist were not realised. Sadly and inevitably the quality of his work diminished. He died in 1958.

Many of his canvases were sold in America, but some of the paintings were subsequently bought by Zermatters or even given back to the village. Examples of Aufdenblatten's work may be seen at the Vereinzentrum.

PAUL SÉCHAUD (1906 - 1982)

Paul Séchaud settled in Zermatt in 1932. It was the year of his marriage to Edmée Guinand, which was to last into its fiftieth year. He was a native of the canton de Vaud and came to the Seiler Hotels as a tennis player and coach. He was an excellent sportsman and teacher. But deep in his heart lay the desire to paint. As a youngster, he had already shown promise by producing striking colour contrasts.

To begin with, Paul Séchaud painted in water colours: Venice, still lifes and gypsies (gitans, as he called them in French, his mother tongue). Flowers remained one of his favourite subjects, and he was often called 'the flower painter'. He painted magnificent vases filled with roses, or iris, misty mimosa or lilac, and pristine daisies, mostly one flower species only.

Then came Zermatt, and an ever deepening feeling for the nature surrounding him. He painted: chapels, including many inspiring pictures of the tiny chapel at Schwarzsee; the Matterhorn from different angles, in summer and winter, full size or seen peeping over the roof of a chapel or a Stadel; wonderful, rich autumn colours: the golden needles of a larch tree in contrast to the evergreen Arolla pine, rising above a carpet of bright red bilberry and whortleberry leaves; a saucer of blue gentians on a wooden table next to a yellow drinking bowl; a plate of wild strawberries beside a glass of Edelweiss.

As a bold painter, Paul Séchaud excelled in winter scenes: the old village houses and side streets, wrapped up in heaps and mounds of snow with blue, grey and pale ochre shadows. He felt the magic of Zermatt so intensely that he even helped to reveal some of it to the Zermatters themselves.

Wherever he went to paint, he was often accompanied by his wife. Paul Séchaud loved Zermatt, and Zermatt loved him. He was warm-hearted and generous, sustained by a deep faith in life and in God, all of which is reflected in his art.

In memory of Paul Séchaud, a carrefour down by the river was named after him. This inauguration had been planned to celebrate the golden anniversary of his marriage to Edmée, as well as his coming to Zermatt. Sadly, he died before the great day, but the small piece of Zermatt soil which bears his name, honours the man and his artistic achievements: a testimony of his friends from the village.

Many hotels and restaurants possess pictures by Paul Séchaud. His distinctive style is easily recognisable.

A catalogue of Paul Séchaud's works may be purchased from:
Hans Lutz, Haus Cervin, Winkelmatten, Zermatt.

JIM KINGWELL
Originally from Alameda, California, Jim Kingwell began his art education at the California College of Arts and Crafts. He then continued on a scholarship to the San Francisco Academy of Art. Jim has travelled and painted throughout the USA, Europe and South America. The cultural diversity of people and their land inspire the 'Romantic Realism' he captures in his paintings. Included in this book are drawings Jim has completed during numerous stays in Zermatt. Some are only studies to be used in future works, whilst others are completed works, in themselves expressing those special moments in his encounters with Zermatt.

SIGISBERT PERREN
Born in Zermatt in 1928, Sigisbert went to the local school before completing his Matura at the Kollegium in Brig. Sigisbert then went on to study at Freiburg University. After completing his studies he was employed as a secondary teacher in the Canton Thurgau, eastern Switzerland. During this time his love of the arts prompted him to study further at the Kunstgewerbschule in Zürich and St. Gallen.

Later he went on to learn the Art of Radiereus in Salzburg. He was awarded the cultural prize of Zermatt 1993.

SILVANO ARMANI was born in northern Italy in the mountainous area of Brescia - Bergamo. He is well known for his water-colour pen drawings which can be seen in many local establishments. He is a versatile artist who has also painted a mural. He is currently painting in oil and acrylic and using pastels whilst moving away from the figurative aspect of his art. He is a member of the Ober Walliser Künstler Vereinigung.

THEO IMBODEN
Religious and Anthropological Glass Reliefs and Glass Sculptures
Many public works of this acclaimed artist, born in Täsch, may be studied in and around Zermatt, as well as in his native village where the Täscherlegende may be seen at the Hotel Täscherhof. The life story of Theo Imboden is one of destiny, how the young lad caring for his ailing father was given his first box of coloured pencils, became an apprentice painter/decorator and was pointed in the direction of working with glass - the material that corresponded best with his creative talents - by a sympathetic teacher. After completing an apprenticeship and studies in this medium, he wandered across Europe to increase his technical knowledge. He returned to Täsch in 1959 and set up a modest studio where he worked, mainly for local restaurants, restoring old windows, painting shields, crests and lamps. His reputation as outstanding craftsman soon obtained for him commissions from eminent artists to realise their designs for church windows, both in the Valais and further afield. It was a logical step for Theo Imboden to go on to create - in unique glass sculptures - his own inspirations, their central theme being the physical, social and cultural aspects of mankind. He was awarded the much coveted Kulturpreis des Staates Wallis 1989.

LISA IMESCH came to Zermatt from Lucerne seventeen years ago. Her work as an artist is almost exclusively in water-colour, representing landscapes and flowers. The variety of blooms in the summer meadows of Hermetje above Zermatt hold no secrets for her.

The sketch of local views by Lisa Imesch which enhances this book emphasises the strong shapes and outlines of mountain, rock and lake in the Zermatt area. The clear reflections of the landscape in the calm waters of mountain lakes perfectly illustrate the crystalline quality of the luminous Alpine atmosphere.

HANS LUTZ originated from Basel (Bâle) where he worked in confectionary. His early creativity expressed itself in the form of exquisite and intricate sugar sculptures.

On retiring from running one of Zermatt's most renowned mountain restaurants he took up drawing, following a skiing accident which kept him immobilised for long enough to try something new. He has not looked back since then and has gone from strength to strength. Leaving his early days as a water-colour painter behind, he now concentrates on pen drawings where his great powers of observation come to the fore. Some of his work can be seen in local establishments such as restaurants and hotels, as well as in Zermatt's old people's home. There are many examples of his work in this book.

ALBERT PILKINGTON was born in Manchester, England in 1932. He studied graphic design and illustration at the Manchester College of Art. In 1950 his training was interrupted by National Service, serving with the Royal Air Force and with the Canadian Air Force. After his release he pursued a career in commercial art. Today he has decided to concentrate his efforts on landscapes in aquarelle. Fascinated by the mountains and Switzerland, Zermatt is one of his favourite places in which to paint.

PAULINE REY was born in 1949 on Vancouver Island, Canada. After finishing her education she left home and tried her skills in numerous jobs, from secretary at the Grand Bahama Hotel to crewing as deck-hand on a yacht in the Mediterranean. She visited Zermatt for the first time in 1971 and has now settled here with her family. During seven years in India with her Swiss husband she set up and helped organize a small cottage industry for displaced and rejected Indian women. She has been taught by numerous highly skilled artists and has adapted her talent to different media, be they pencil, oil, acrylic or aquarelle. The chapter on the flora of Zermatt is illustrated by her pencil drawings.

JOHN CORBETT FCSD FRSA
Architect, Designer
Studied architecture at Birmingham College of Architecture. John Corbett compiled the Zermatt - Furi map for this book.

GEOFFREY HUBAND N.D.D. A.T.C.
Born in Worcestershire, England, in 1945, Geoffrey Huband studied at Stourbridge College of Art and completed his training at Victoria College, Manchester University. He settled in Cornwall to paint in 1970. His work has been featured on Independent Television and is in numerous private and public collections worldwide. He exhibits with the Royal Institute of Oil Painters, the Royal Society of Marine Artists and is a member of the Federation of British Artists. Excellent draughtsman and artist, he is currently drawing the covers for Alexander Kent's series of books. Having enjoyed a 'unique, wonderful and inspirational' summer holiday in Zermatt, Geoffrey Huband was delighted to be involved in this book.

PHILIP SIEGENTHALER
Illustrator, Physician and Qualified Homeopathic Practitioner
Studied Medicine at the University of Lausanne (Vaud, Switzerland). In his precious spare time Philip Siegenthaler creates terracotta sculptures. The instantly appealing and amusing character studies of the youngsters in the chapter on Children in the Mountains were executed by him.

HANNES TAUGWALDER

This well-known author (born in Zermatt) spent all the war years in London, recorded his experiences both of London and his childhood in Zermatt in autobiographical works. *The Lost Valley* (Das verlorene Tal) is due to be published in English in 1995.

CIVIC ART IN ZERMATT

Zermatt has a wealth of works of art by other artists in numerous different media, regretfully not represented in this book. Many of them have most generously donated their work for the benefit of Zermatt and all who live in and visit the village.

HOTEL★★★★ *Butterfly* CH-3920 ZERMATT

The Hotel With The Smiling Face.

We welcome our guests into the
Heart of our Hotel.

Our comfortable entrance houses
a collection of Outstanding Paintings,
An Introduction for our visitors to the riches and beauty of
the world of Zermatt and its Cultural Heritage
A Private viewing "At Home".

Cosy Bar where Coffee and Apéritif go hand in hand.

Intimate Dining Room with separate alcoves.
Privacy to enjoy our carefully chosen menus
The Emphasis:
Fresh Produce and Garden Herbs
Extensive Wine List

For your comfort we have updated and refurbished
our Hotel whilst retaining our individual Welcome

Tel. (028) 66 41 66   Fax (028) 66 41 65

GETTING TO ZERMATT

I T MAKES LIFE easier, whatever means of transport is used, to have a number of Swiss coins with you to pay for porter, luggage trolley, luggage lockers, airport bus, telephone, toilet facilities. 1, 2 and 5 SFr. coins, as well as 50 and 20 centime pieces, are the most useful.

BY AIR AND TRAIN

FLIGHTS

Up to twelve scheduled flights daily - by British Airways, Crossair, Swissair

| London Heathrow | - | Geneva | London Heathrow | - | Zürich |
| London Gatwick | - | Geneva | London Gatwick | - | Zürich |

Connecting flights via London Heathrow
from Aberdeen, Belfast, Birmingham, Edinburgh,
Glasgow, Inverness, Manchester and Newcastle.

Daily scheduled flights by British Airways, Crossair, Swissair

| Manchester | - | Geneva | Manchester | - | Zürich |
| Birmingham | - | Zürich | Birmingham | - | Basel (Bâle) |

Daily scheduled flight by Aer Lingus

Dublin - Zürich

Many charter flights are available from within the UK to Switzerland.

ONWARD TRAVEL BY TRAIN
(with SBB/CFF, Swiss Federal Railway and BVZ, Brig - Visp - Zermatt line)

SBB offer good train facilities, buffet or restaurant cars, telephone service and, on some trains, nursery facilities.

TRAIN FARES - CONCESSIONS

A half day pass, 100 SFr. valid for one year, gives 50% reduction on most fares. Family cards allow children under 16 to travel free if accompanied by a parent. Application forms must be completed before purchase of family card. Reductions for children and pensioners.

TRAVEL TIMES

Geneva - Zermatt: 4 hours
> Geneva airport has its own SBB station with regular trains to Brig or Visp.
> Change at Brig or Visp onto BVZ for Zermatt.

Zürich - Zermatt: 5 hours
> Zürich airports has its own SBB station with regular trains via Bern (change) to Brig.
> Change at Brig onto BVZ for Zermatt.

Basel (Bâle) - Zermatt: 5 hours plus.
> Airport bus from Basel (Bâle-Mulhouse) airport to Basel (Bâle) SBB station.
> Regular trains, some direct, some via Bern (where you change).
> Change at Brig onto BVZ for Zermatt.

LUGGAGE

Some train connection times are very short. A good solution to all the problems of hauling luggage around stations is to make use of the fly baggage service offered by Swissair/Crossair.

For first class and business class passengers there is no charge for this service. The cost to Economy class passengers is 20 SFr. per item. The luggage arrives one to two trains later than the passengers, and the collection office in Zermatt generally closes by 20.00h except in high season. It is essential to check for details.

BRIG - (VISP) - ZERMATT - rack and pinion railway

In both Visp and Brig the Zermatt train has its own platform outside the main SBB station.

The journey takes about an hour, depending on the number of stops. The route is very scenic and most enjoyable in daylight.

The last trains from Brig to Zermatt run as follows:

Throughout the year	Brig	19.36h.	arrives Zermatt	20.47h.
High season only	Brig	21.30h.	arrives Zermatt	22.14h.

The trains between Täsch (the village where all cars are left) and Zermatt run every twenty minutes,

the last train leaving	Täsch	23.35h.	arrives Zermatt	23.46h.

Should you miss your last train connection to Zermatt from Brig or Visp, you may wish to hire a taxi to take you to Zermatt. The cost will be the about the same as an overnight stay at a Brig hotel. The taxi rank is outside the main entrance of both stations.

BY CAR

If travelling by car, one can only go as far as Täsch, the village below Zermatt. From there you can either take a train or a taxi to Zermatt. The car can be left at the car park next to the station or with some of the taxi companies which will also drive you to Zermatt. In the very busy season, normally only in the winter, there is an overspill car park about half a mile away from the station.

When taking the train, it is useful to have 5 SFr. coins for the deposit on the luggage trolleys, which can be wheeled straight on board.

TAXI FREDY

028 67 33 66

24 hour service
Indoor and outdoor parking facilities
Collections from Brig and Visp
Transport to Zermatt

ARRIVAL IN ZERMATT

Many hotels collect their guests by their own electro taxis or by horse drawn carriage.

There are trolleys available (as in Täsch) to help you ferry your luggage to the electro taxis parked outside the station, opposite the Gornergrat Railway Station (5 SFr. deposit required).

Some hotels in Zermatt lock their doors at 22.00h, so that late arrivals may have difficulty finding anywhere to stay. Arrangements with hotels can be made in advance. The larger hotels provide an all-night service. (NB: always take your room key with you when leaving the hotel so as not to be locked out!)

FROM AIRPORT TO ZERMATT BY HELICOPTER

The helicopter company at Zermatt offers a 'taxi' service from all main airports in a 4 to 12 seater helicopter. Price on request. Flying time from Geneva = 50 minutes, from Zürich = one hour.

Additional information can be obtained from the Swiss Tourist Office,
Swiss Centre, Leicester Square, London.

ACCOMMODATION

There is a huge variety of hotels and self-catering apartments available. Even in the summer months there will be times when accommodation is not available and therefore it is advisable to book. For those who have not made reservations, there is a board in the railway station equipped with telephones and press buttons which enables the visitor to see which hotels have rooms to let and their corresponding price.
Details of self catering apartments can be obtained from
the Zermatt Tourist Office (0041 28 66 11 81).

Switzerland prides itself on high standards, cleanliness, hospitality and excellent value for money.

ZERMATT

Zellner's of Zermatt

The meeting place for coffee and the real "Butter Croissants"
Mouthwatering Cakes - Local Bread Specialities - Chocolate
Made In House By Zellner Master Baker and Confiseur
With Traditional and Health Conscious Methods
Welcoming Shop
Warm Comfortable Traditional
Breakfast and Coffee Shop - Lunch - Tearoom
At the Heart of the Village

HEIDI'S GERSTENSUPPE – BARLEY BROTH
FROM THE RESTAURANT FINDLERHOF

Serves 4

100 g pearl barley
2 carrots
2 small leeks
1 celery
2 onions
1 bayleaf

130 g smoked bacon
50 g margarine
2 ltr beef or chicken stock
100 ml double cream
flour, parsley, chives, salt and pepper

Cut the carrots and celery into small cubes, the leeks into fine rings. Chop the onions finely and cut the smoked bacon into thin strips. In a large saucepan fry the bacon and then cook the vegetables in margarine, dust with flour, season with salt and pepper, add the barley and meat stock and leave to simmer for 3 hours. Just before serving add the double cream, parsley and chives, but do not cook again.

RIVER TROUT MEUNIÈRE WITH POACHED FRESHWATER CRAYFISH AND FRESH HERBS
FROM VINCENT FAVRE, HEAD CHEF, SEILER HOTEL, MONT CERVIN

Serves 8

4 salmon trout (280 g each) to
give 8 fillets
24 whole freshwater crayfish (these
can be replaced by crevettes,
tiger prawns or crab)

40 ml fish stock
150 g butter
2 ltr court bouillon
1 large tbs each of chopped parsley,
tarragon, basil and chervil

Wash the trout fillets, remove the skin and bones. Use the skin and bones to make a fish stock. Clean the crayfish. Bring the court bouillon to boil, add the crayfish, bring back to boiling point and remove from heat. Now boil the fish stock then, on a reduced flame, stir in the butter and chopped herbs, season to taste and keep warm. Quickly fry the seasoned trout fillets in a non-stick pan and keep warm. Remove the freshwater crayfish from their shells. Serve on individual warmed plates, place the trout in the middle, coat generously with the herb mixture. Surround with the crayfish and serve hot.

CARPACCIO OF TROKENFLEISCH
WITH OLD GOMSER CHEESE
FROM THE NICO TEAM, HOTEL NICOLETTA

Serves 4

200 g trockenfleisch, sliced very thinly
(if not available use Bressola)
50 g old gomser cheese
(Sbrinz or Parmesan)
100 ml thistle oil (olive oil)
8 mushrooms, seared

5 tbs white wine vinegar
Salt, pepper, basil, parsley and chervil
8 asparagus spears, cooked
8 mushrooms, seared

Arrange the slivers of trockenfleisch on a flat platter. Cut the old gomser cheese into thin slices and sprinkle over the meat. Make a vinaigrette with the oil, vinegar, salt, pepper and finely chopped herbs. Pour over the carpaccio, garnish with the asparagus spears and mushrooms.

TERRINE OF VEAL SWEETBREADS WITH WILD GARLIC
FROM THE RESTAURANT CORBEAU D'OR, HOTEL MIRABEAU

400 g veal sweetbreads
30 g butter
1 onion, finely diced
150 g finely diced leeks, celery,
apples and carrots
100 ml dry white wine
5 tbs noilly prat
3 leaves of gelatine
300 ml cream

1 garlic clove, crushed, white pepper
and garlic vinegar
20 g butter

for the garlic sauce
1 tbs cream
4 tbs soured cream
100 g wild garlic, chopped

Blanch the sweetbreads in boiling saltwater, drain and rest. Using a copper pan, heat the butter with the onions and vegetables until soft, making sure they do not burn. Over a low heat add the sweetbreads, douse with white wine, then let the mixture cool. Work the mixture into a smooth mousse, add the noilly prat and the softened gelatine, season with crushed garlic and salt. Place the mixture in a greased terrine, to ¾ full, and leave to rest in the fridge for at least 5 hours. Whip the cream, until thick, stir in the sour cream and wild garlic, cool well. To serve, turn the terrine onto a large platter or cut slices onto individual plates, top with the cream sauce and decorate.

WINTER SALAD WITH DUBLIN BAY PRAWNS AND SESAME
FROM KOBI AND MARIANNE, MOUNTAIN RESTAURANT ROTHORN

take a mixture of winter salad,
  like lollo rosso, endives,
    radicchio and lamb's tail lettuce
large fresh prawns
roasted sesame

for the vinaigrette
lemon juice
aceto di modena (balsam vinegar)
olive oil
mustard
salt, ground pepper and fresh herbs,
  basil, sage, parsley and chives

Make up the vinaigrette, mixing all the ingredients together. Wash the salad and dry well, arrange decoratively on a plate. Season the prawns with salt and pepper, coat them in the roasted sesame. Cook on both sides until golden brown. Place the prawns on the plate with the salad and sprinkle with the vinaigrette.

TORTELLONI ALLA PANNA
FROM MAX AND GRETI, RESTAURANT ZUM SEE

Serves 4

for the pasta dough
400 g flour
4 eggs, beaten
1 tbs olive oil
1 tsp salt

for the filling
100 g riccotta (not quark)
100 g cooked, well drained spinach
1 egg beaten

50 g grated parmesan
salt, pepper and nutmeg to taste

for the sauce
1 tbs butter
1 clove finely chopped garlic
20 ml double cream
10 ml milk
100 g parmesan
salt, pepper and nutmeg to taste

Firstly prepare the pasta dough. Mix all the ingredients together (if needed add a little water) and leave to rest. Then prepare the filling, mixing all the ingredients together, making sure that the spinach is completely dry. Leave to rest in the fridge. Next roll out the dough. Preferably with pasta machine, cut 10 cm squares. Place a little filling on the squares. Now fold the pasta in half to make a triangle and roll up like a croissant, pressing both ends together. Cook the tortelloni in boiling water for 5 minutes. To make the sauce, gently heat the butter and garlic together, then add the cream, milk and seasoning. Now add the tortelloni and cook for a couple of minutes, lastly adding the grated parmesan. Serve in warmed soup plates, with fresh grated parmesan. All the work for this dish can be done a day in advance, so the final preparation only takes 10 minutes or so.

FETTUCCINE ALLA VODKA
FROM ANTONIO, THE SPAGHETTI FACTORY, HOTEL POST

Serves 4

400 g mixed green and white noodles
160 g sliced mushrooms
120 g cooked ham, chopped into pieces
60 g finely grated parmesan

40 g butter
400 ml cream
2 tbs mild curry powder
80 ml vodka or more to taste

Boil the pasta in slightly salted water until cooked (*al dente*). In a large frying pan melt the butter, add the ham and mushrooms and lightly fry. Now add the cream and curry powder and simmer until the sauce thickens. Drain the pasta and mix with the sauce. Toss together, pour over the vodka and ignite, add the parmesan, toss again and serve on warm plates.

BUON APPETITO!

LINGUINE ALLA LACRIMA DI MARE
PASQUALE'S PASTA, FROM THE HOTEL DERBY

Serves 4

use a mixture of prawns, squid,
*   cockles and mussels (vongole)*
fresh, chopped tomatoes (skins removed)
oregano, garlic and basil

olive oil
300 ml white wine
linguine (thin strips of tagliatelle)

Cook the linguine in salted boiling water until al dente. In a large copper pan, over a low heat pour a few drops of olive oil, add the seafood, cook and douse with white wine. Add the tomatoes and simmer for 6 to 7 minutes. Sprinkle with the herbs and garlic. In warmed serving plates, place the linguine, cover with the sauce and serve.

Lacrima di mare – the tears of the sea, memories of Italy

BUON APPETITO!

NOODLES WITH SAFFRON, AND FRESH LANGOUSTINE
FROM KOBI AND MARIANNE,
MOUNTAIN RESTAURANT ROTHORN

*fresh langoustine or Norway lobster
    or lobster tails*
noodles

for the sauce
saffron
cream

fish stock
chopped shallots
lemon juice
butter
white wine
salt and ground pepper

Season the langoustine. In a frying pan, melt the butter and lightly fry the langoustine with the shallots, douse with white wine, fish stock and saffron. Remove the langoustine and keep warm. On a reduced flame stir in the cream and lemon juice and simmer. Cook the noodles *al dente*. Pour the sauce into hot plates, add the linguine, top with langoustine and serve.

QUICHE LORRAINE WITH LAMBS LETTUCE
FROM BERNIE AND ANDREA, RESTAURANT OLYMPIA STÜBLI

Serves 4

250 g short-crust pastry
100 g chopped bacon
100 g gruyère cheese
2 eggs

20 ml cream
10 ml milk
salt and pepper

Line a pie dish or baking tray with the pastry and prick several times with a fork. Fry the bacon, drain the fat and place in the shell with the grated cheese. Beat the eggs, cream and milk together and season. Pour the mixture into the shell and bake for 30 to 40 minutes at 200°C. Serve with the fresh lamb's lettuce or other fresh green lettuce.

RIFFELALPER KÄSESCHNITTE
FROM THOMAS MOOR, HOTEL RIFFELALP

Serves 4

300 g gruyère cheese
100 g appenzeller (or cheddar)
2 eggs, beaten
6 tbs dry white wine

grated nutmeg, salt
4 chunky slices white bread
2 pears, peeled, halved and cored
gherkins and pickled onions

Heat the oven to 200°C. Grate both cheeses and mix well with the beaten eggs and 2 tbs of the wine. Season with nutmeg and salt. On a baking tray, sprinkle the slices of bread with the rest of the wine, place half a pear on each one and cover with the cheese mixture. Bake until golden brown and bubbly. Serve with the gherkins and pickled onions.

DEEP FRIED CHICKEN BREAST IN THE RUSSIAN MANNER
FROM RENE LUCAS, HEAD CHEF, HOTEL ZERMATTERHOF

Serves 4

4 chicken breasts, skinned, bone attached

for the duxelle
25 g butter
16 mushrooms
4 shallots
80 g mousse de foie gras

for the coating
flour
seasoning
1 beaten egg
white breadcrumbs

for the sauce perigueux – truffle sauce
to 300 ml demi-glace sauce (brown sauce)
add 1 truffle

To make the stuffing: chop the mushrooms and shallots finely and sweat in a copper pan with a little butter until transparent. Cool and mix in the mousse de foie gras, season to taste. Make a slit in the chicken breast, stuff with the duxelle and seal the slit. Roll the chicken breasts in flour, coat with the beaten eggs and cover in the white breadcrumbs. Fry in a deep fat fryer at 180°C until golden brown. Serve with the perigueux sauce.

A good quality chicken liver paté, thinned with a little brandy, can be substituted for the mousse de fois gras.

RACK OF LAMB COATED IN FRESH HERBS
FROM ROGER MUTHER, RESTAURANT LE MAZOT

Serves 4

4 x 150 g best end of neck
   (rack) of lamb
salt and pepper
mild mustard
olive oil

for the herb coating
100 g breadcrumbs
1 clove garlic

1 small shallot
1 tbs mild mustard
fresh rosemary, parsley, thyme and
   oregano, finely chopped
1 tbs white wine
50 g melted butter
juice of half a lemon
pinch of salt and pepper

Mix all the ingredients for the coating together and leave to stand in a cool place for 1 hour (not in the fridge). Season the lamb and sear on the grill or in the frying pan (not too hot) until medium rare. Now coat the topside of the meat with the herb mixture and cook in a warmed oven at 180°C for 1 to 2 minutes. Serve with a sauce made from lamb stock, gratin dauphinois, green beans and ratatouille.

GUTEN APPETIT!

RACK OF ZERMATT LAMB IN FRESH HERBS, WITH BREADCRUMBED LAMB
FROM ALBERT WYSSEIER, CHEF DE CUISINE, SEILER HOTEL, MONTE ROSA

Serves 10

for the breadcrumbed lamb
3 kg boned shoulder of lamb
1 calf's foot (substitute pig's trotter)
200 g browning vegetables
   (onions, celery, carrots, garlic)
50 g tomato purée
salt, pepper, garlic and thyme

1 bouquet garni (bayleaves, cloves,
   ground pepper, rosemary,
   thyme and sage)
30 ml red wine
80 ml lamb stock (see below)
2 beaten egg yolks
white breadcrumbs

Season the boned shoulder of lamb, with salt, pepper, garlic and thyme. Together with the calf's foot sear in a large ovenproof pan. Remove the meat, and drain the fat off. Now brown the vegetables and the tomato purée to a dark reddish brown. Next add the meat, cook a little and douse with red wine, let the mixture reduce and add the lamb stock. Cover the pan and leave in the oven for 3 hours on a low temperature, 80°C to 120°C. Take the meat from the pan and remove the bone from the calf's foot. Sieve the vegetables and juices. Cut all the meat into squares. In the frying pan, on a low heat, cook the meat and juices, season and reduce a little. Now pour onto a baking tray, about 2 cm thick, cover and weight. Leave in the fridge for 12 hours. Once the mixture is pressed, cut into 6 by 4 cm triangles. Coat in beaten egg yolk and breadcrumbs. Cover both sides in clarified butter and cook in the oven at a low temperature, 70°C, for 15 to 20 minutes.

VEAL AND BEEF WITH BASIL
FROM RENE LUCAS, HEAD CHEF, HOTEL ZERMATTERHOF

Serves 4

400 g fillet of beef
400 g thin veal steak
15 basil leaves
salt and pepper

10 tbs vegetable brunoise made with
finely diced onions, carrots and celery
250 ml white wine
1 tbs tomato purée
net or string to hold the rolls together

Lightly brown the fillet of beef, cut open lengthways. Flatten out, season and cover with basic leaves. Place the veal steak on top and roll up, tie with string at 3 cm intervals. Preheat the oven to 250°C. The roasting is done in three stages, always at 250°C.

1 Roast for 10 minutes and then cool for 15 minutes.
2 Roast again for 10 minutes and cool again for 15 minutes.
3 Place the meat on the vegetable brunoise and roast again at 250°C.

Remove from the oven and check the temperature of the meat: it should read 45°C in the middle, ie, pink inside. Let the meat rest in a warm oven for 10 minutes.

To make the sauce, boil the vegetable brunoise with white wine and add 1 tbs of tomato pure, season, strain and remove the surplus fat. To serve, pour the sauce onto warmed plates and arrange the slices of meat.

Variations: Lamb and pork: same as above, the temperature should be 50°C at stage 3.

Chicken breasts and rabbit fillet: temperature should be 60°C at stage 3.

The beauty of this recipe is that it may be served with any choice of vegetables, rice, pasta or potatoes.

BASIC FONDUE RECIPE

Serves 4

350 g gruyère cheese
350 g emmental cheese
1 clove garlic
300 to 400 ml white wine

20 ml kirsch
10 to 20 g cornflour
ground pepper and nutmeg
600 g white bread, cubed

Rub the inside of an earthenware fondue dish with the garlic clove. Pour in the white wine, cook but do not boil, add the grated cheese, stirring all the time with a wooden spoon. When the mixture is bubbly but not burning, stir in the cornflour blended with the kirsch. Continue stirring and add the pepper and some nutmeg. Transfer the fondue pot to a réchaud waiting on the table. Serve with the cubed bread, gherkins, pickled onions and ground pepper. Watch out that the fondue does not burn! The trick is to make sure that the fondue is always stirred. Accompany with white wine, plain black or peppermint tea. The locals suggest a small glass of kirsch to help with the digestion.

FONDUE WITH CEPS (WILD MUSHROOMS)
FROM RALPH BUSH, RESTAURANT CASA RUSTICA

Serves 4

300 g gruyère cheese
300 g freiburger vacherin cheese
300 g valais cheese
20 g ceps (wild mushrooms)
50 g butter
1 clove garlic

45 ml white wine
20 ml kirsch
10 to 20 g cornflower
pepper and nutmeg
600 g bread cut into cubes

Grate all the cheeses and mix together. Rub the fondue dish with the garlic clove, slice the ceps and fry in butter, reserve. Warm the white wine in the fondue dish with a wooden spoon, stir in the cheese bringing almost to the boil. Dissolve the kirsch with the cornflour. Stir into the cheese mixture, season and cook (do not boil). Take the pot to the table and place on the réchaud, take chunks of bread and stir in the fondue. Dry ceps are available from specialist shops, otherwise use other mushrooms.

SMALL DUMPLINGS OF CHILLED FROMAGE FRAIS WITH ELDERBERRY COULIS
FROM HELMUT SCHINWALD, CHEF DE CUISINE, HOTEL LA GINABELLE

Serves 4

200 g fromage frais
76 g icing sugar
egg yolks, beaten
half a lemon (juice and grated rind)
250 ml cream, whipped
2 leaves gelatine
pinch of salt

for the coulis
250 g elderberries
2 cooking apples
150 g damsons or plums
vanilla sugar and cinnamon powder
amaretto

Soften the gelatine leaves, mix the fromage frais, sugar, egg yolk and flavourings together. Carefully add the gelatine and the whipped cream. Leave to set in a fridge for about 2 hours. For the elderberry coulis: wash the elderberries and remove the stalks. Peel the apples and slice thinly. Wash the damsons or plums, remove the stones and slice thinly. Sprinkle with the vanilla and cinnamon, add a few drops of amaretto. Cook all the ingredients over a low heat for about 30 minutes, add a little sugar if needed. To serve, place the coulis on individual plates, scoop out the quark dumplings and arrange on top of the coulis.

APPLE CRISP
FROM BERNIE AND ANDREA, RESTAURANT OLYMPIA STÜBLI

Serves 6 to 8

8 large cooking apples
100 g white sugar
100 g brown sugar
500 g oatmeal
500 g white flour

2 to 3 tsp salt
200 g butter
3 tsp cinnamon
½ tsp nutmeg
juice of 1 lemon

Combine the dry ingredients, knead the butter into the mixture until it resembles breadcrumbs. Peel, core and slice the apples, place in a greased baking dish. As the apples have a tendency to 'bake down' pack the topping tightly over them, bake at 180°C for 35 minutes or until the topping is golden brown. Serve with a scoop of vanilla ice cream and/or whipped cream.

ZERMATT WALNUT TART
FROM CAFÉ ZELLNER

Quantity for 4 tarts of 20 cm diameter

for the pastry
750 g flour
300 g butter
300 g sugar
3 to 4 eggs, beaten
1 egg yolk, beaten
grated rind of 1 lemon

for the filling
500 g sugar
500 ml cream
50 g honey
500 g shelled walnuts
icing sugar

Beat the butter and sugar together until light and fluffy, add the eggs and mix well. Stir in the flour and lemon rind. Knead to a smooth dough. For the filling, heat the sugar in a copper pan until golden brown. Warm the cream and mix with the sugar, add the honey and boil to soft ball stage 115° (use a sugar thermometer). Stir the walnuts into the mixture and leave to cool slightly. Roll out the pastry to 4 mm, place in the greased baking trays. Spread with the filling, dampen the edges of the pastry with egg and cover with a pastry lid. Prick all over with a fork and bake at 220°C until golden brown. Sprinkle with icing sugar.

GRATIN OF APRICOTS WITH FOREST-FLOWER HONEY ICE CREAM
FROM THE NICO TEAM, HOTEL NICOLETTA

Serves 4

for the gratin of apricots
12 ripe apricots
20 ml abricotine (apricot Schnapps)
50 ml white wine
2 egg yolks
1 egg
50 g sugar
100 ml orange juice
rind of 1 orange

100 ml whipping cream
50 g icing sugar
50 g roasted almonds

for the ice cream
300 ml milk
100 ml double cream
1 vanilla pod
100 g forest-flower honey

For the gratin: halve the apricots and remove the stones. Poach in white wine, abricotine and a little water and sugar to taste. In a bowl placed over hot water, whisk together the egg yolks, egg, sugar, orange juice and rind until pale and foaming. Remove from the heat and continue beating until cool. Arrange the apricots, fan like, on a deep ovenproof plate. Mix the whipped cream into the egg mousse, and coat the apricots with the mousse. Put under a hot grill to brown, sprinkle with icing sugar and almonds, serve hot with the forest-flower ice cream.

For the ice cream: infuse the milk and cream with the vanilla pod and bring to the boil. Remove from heat, add the honey, stir well and cool quickly in a bowl of chilled water, stirring often to prevent a skin from forming. Cool the mixture in a fridge or freezer, stirring from time to time. Pour the mixture into an ice cream maker and leave to freeze. Freezing time 20 to 25 minutes.

LIGHTNING CAKE WITH APPLES
FROM GUNDA, HOTEL BUTTERFLY

Serves 12

1 kg cooking apples, peeled,
   halved and cored
3 tbs sugar
juice of 2 lemons

for the cake
60 g butter
150 g sugar

juice and rind of half a lemon
8 g baking powder
200 g plain flour
10 ml milk
1 tbs rum
2 egg yolks
2 egg whites, whisked
3 tbs icing sugar

Score the halves of the apples on the rounded side. Sprinkle with sugar and lemon juice, set aside. Make the pastry by beating the butter and sugar until light and fluffy, slowly mixing in the beaten egg yolks, then the lemon juice and rind, with the flour and baking powder. Stir in the milk and rum. Fold in the stiff egg whites. Spread into a well greased spring cake tin. Lay the apples (scored side up) on top and brush with butter. Place in a preheated oven at 180°C and bake for 35 to 40 minutes until golden brown. Remove from the cake tin while still warm, sprinkle with icing sugar.

'KAISERSSCHMARREN' WITH A COMPOTE OF PLUMS
FROM HELMUT SCHINWALD, CHEF DE CUISINE,
HOTEL LA GINABELLE

Serves 4

for the pancake
100 g plain flour
120 ml milk
2 egg yolks, beaten
50 g sugar
2 egg whites, whisked
25 g raisins

for the compote
200 g plums
400 ml orange juice
50 ml lemon juice
30 g sugar
cornflower
cinnamon and nutmeg to taste

For the compote: put all the ingredients into a pan and simmer until the plums are soft. Mix a little cornflour with water and thicken the compote, keep warm. For the pancake: mix the milk, flour and half the sugar to a smooth paste. Beat the egg whites with the sugar until stiff, stir them into the paste. Preheat a frying pan, melt a little butter, pour in the mixture and sprinkle with raisins. Cook on both sides, until golden brown. To serve, break up the pancake, place on warmed plates with the compote on the side.

VEGETABLE PANCAKES IN A CREAM SAUCE
FROM URS ZUMTAUGWALDER, RESTAURANT FINDELGLETSCHER

Makes approx. 20 pancakes

for the pancakes
1 lt milk
16 eggs
300 g flour

salt, pepper and nutmeg
sauce béchamel
sauce béarnaise
a choice of vegetables, chopped and blanched

Make up a batch of pancakes and leave them to cool. Prepare the vegetables and blanch. Next make the cream sauce, using ⅔ sauce béchamel and ⅓ sauce béarnaise. The sauce béarnaise gives the pancakes a special taste. Now reheat the vegetables in the cream sauce, place a little filling in each pancake and roll up, sprinkle with a little cheese, if desired, and cook in a medium oven for 2 minutes.

SALMON MOUSSE
FROM JACQUES DARIOLI, RESTAURANT LE GITAN

250 g smoked salmon, puréed
20 ml cream
finely chopped fresh dill
lemon juice
pepper and cayenne pepper

for the sauce
10 ml oil
10 ml bouillon
5 ml lemon juice
20 ml cream
salt, pepper and cayenne pepper

Firstly purée the smoked salmon, then beat the cream until thick. Mix them together and season with pepper, dill, lemon juice and cayenne pepper. Leave to set in the fridge. Make the sauce by mixing all the ingredients together and season with salt, pepper and cayenne pepper. Serve on individual plates, pouring a little sauce on the plate and adding a scoop of the mousse.

ACKNOWLEDGEMENTS

The author wishes to thank all the people of Zermatt and elsewhere who have contributed to and collaborated with my work.

Thérèse Stembridge-Fürer, Chantal Perren-Norman, Leo Imesch without whose help this book could not have been written.

The Zermatt Tourist Office under the Directorship of Mr. Amédé Perrig who was kind enough to recommend my work.

Mr. Gabriel Taugwalder, President of the Tourist Office Zermatt.
Mr. Edwin Aufdenblatten, President of the Burgergemeinde Zermatt.
Mr. Robert Guntern, President of the Municipality Zermatt.
Mr. Sepp Julen of the Hotel Mirabeau, President of the Hotelier Association.

Dr. H. Biner, Mr. Y. Biner, Mrs. Gigi Biner, Dr. D. Collins, Mme Marie-Thérèse Furrer, T. Fux, Dr. P. Heinzmann, Mr. W. Hofstetter, Mr. M.A. Houmard, Mr. M. Johnson, Mr. L. Jörger, Mr. A. Kronig, Mr. Ivo Kronig, Mr. Kurt Lauber, for improving my knowledge.

Victoria Linklater (MA Hons, M Litt Oxon) for editing the book.
Richard J. Wise for layout design and typesetting.
Melanie Clay for her help with computer work.

Mr. Perren/Barberini for his invaluable help with the artwork.
Mr. M. Crettenand (Galerie Du Rhône SA, Grand-Pont 17 - CH - 1950 SION. Tel: 00 41 27 22 00 50, Fax: 00 41 27 22 02 50) for his help with the artwork by François Gos.

A special thank you for the staff of the Seiler Hotels, the Municipality of Zermatt, the Burgergemeinde and the Zermatt Tourist Office for their invaluable assistance.

The Swiss Alpine Club, Fenchernweg 41, 3252 Worben. Tel: 00 41 32 85 15 44, Fax: 00 41 32 85 15 32 who supplied the photograph of the Matterhorn and route up the Hörnli Ridge from Dr. H. Biner's book *Hochtouren im Wallis, Vom Trient zum Nufenenpass.*

The Alpine Club, 55 Charlotte Rd, London EC2 A3QT. Tel: 0171 6130755

The Nestlé Foundation Pro Gastronomia and its President, Mr. G. Valterio.

The Artists.

The Children.

Published by Elisabeth Upton-Eichenberger
U GUIDES
The Bishop's Croft, Rowney Green, Alvechurch, Nr Birmingham B48 7QG
ISBN 0 9525371 0 9

Printed by
Warwick Printing Co Ltd, Theatre Street, Warwick CV34 4DR, England